SHOWMAN
OF THE
SCREEN

Showman of the Screen

JOSEPH E. LEVINE and His Revolutions in Film Promotion

A. T. McKENNA

UNIVERSITY PRESS OF KENTUCKY

Scholarly publisher for the Commonwealth,
serving Bellarmine University, Berea College, Centre College of Kentucky, Eastern Kentucky University, The Filson Historical Society, Georgetown College, Kentucky Historical Society, Kentucky State University, Morehead State University, Murray State University, Northern Kentucky University, Transylvania University, University of Kentucky, University of Louisville, and Western Kentucky University.

Editorial and Sales Offices: The University Press of Kentucky
663 South Limestone Street, Lexington, Kentucky 40508-4008
www.kentuckypress.com

Unless otherwise noted, photographs are courtesy of the Joseph E. Levine Collection, Howard Gotlieb Archival Research Center, Boston University.

Cataloging-in-Publication data is available from the Library of Congress.

ISBN 978-0-8131-6871-5 (hardcover : alk. paper)
ISBN 978-0-8131-6872-2 (epub)
ISBN 978-0-8131-6873-9 (pdf)

This book is printed on acid-free paper meeting the requirements of the American National Standard for Permanence in Paper for Printed Library Materials.

Manufactured in the United States of America.

Member of the Association of
American University Presses

For Pat, Tony, and Tianqi

Contents

Introduction

An Unfettered Hustler

> I certainly don't believe in letting a picture walk in on rubber heels. I think that any picture worth making is worth promoting.
>
> —*Joseph E. Levine*

Short, ovular, immaculately dressed, and foul-mouthed, Joseph E. Levine was a showman. Joe's story is a particularly American story. He came from grinding barefoot poverty to become one of the most important men in American cinema. He was the most recognizable showman in America, yet he is now all but forgotten. He was a streetwise hustler, hawker, and flim-flam man from immigrant stock. He met politicians, presidents, and royalty and was granted a private audience with Pope Paul VI in Rome in 1964. It was said of Joe that he could sell a sack of shit to a ladies' group. *Variety* called him the "Boston Barnum."

P. T. Barnum is the touchstone of showmanship. He established the American showman as an outlaw, antielite figure, coming to prominence as he did in the decades following the American Revolution, when the colony had rejected British law and British elites. Neil Harris, Barnum's biographer, writes that Barnum grew up in an age of "social confidence . . . irreverence [and] happily exploding social rituals."[1] Adopting a similarly antielite pose, Joe would merrily antagonize critics and intellectuals. His use of the term *eggheads* to describe members of America's cultural elite was repeated, and often. An interview from 1970 shows Joe in fiery form as he attacks the critics of the day: "Renata Adler? Ah, for Crissakes. Did you read her reviews? Did you understand them? She don't like movies. Vincent Canby seems to like pitchas made in Czechoslovakia. What the hell do I know about pitchas made in Czechoslovakia? Pauline Kael is a sonafabitch. You think she loves movies? When was the last time she said anything good? OK, about some pitcha made in Czechoslovakia."[2]

The showman objectifies. Customers did not patronize Barnum's shows merely to see the Smallest Man Who Ever Walked Alone, General Tom Thumb (who was, in fact, a child with dwarfism), or the Feejee Mermaid (a monkey's head attached to a fish's body); they went for the show, the attendant ballyhoo. The showman provides a way of seeing. Showmanship is about objectification, not the object. The object may not be extraordinary, but the showman's job is to *render* the object extraordinary.

Movies were Joe's objects. He set up his own independent movie company, Embassy, in 1938 and began working as an exhibitor and distributor. He achieved fame and notoriety in 1959 with *Hercules,* a bargain basement sword-and-sandal movie he picked up cheaply in Italy and then opened all over America with an unprecedented saturation opening and blunderbuss ballyhoo campaign. "We're reminding everyone that this is a circus business," he declared,[3] as if chastising the film industry as a whole for its timidity. In this circus, Joe was ringmaster. He promoted himself alongside *Hercules* and became famous. He was famous in the true sense of the word. He was known by the man in the street.

Joe was an exploitation man. *Exploitation* is a term with a variety of interrelated meanings in the film world. Movie studios and film companies now have marketing departments, but up until the middle of the twentieth century they had exploitation departments. Exploitation basically means advertising and promotion, often with an added sense of urgency. Marketing invites you to see a film; exploitation *tells* you that you *must* see *this* film. But exploitation is also a collection of genres with the common denominators of low budgets and exploitable elements—shocking, timely, taboo, or lurid subject matter to attract an audience in lieu of stars and production values.

Exploitation historian Eric Schaeffer draws a distinction between the classical exploitation films of the first half of the twentieth century and those that came later.[4] Classical exploitation films dealt with taboo or "forbidden" themes such as unwed mothers, drug use, miscegenation, and wartime atrocity, all of which were ballyhooed with a moralistic, tabloid fervor. Later exploitation films were, by contrast, often aimed at teenagers. They were low-budget sci-fi, horror, teen-gang, and rock-and-roll flicks. Like their classical forbears, these exploitationers were microbudget attractions distinguished by advertising—exploitation—that promised the audience much more than the film would deliver in terms of lurid and horrifying delights. Joe dealt in both classical exploitation and teen "weirdies" at various times, so I use the term *exploitation* in its broader sense for this book, encompassing the various genres, and as a synonym for the term *promotion.*

During the 1950s, Joe spent much of his time dealing in exploitation movies. It was with this kind of film, he said, that "I could give vent to my peculiar talent."[5] He subsequently diversified to an astonishing degree. He dealt in exploitation, art house, horror, teen pics, peplum, children's films, family films, counterculture films, Westerns, documentaries, studio spectaculars, and blockbusters. He dealt in films from all over the world and from all over the cultural spectrum, becoming the most versatile movie promoter of his generation. My own interest in Joe was piqued when I noticed that he had released the Euro-art classic *Contempt,* the action spectacular *Zulu,* and the cult classic Bad Film *Santa Claus Conquers the Martians* all in the same year, 1964. "I like movies," he boasted, "all of them, I find something good in almost every movie."[6] A bold declaration, to be sure, but the extraordinary diversity of his output bolsters his claim.

The films that initially brought Joe fame were ready made, as were many of the films he dealt in throughout his career. Films such as *Godzilla: King of the Monsters* (1956), *Hercules* (1957), and *Two Women* (1960) had been completed by the time they fell into Joe's hands, though the first two were spruced up a little for the American audience. Some production investments in the 1940s notwithstanding, Joe did not really enter the production side of filmmaking until the 1960s. His name is on hundreds of films, on publicity materials, and on opening credits via the legend "Joseph E. Levine Presents." He also has dozens of producer and executive-producer credits, and his status as investor, presenter, producer, and/or executive producer oftentimes does not fully indicate the level of his involvement in a particular project. Unlike Irving Thalberg, the boy wonder producer of Universal and MGM who oversaw hundreds of films yet received only one posthumous credit (for *The Good Earth* [1937]), Joe would try to slap his name on just about any film that came into his orbit, causing some confusion.

What a producer or executive producer actually does is something of a mystery for those outside the film world, but it often depends on the producer, and it often depends on the project. It is fair to say that, having entered the production side of filmmaking in the 1940s, Joe did not really become a "working producer" until he was in his seventies with *A Bridge Too Far* (1977). Prior to that, his level of production involvement varied from project to project, but he could be described mostly as package producer or participant investor.

Joe was extremely adept at "packaging" productions in terms of casting—both acting talent and production personnel. He could match the right project (book, script, or idea) with the right director and screenwriter. He would often have a hand in casting stars and intervene at the scripting stage with ideas, suggestions, and sometimes demands. When the package was completed, Joe preferred to step back and allow the production to take care of itself. This way he could oversee up to a dozen projects at a time, keeping a watchful eye on progress from a distance, always ready to swoop down with an explosive intervention if things were not going to his satisfaction. A working producer, by contrast, works on one project at a time, keeps a much closer eye on production matters, and is often on set every day. Joe was not so interested in such minutiae, and, as a general rule, the better the package or the more he trusted the director and production personnel, the less likely he was to intervene.

The contractual terms for Joe's aborted production of *Will Adams* from 1964 provide some insight into his attitude to credits:

> 1. Production credit will be "Produced by Eugene Frenke and Jules Buck."
> 2. Mr Levine will receive credit as Presenter and Exec-Producer.
> 3. In the event a director is secured who insists on a production credit then, provided Buck will also agree, Mr Levine will receive credit only as a presenter and Frenke and Buck will receive credit as Exec-Producers.[7]

Specific credits were sometimes negotiable. The legend "Joseph E. Levine Presents" was, however, nonnegotiable. Also, when working in collaboration with another organization (*Will Adams* was to be made through Joe's Embassy and Paramount), Joe would always retain the advertising and promotion rights—an arrangement that suited both parties. Joe's ability to put a movie over to an audience was what organizations, from boutique production outfits to major Hollywood studios, were keen to capitalize on in their collaborations with Joe.

By his own dubious account, Joe was involved in some way with nearly five hundred films during the course of his life: "'*A Bridge Too Far* is the 493rd picture I have either produced or imported,'" he told Victor Davis in

1977, adding, "'Carlo Ponti says I stole two from him.' Pause. Triumphant grin. 'It's possible!'"[8] Such hints at ethical or legal transgressions were very much part of Joe's outlaw-showman persona and point to another factor that makes assessing his contribution to the vast amount of films that formed his inventory even more difficult: Joe Levine was a notorious credit stealer.

Cary Grant, on the subject of *A Touch of Class* (1973), told Guy Flatley in 1973, "Despite what it says on the billboards, Joe Levine did *not* produce the movie. . . . If anyone is responsible for *A Touch of Class,* it is Mel Frank, the man who wrote it and directed it. I like Joe Levine but I do believe it is a habit of his to take credit where he really shouldn't, something that applies even to *The Graduate.*"[9] Film importer Arthur Mayer also expressed anger at Joe's credit stealing,[10] and Lawrence Turman, the producer of *The Graduate* (1967), has said that Joe tried to "obliterate" him after the film's success.[11] But Joe could also be very supportive of creative talent and be fulsome in his praise for the talents he was backing when talking to the press. Indeed, one of the ways Joe sought to "obliterate" Turman was to ascribe all the credit for *The Graduate* to director Mike Nichols and thereby tangentially to himself for having "discovered" Nichols.

Exhibitor, distributor, producer, executive producer, promoter, and presenter, Joe Levine had many roles in the film industry. The press often referred to him with the catch-all moniker *mogul.* He claimed to hate the term, but the press books for his later productions called him "minimogul"; the U.K. journal *Films and Filming* called him "mogul of the mediocre";[12] and his *New York Times* obituary in 1987 stated that "the term *movie-mogul* could have been invented for him."[13] In many ways, Joe harked back to the old-time movie moguls, the bosses and heads of production of the studio era. But as the studio system crumbled through the 1950s and 1960s, he was a mogul for the postmogul era. "My business is loose," he once said. "I can go anywhere, do anything, and do it right away. Who needs a board of directors? Five years ago I had only three people in my office—four including my wife."[14] Joe loved his independence and hated losing it when he sold his company to the Avco Corporation in 1968. For most of his career Joe was independent and gadfly, an entrepreneur unbound by studio constraints who created a truly byzantine web of partnerships, associations, and collaborations as befitted his extraordinary talent for keeping movie product flowing from multiple sources. Importantly, it was not necessarily direct involvement with the filmmaking process that earned the moguls this moniker. The moguls were not always filmmakers; they were the men who created the conditions whereby filmmaking could flourish. They, like Joe, were expeditors of cinema.

In public, Joe strongly subscribed to what film scholar Robert Sklar has called "the traditional conception" of the moguls, in which "the intellectuals" were their enemies and "the people" their friends.[15] He was fiercely defensive of the audience for his more populist fare and strongly critical of the "eggheads" who criticized him and his ballyhoo approach. Like many of the moguls, he would often affect ignorance and downplay his intelligence. Samuel Goldwyn, for example, was happy to be thought of as a buffoon due to his highly publicized mangling of the English language and lexicon of malapropisms composed by his press agents; Harry Cohn also would downplay his excellent command of the English language in public and once told a young screenwriter, "If you don't learn anything else from me, learn this: Always let the other fellow think he's smarter than you."[16] Joe adopted similar tactics, as Richard Attenborough recalled: "He enjoys greatly giving the impression that many things are beyond his comprehension. 'No use sending me the script. I can't read,' he is always saying. Nothing is farther from the truth. He studies every subject in which he is involved meticulously, whether it be his next production or the most recent acquisition for his walls."[17]

There was a sly humor to Joe's posing as a philistine. The filmmaker Peter Rosen once wrote a script for Joe based on the novel *The Case against Org* by Mark Dintenfass—a left-field proposal even for Joe's eclectic tastes. At their meeting to discuss the project, Joe entered Rosen's office with a copy of the script, full of paper clips acting as markers. Rosen was thrilled that Joe had read it in such detail. Opening the script, Joe pointed to a word and asked, "Why did you use this word? Why not another?" He repeated this question for various other parts of the script until Rosen realized that Joe was highlighting all the multisyllable words, thereby emphasizing his own lack of education, which was cut short due to poverty, and gently mocking Rosen's status as a Yale alumnus.[18] Rosen, a good friend of Joe's, took the comments in the way they were intended, as badinage.

Joe's sly humor and mogulish posturing were very much a part of his public image. In his dealings in art cinema, he ostentatiously and gleefully trampled over the cultural borders that dictated that the world of arthouse cinema should remain sacrosanct and free of the kind of vulgar promotional overtures associated with other, supposedly lesser film forms. He gloried in the consternation such cross-pollination would cause as he dealt across the board, catering to highbrow, lowbrow, and middlebrow tastes. Joe genuinely enjoyed the criticism aimed at him from self-appointed cultural gatekeepers, not least because that criticism brought him free publicity and bolstered his reputation as a maverick outsider. But beneath the provocations and his regular denunciations of "eggheads" lay the most important element of his peculiar talent for movie exploitation: his versatility. He once said of his career-defining import, "*Hercules* was lousy, wasn't it? Still, I'm not ashamed of it. I'm in this business to survive, you naturally have to cater to different levels of taste."[19] While his comments may appear mercenary, catering to different levels of taste is no mean feat, and Joe's wide-ranging appetites and abilities meant that he was unbound by the cultural borders that fettered the intellectual community of postwar America.

Reports of Joe's vulgarity are so legion that it cannot be dismissed as a mere pose. He could be, as Paul O'Neil of *Life* magazine reported, "splendidly profane" in his creative use of obscenities,[20] and he could also be downright offensive. He had a stupendous temper. Bodybuilder Steve Reeves remembered Joe throwing a plate of spaghetti at a chandelier when Reeves reminded him that, according to the terms of their *Hercules* contract, it was Reeves, not Joe, whose name was to be given above the title billing as the film's star on posters and advertisements.[21] Later in his career, the seventy-six-year-old Joe attacked Tom Canford, a press agent, in the production office of *Tattoo* (1981). "He raised his walking stick like a wand," recalled Canford, "and advanced on me like something wicked come this way from Oz, shouting, 'I've caught you at last!'"[22] But Joe was also extremely sensitive, his feelings were easily hurt, and, like many whose feelings are easily hurt, he could often be inconsiderate of the feelings of others.

Joe once claimed to have "gotten along with most people along the way, except that actress, what's her name? Who I starred in *Harlow*."[23] But Carroll Baker, to whom Joe was referring, was certainly not the only enemy he made during his career. His feuds were innumerable, with victims and adversaries including Carlo Ponti (on and off for many years), Robert Aldrich, George C. Scott, Larry Turman, Richard Attenborough, Peter O'Toole, Jean-Luc Godard, and many more besides. Joe invested in eight of Sophia Loren's films, and they became very close friends, but he is conspicuously absent from both of her autobiographies. Joe feuded with the British producer Michael Klinger over the lackluster campaign for Klinger's production of *Baby Love* (1968) and with sometime partner Max Rosenberg over an unpaid debt. Both Klinger's and Rosenberg's children, however, remember a warm side to Joe. Tony Klinger recalls helicopter trips over Manhattan with Joe,[24] and Rosenberg's daughter, Elizabeth, fondly remembers "a toy kitchen he gave me for a Christmas present. I remember it in detail—a great toy."[25]

Joe was an unconscionable name-dropper, and his sphere of influence was extensive. President-elect John F. Kennedy, a fellow Bostonian, praised Joe in a letter to *Variety;* President Lyndon Johnson invited him to the White House for the signing of the National Endowment on the Arts and the Humanities Act in September 1965, afterward presenting him with the pen he used; and as president-elect, Kennedy's former rival Richard M. Nixon wrote to Joe for advice: "As you may know, I have pledged to bring into this administration men and women who by their qualities . . . can make a significant contribution to this country. You, as a leader, are in a position to recommend exceptional individuals."[26] Who, if anyone, Joe recommended to serve in Nixon's administration is not known.

It is difficult to ascertain precisely what Joe's politics were. He spoke highly of President Kennedy, became friends with the Kennedy clan, and distributed the documentary *John F. Kennedy: Years of Lighting, Day of Drums* (1966) for free. He donated to both the Democratic and the Republican Party. One can imagine him responding positively to Nixon—both were raised in poverty, both expressed a distaste for the cultured liberal elite, and both were famously foul-mouthed. An aspirational Republican message would have resonated with Joe, too, but I would suggest that politically he leaned to the left. In the late 1970s, when the unions were coming under heavy fire from the film industry, he expressed sympathy: "Sure, production costs are high . . . but how can you get away from that? You can't blame the unions. Their people have to make a living too."[27] Most importantly, he envisaged the audience for many of his films to be the working class, and he was very defensive of them. No doubt, such support worked in his favor, yet he was always sympathetic to "the people"; he never patronized them and attacked those who did—whether those attacks be real or imagined.

By the mid-1960s, Joe was one of the most powerful and influential men in American cinema, yet composer Maury Laws says, "I think I've always considered him a little man who got in over his head,"[28] and Michael Klinger, who remained fond of Joe despite their feuds, thought Joe "a bit of clown."[29] These claims are not as contradictory as they appear. Joe's love of deal making and his boundless energy were often unfocused, a manifestation of his street-urchin hustler origins. For all the wealth he accumulated, his insecurity never left him, and he could be extremely reckless. Throughout his career, he was often one or two bad decisions away from ruin, and equally, one or two good decisions away from yet more millions. Less than a month before his death, Joe reflected on his gambler's approach: "Anything can happen in this business. It's all a giant crap shoot and I intend to keep playing. . . . I was the fastest decision maker in the business and my credo still is 'Do it!'"[30]

Standing only five foot four in his socks, Joe was larger than life. So it is little surprise that he was fictionalized on numerous occasions. There is a script based on Joe's life doing the rounds of Hollywood, entitled *The Abominable Showman,* which has not yet been produced. *Slipstream* (2007), written and directed by Anthony Hopkins, features a film producer based on Joe and played by John Turturro. Joe was lampooned as "Joe LeVenal" in *Mad* magazine,[31] and Harold Robbins based the character Sam Benjamin in his novel *The Inheritors* on Joe. One scene in the novel shows Benjamin on the telephone to Europe, demanding a "big exploitation picture in color. I want a lot of production values, costumes, and naked broads. Something I can buy cheap and promote the hell out of in the States"; significantly, the omniscient narrator says of Benjamin, "He loved movies. Every one of them. Good or bad."[32]

Most famously, Joe was caricatured as the vulgar, philistine American producer Jeremy Prokosch in Jean-Luc Godard's film *Contempt* (1963). Joe may be largely forgotten, but Godardians know well who he is, and it is a shame that Godard's in-joke has gained so much traction at the expense of Joe's wide-ranging abilities. Joe was no philistine. Nor was he anti-intellectual, despite his occasional outbursts. He brought many of the best-regarded films of the postwar period to the United States, many of which he donated to museums such as the Museum of Modern Art; he was a keen collector of art ("I like to say I've collected all the French Impressionists from Van Gock to Van Go," he once Goldwynesquely remarked[33]); he gave speeches and funded programs at universities and supported many productions in the legitimate theater. Predictably, the more Joe became involved in respectable culture, the more he was accused of being a nouveau riche dilettante, accusations he relished.

In his 1941 study of Hollywood, Leo Rosten outlines the snobbery associated with the film world. "Aristocracies have always detested the *nouveaux riches:* the war between society and the parvenus has run through history. Self-made men have never 'rated' in the rarefied circles of pomp and prestige. . . . Hollywood, the very quintessence of the *nouveaux riche,* is the most fertile incubator of parvenus in our time. As such, it symbolizes all that is obnoxious to the old and austere social cliques in the land."[34] Such snobbery was still very much in evidence during the years Joe was active and famous. He was frequently accused of attempting to improve his standing among critics and cultural elites by moving toward more high-brow fare at the expense of the people-pleasers, but the accusation was never true; for every *8½* (1963) there was a *Billy the Kid versus Dracula* (1966); for every *Lion in Winter* (1968) there was a *Terrornaughts: The Virgin Sacrifices to the Gods of the Ghastly Galaxies* (1967).

In many auteurist film histories, commentaries, and director studies, Joe is cast as a foil, a philistine oaf who provides greater glory for the director by comparison. An authentic artist, runs the cliché, must suffer for his or her art, and many writers imply that the reputable subjects of their studies worked with or for Joe on sufferance, and emphasize the supposed inappropriateness of Joe's involvement by implying a cultural gulf between an artist's creativity and the producer's mendacity. Philip Lopate, for example, in his essay about *Contempt,* dismisses Joe as "the distributor of *Hercules* and other schlock";[35] Paul Sherman's review of *Boccaccio 70* (1963) belittles him as a "social climbing vulgarian";[36] and J. W. Whitehead writes in his book about Mike Nichols that funding for *The Graduate* was provided by "Joseph E. Levine's independent production house that imported racy European art films and made B-movie exploitation films."[37] None of these claims is factually incorrect, but they are reductive, accusatory, and given the context, snobbish.

The financial side of art, the business of show business, has long been problematic for film scholars and historians. Notions of artistic purity have led to the privileging of text over context and of object over objectification, which in turn has led to hugely important industrial figures such as Joe being disparaged or overlooked at best and forgotten at worst. In 2004, Dade Hayes and Jonathan Bing noted, "Levine's legacy is all but erased from the record books,"[38] a justifiable assertion that is less true now than it was then. During the writing of this book, more Levine-related material has appeared. In their book *Open Wide: How Hollywood Box Office Became a National Obsession,* Hayes and Bing position Joe as a key figure in the development of the modern-day blockbuster, as do Steve Neale and Sheldon Hall in *Epics, Spectacles, and Blockbusters: A Hollywood History;* Pauline Small's study of Sophia Loren, *Sophia Loren: Moulding the Star,* acknowledges Joe's contribution to Loren's career; and Tino Balio's book *The Foreign Film Renaissance on American Screens, 1946–1973,* recognizes Joe's pioneering work in promoting foreign films in the United States during the postwar years.[39]

Two other important books have also appeared in recent years, both meticulously researched studies of single films that provide balanced and fascinating accounts of Joe's work as an executive producer: Sheldon Hall's *"Zulu": With Some Guts behind It—The Making of an Epic Movie* and P. B. Hurst's *The Most Savage Film: "Soldier Blue," Cinematic Violence, and the Horrors of War;*[40] but the fuller story demands to be told. This book seeks to act as a corrective to the many misunderstandings, assumptions, and prejudices about Joe and to rectify his absence from most histories of American cinema. It also tells the tale of his peculiar talent for movie and self-promotion and his extraordinary career in the motion-picture business.

One popular misconception about Joe is that he was a cigar smoker. Hollywood folklore dictates that a big cigar always must be either gripped between a mogul's molars or clutched in his stubby fingers, and Joe was regularly described as a "cigar-chomping movie producer" in the press. In his memoirs, Michael Caine recalls: "If you wanted to cast a caricature of a Hollywood movie producer, Joe would have been it. He was short, fat, loud and he always smoked a big cigar."[41] Caine knew Joe well, made three movies with him, and would have known that Joe did not smoke cigars, but poetic license is justifiable in sketching Joe as an archetype. Joe, however, did not care for that particular image of himself: "I never smoked a cigar in my life," he told Gary Arnold of the *Washington Post,* railing against stereotype, "I can't stand them."[42] Nonetheless, the very fact that I felt compelled to double-check this particular piece of trivia with people who knew and worked with Joe gives some indication of how much credence we can give to Joe's claims, even on ephemeral details.

Joe may have been archetypal, but he was not a cliché. He was too independent and his approach too original for him to conform fully to stereotype. He appeared, as Caine suggests, as a caricature of a Hollywood producer, but he never moved to Los Angeles. Embassy had offices in Boston, London, Paris, and Rome, and from the 1960s on Joe conducted most of his business from his New York office. Throughout his career Joe worked often in Hollywood, but he remained determinedly and defiantly outside the Hollywood system, which afforded him both the independence he craved and the maverick-outsider reputation that his public image demanded.

Joe could be different things to different people. The producer Edward Feldman, who worked as a press agent for Joe, remembers him having "one of the biggest egos in the Western or any other hemisphere."[43] However, Maury Laws remembers that Joe "wasn't rude or arrogant,"[44] and Mel Brooks, who made *The Producers* (1967) with Joe, recalls that Joe was "never arrogant or egotistical like a lot of other studio executives."[45] Joe was certainly not the nicest man in show business. He was not a gentleman producer in the mold of Hal Wallis, but he did not have a monstrous reputation, as Harry Cohn did. He was a tough and shrewd businessman who could be fantastically generous or gratuitously brutal in his business dealings. He was more of a rascal than an ogre. A scoundrel showman, capricious and contradictory.

Joe famously insisted that extra nude scenes of Brigitte Bardot be inserted into *Contempt* and ballyhooed *The Carpetbaggers* (1964) with a well-publicized Carroll Baker nude scene, which was excised at the censor's request. To promote *The Nightcomers* (1971), Joe demanded that the star Stephanie Beacham strip for a *Playboy* shoot—and was reportedly bemused at her refusal because she had appeared naked in the film.[46] By contrast, Peter Rosen remembers, "I accompanied him for several trips up to New Haven to see plays at the Yale Rep. He didn't like the avant-garde theater of the times, because there was so much nudity."[47]

Joe said that he had been blessed by poverty and insecurity and had learned their lessons. He hated the very memory of his childhood poverty yet seemed to crave insecurity throughout his later life. He took a gambler's approach to filmmaking and promotion, often incurring frightening amounts of debt. When Avco bought Embassy in 1968, he was appointed president of Avco Embassy and had the security of the corporation's billions to back him up, but he was miserable: "I felt like I was in jail," he said of the experience.[48]

If he craved security, his wife, Rosalie, provided it. He worshipped Rosalie; she was his partner and business adviser until his death, and he named his huge pink yacht after her. He was broadly faithful, though he was partial to prostitutes. Joe and Rosalie adopted two children, Richard and Tricia, whom he spoke warmly of in interviews. As with any family, there were stresses and strains, and Joe's surviving family declined to be involved in the writing of this book.

"I rated Joe a terrific film businessman and a great showman, one of the last of his breed," says Tony Klinger. "He wasn't really a producer. He was a deal maker who dealt in films."[49] For Peter Rosen, Joe "represented the only mogul who was not in Hollywood, so as the first truly independent producer he led the way for people like Harvey Weinstein . . . who could make major films outside the Hollywood system."[50] Edward Feldman says that Joe was "easily one of the most important and visible single individuals in the industry. . . . He was a terrific showman and had a real knack for being a movie executive.[51] Mel Brooks believes Joe to be "very important. He is responsible for some ground-breaking films that might never have been made—like *Godzilla, The Producers, The Graduate,* and *The Lion in Winter,*" concluding that "today more than ever we need more Joseph E. Levines rather than corporate overlords deciding what we see at the movies."[52] For screenwriter William Goldman, "It's my guess that when the long term history of the sound era is written, Levine's importance will be that, in a crazy way, he helped keep [the industry] alive."[53]

Joe was a noisy man who made his presence felt. He did not believe in allowing a picture, or himself, "to walk in on rubber heels."[54] He loved movie promotion, and he loved movies, and therein lay the source of his peculiar talent. Even as a successful and wealthy independent, Joe continued to seek out cinematic curios of limited appeal—films that may have turned a small profit or, just as likely, incurred a small loss. His catering to "different levels of taste," then, was not simply about survival but also about promoting the medium he loved in all its forms. His output was multifarious to the point of being scattergun, and there is no key to understanding the internal logic of his vast inventory of films, which reads like the wet dream of the most contrived postmodern eclecticist.

Joe believed in grand gestures to promote his films. He held the world premiere of *The Adventurers* (1970) on board a cross-country jet flight. At an industry luncheon to launch *Jack the Ripper* (1959), he promised he would spend $1 million on promoting the film in America; then he unveiled $1 million in cash for all to see. When Carroll Baker was unable to attend a tour of Australia to promote *The Carpetbaggers,* Joe sent along one of the dresses she had worn in the film with instructions for Carroll Baker look-alike contests to be held. Press books for Joe's later films began: "God didn't create Hercules or Mike Nichols or Sophia Loren or Mel Brooks or Dustin Hoffman or Julie Christie or Marcello Mastroianni or countless others of the biggest and brightest names in the entire entertainment industry. No, it wasn't God, it was some guy from Boston—a guy named Levine, Joe Levine."

Joe also thrived in intimate settings. He was a witty man and an entertaining raconteur. His most famous line is, "You can fool all of the people all of the time if the advertising is right and the budget is big enough." Countless profiles cite this line, yet I am unable to find a reliable source that proves he actually said it. This does not mean that he never said it, though he was very fond of repeating his favorite maxims, but it does seem oddly fitting if the quip he is most famous for is a misattribution.

Above all else, Joe was a showman. His enthusiasm for showmanship never waned, and he remained convinced of its importance in the film world, whether it be manifested through the lavishing of millions on an explosive marketing campaign or simply the delivery of a well-timed bon mot to a sympathetic interviewer from a local rag. Among all those who knew Joe—those who loved him and those who hated him—nobody ever questioned his abilities as a showman.

In 1974, Joe wrote about the industry he loved: "I love this business which is not really a business. The film industry is composed of an indescribable collection of dreamers and schemers, geniuses and phonies, sharpshooters and lunatics. It's action, on the screen and off. I hope that when my time comes it'll happen not in bed, but in that suite in Rome, or on a plane, or on the back lot of a studio in Hollywood, Paris or London."[55]

As if to demonstrate his prominence and maverick nature, the bio that accompanied this article from the *New York Times* is revealing. Underneath the article, in the space reserved for a short biography of a guest author, read the words, "*Joseph E. Levine is . . . well . . . Joseph E. Levine.*"[56]

1

Barefoot Boston Boy Becomes Movie Man

> When I was little we were in the iron and steel business. My mother did the ironing and I did the stealing. We were so poor I didn't eat a thing until I grew up.
>
> —*Joseph E. Levine*

Joseph Edward Levine was born on 9 September 1905 into the horrible poverty of Boston's West End. His earliest years were spent on Spring Street, where he was born in a small apartment above a fish market. Joe would later joke that as the youngest of six children in a crowded apartment filled with the smell of fish, he had to go into the bathroom if he wanted a breath of fresh air.[1] Joe's family moved from tenement to tenement in the slums of the West End often during his childhood, at various times living on Hollander Street, Poplar Street, Minot Street, and Billerica Street, among others. But it was Billerica Street he mentioned most often, as if that one street symbolized all the misery of his early years. When he was an adolescent, his family moved to Roxbury, a slightly more comfortable neighborhood, but still rough: "I was a tough kid, but also I wasn't tough. I hated to fight. But I'd fight. I had to fight a tough kid called Edgy when we moved to Roxbury. Edgy got off the sidewalk the next time we met. Things were better in Roxbury. We had a porch."[2]

Joe's parents were Russian Jewish immigrants. There had been an influx of Jewish immigrants into Boston between 1880 and 1917, and almost all came from Russia. They were fleeing the violence and pogroms of their homeland as well as the anti-Semitic laws instituted during the reign of Czar Nicholas II. In 1880, there were around one hundred Jews living in Boston's West End; by 1910, this number had grown to around forty thousand. The typical Russian Jewish immigrant family was "a literate male with a skilled trade who arrived with an illiterate wife and illiterate children."[3]

Like many Jewish immigrants to Boston, Joe's father was a tailor and was able to find work in Boston's thriving garment trade, but he died when Joe was four. His mother remarried to a widower, another tailor who earned four dollars a week, gambled, and brought an additional five children into the household ("years later we used to refer to it as a merger"[4]), but that marriage broke up when Joe was seven. At a meeting of Boston's West Enders in 1962 at which Joe was the guest of honor, he described a typical day in his childhood, as recorded in Joseph A. MacDonald's account of the evening:

> [Joe] depicted an average day when he was young by saying that after school he would rush in town to Filene's Corner where he sold papers for "Dummy" Miller. After selling papers he would go over to Schraft's Bakery where he would buy a nickel's worth of broken cakes. Then he would go down to Hawley Street where he would collect whatever broken crates and boxes he could take home for the kitchen stove. This was the only fuel that the family had for cooking and heating the flat.
>
> His family by then consisted of eleven children and a boarder and providing for all was a problem.[5]

His other activities around this time included shining shoes and hanging around the train station area insisting to travelers that they wanted their bags carried in exchange for a small fee. "As a kid I never had time to think about what I wanted to become," Joe told Gay Talese. "I went around Boston shining shoes, selling papers and carrying people's bags. I used to pull those suitcases out of their hands and say 'Let me carry your bag mister, oh, let me carry your bag!'"[6]

In addition to the legitimate and semilegitimate ways Joe had of earning a few bucks, he also indulged in some petty larceny. "We were in the iron and steel business," he would joke. "My mother did the ironing and I did the stealing."[7] In Albert and David Maysles's documentary *Showman* (1963), which covers some of the Boston West Enders dinner in 1962, Joe tells his staff a story about his friend Hilkey Alpert. Joe considered him a "rich kid . . . he had shoes, y'know?" On a mission to steal firewood, Hilkey began to cry. When Joe asked him why he was crying, Hilkey said he was cold. Joe was puzzled: "It never occurred to me to be cold before . . . so I started crying too!"

At the dinner, Joe spoke warmly of Hilkey and said he would very much like to meet with him again. Fortuitously, Hilkey was there, as Joseph MacDonald recounts:

> [Joe] asked if his old friend Hilkey Alpert was present and a voice in the rear of the hall said "Here Joe" and he stood up. Dramatically Joe Levine became the little boy from Billerica Street in the West End and he told Hilkey that he had been wanting to see and talk to him for over forty years and he was glad he had found him. He said "Hilkey, your troubles are over. I'll take you to Hollywood and put you in my next picture!"
>
> This was a tense and human moment when two boys who had shared their youthful experiences met after many years. The entire group felt that they were part of this drama and applauded loud and long. Horatio Alger had come to life at this dinner.[8]

In *Showman,* Joe speaks movingly and sincerely about Hilkey and his wish to meet him again, having received a letter from him some time earlier. The moment they were reunited after so many years was undoubtedly an emotional one. But when Joe and Hilkey met later that evening in a more intimate setting, the meeting was awkward. Neither knew quite what to say to the other.[9] They were living in different worlds.

Joe was the living embodiment of the American Dream. He came from nothing and rose to accumulate enormous wealth, influence, and power. Rags-to-riches tales demand a romanticization of the rags as a necessary precursor to the riches, but Joe never, ever romanticized his poverty-stricken childhood, though he did have a dark sense of humor about it: "I can remember dinner: one bagel and a piece of baloney. But I always knew what I weighed. They were weighing me at school because I was undernourished."[10] He would sometimes jokingly request a violin when talking about his past: "Have you got a fiddle? Have you got a hearts-and-flowers record?"[11] But beneath the jokes, he was defiantly unsentimental about his childhood: "I remember the stink of it. When they had a pogrom in

Poland, we'd have one on Billerica Street the next week. . . . I remember nothing good about Billerica Street."[12]

On the streets and within the institutions of Boston (as well as of the United States as a whole), anti-Semitism was rife. One resident of Boston, Isaac Goldberg, recalls his childhood friends at the turn of the century thus: "We were a cosmopolitan gang. . . . There were Italians, Scotch, Irish, Bohemians, Jews and nondescripts. . . . We knew nothing of racial prejudice. . . . Later our education would be completed by our parents; we would learn to hate each other as befits members of a Christian civilization."[13] The tensions caused by the mixing of different groups would later be replaced by tensions from Boston's Balkanization as different ethnicities created their own neighborhoods or demarked their own territories. Later still came the Depression and ethnic resentments intensified by hopelessness and the scapegoating of Jews. "The man who fully exploited these tensions," writes Jonathan D. Sarna,

> and in the process attracted a large local following was Father Charles E. Coughlin, a demagogic radio priest. . . . His call to "drive the money changers from the temple," his scurrilous attacks upon New Dealers, and his fulminations against "International Bankers" struck sympathetic chords in Catholic Boston. . . . In 1935, Coughlin was a guest of Boston City Council . . . a year later his Union Party ran stronger in Boston than in any other American city. Thereafter, beginning in 1938, his anti-Semitism became increasingly overt and raucously strident. He linked communism and atheism with "Jewish internationalism," reprinted the *Protocols of the Elders of Zion,* and embraced fascism. He also established the Christian Front, a quasi-military pro-fascist organization . . . The brutal attacks on local Jews that took place in Boston over the next five years were frequently carried out by Christian Front members.[14]

"Being Jewish is like being black," Joe once told Peter Dunn of London's *Sunday Times.* Dunn further writes: "it is a subject he never mentions in his interviews with American writers," observing, "For so garrulous and joyously indiscreet a man it is perhaps a mark of how deeply it hurt him."[15]

It is true that Joe rarely mentioned in interviews the anti-Semitism he had encountered as a youth and young man, but he was proud of his background, and his Jewishness was a key part of his public persona as well as of his personal and professional life. He often peppered interviews with Yiddish words and Jewish stories and humor. But concern about how his Jewishness might be interpreted by the unsympathetic was in part responsible for his suppression of the documentary *Showman.* Later, he discontinued the booking of his favorite suite in London's Dorchester Hotel when it was taken over by a consortium of Arab businessmen in 1977, and his decision to pull out of the production of *Gandhi* (1982) was, suggests Richard Attenborough, in reaction to the Indian government's diplomatic recognition of the Palestinian Liberation Organization in 1981.[16]

The years of hardship in Boston's West End helped to form the man Joe became, something he duly recognized. He once joked that if Hercules had come from the West End, "he would have been a stronger and better hero."[17] As a child, Joe showed enormous energy, holding down various jobs, learning ways to hustle an extra dollar, and developing the chutzpah that would mature into his defining gift for self-promotion. His upbringing was tough, and alongside the charm and persistence he developed during this time came other more defensive characteristics. The unforgiving nature of his formative years would manifest itself in his less-attractive side, wherein he was abrasive, scheming, unscrupulous, and unpleasant.

These years also shaped Joe's attitude to money. Bernard F. Dick argues in his book about the producer Hal Wallis, Joe's contemporary, that Wallis's poor background explained his nervousness about spending money, whether his own or others', on movie budgets and in his personal life.[18] Joe was the opposite. He kept a reasonably tight control of movie budgets and sought to make many, many cheap films, but his promotional budgets were notoriously lavish, and in his personal life he was massively ostentatious to the point of recklessness. Joe threw money around and did so with joy. "The way I operate," he told Gay Talese, "I gotta think of money as chips. If I think about it as money, I'm lost."[19]

"My mother always called me the *brategiber*—the bread giver," Joe told Talese. "When I reached fourteen, I was finally able to quit school."[20] Joe then drifted between jobs. His first job was as a floor sweeper and general errand boy in a dress factory, and then he went on the road as a dress salesman, an experience he did not care for: "I was shy and I hated standing around with my hat in my hand waiting for some jerk to decide if he would talk to me."[21] He also sang in choirs and performed as a drummer. Within a few years, he was able to go into business with two of his brothers, opening up a dress shop called Le Vine's ("a sort of French name"[22]). Business was good enough for them to open up two more shops, but Joe grew restless. Selling his share to his brothers, he went to New York City, where he worked briefly as a driving instructor and ambulance driver.

An introduction to showmanship came through a sculptor friend who enlisted Joe to help him sell statues of the evangelical preacher Daddy Grace in New York's Harlem. Daddy Grace was the enormously flamboyant founder of the United House of Prayer for All People. He wore loud, colorful suits, shimmered with jewelry, performed faith healings, and preached with gusto to a largely African American congregation. Joe was impressed: "Oh they loved Daddy Grace. He used to baptize them and afterward sell them everything from tooth paste to jock straps. He made millions. When he died he left millions. His long hair flowed over his shoulders and his fingernails were long like Fu Manchu's. What a fascinating son of a bitch he was . . . we sold a lot of statues."[23]

Upon returning to Boston in the 1930s, Joe became part owner of the Cafe Wonderbar on Massachusetts Avenue. "The restaurant business is a funny racket," he said of the Wonderbar. "At 8 p.m. a nicely dressed man comes in and says 'Hi Joe, howaya?' And at 1 a.m. he's drunk and calling me a dirty Jew bastard. Funny business."[24] Nonetheless, the experience was a positive one: "it taught me a lot about meeting the public. I liked meeting the public."[25] It was at the Wonderbar that Joe had his first brush with a minor sort of fame: his name occasionally appeared in the pages of Boston's local press, and he gained a small reputation in the society pages as a "face" in Boston.

It was also at the Wonderbar that Joe took his first steps into the film world when he met "people who helped me in the movie business later. I got to know Mayor Tobin of Boston, who beat [James Michael] Curley. And through the friendship with Tobin I got to know John J. Spencer, who was the movie censor. Spencer the Censor they called him. He's now an undertaker."[26] Joe's earliest venture into the film world was not a successful one. Emboldened by promises from an exhibitor acquaintance, he bought prints of a number of Westerns starring Ken Maynard for $4,000. There are two conflicting versions of this tale. Joe told Paul O'Neil of *Life* that he acquired twenty-five films based on a promise from a grind house cinema operator to pay Joe $12.50 per picture per day: "I started multiplying and I thought I was going to get rich. It never occurred to me that the guy might just run one picture or that he was talking to me just to help out a friend. I never made a nickel out of those westerns."[27] But then Joe told Katherine Hamill that he had acquired only eight Maynard films because an exhibitor friend promised him that he would play one in each of his seven cinemas, but then reneged on the deal. "Nobody honors a contract in this business," Joe said of the affair, "I got stuck." Whether one is to believe either or neither of these tales, it does appear that there was a positive side to the failure. "After that," said Joe, "I took on only exploitation pictures where I could give vent to my peculiar talent."[28]

In the late 1930s, the exploitation trade beckoned Joe with a sex-hygiene film titled *Body Beautiful.* Sex-hygiene films were a staple of the exploitation trade from its beginnings until after the Second World War, when Kroger Babb would refine the presentation of such films into a fine art with *Mom and Dad* (1945), which became, thanks to its low budget, one of the highest-grossing films of the 1940s. *Body Beautiful*, made around 1938, was even less slick, composed of graphic footage of childbirth from an angle few outside of the medical profession would have seen, and supplemented with shots of suppurating genitalia culled from army films warning recruits about the dangers of prostitutes and venereal diseases. Joe spotted an opportunity:

> One day I asked Eddie Klein, the Boston film man, if I could go along with him while he tried to sell these films to theatres. We went up to see Mike Daly, who owns the Daly theatre in Hartford, and after lunch Daly said, "Why don't you guys stick around til tonight. I got a sex picture on here."
>
> That night Klein and I returned and saw a line of people a block long waiting to see a sex-hygiene picture called *Body Beautiful.* The picture showed the birth of a baby, guys getting treated and lots of other stuff the army shows its soldiers. It made me sick, so I bought it. I gave Daly a $4,000 dollar advance for the rights to show the film through the rest of New England. He said all right, and we made $20,000 from that film.[29]

With *Body Beautiful,* Joe entered the exploitation business and "played it up big."[30] He was an exploitation man, and the tactics of the exploitation trade would define him. As Eric Schaeffer notes, "A film could be completely misrepresented by the advertising and could disappoint spectators, yet the ballyhoo that preceded it was part of the overall entertainment experience, a fact that the audience evidently recognized and appreciated and in which they were complicit."[31]

It is difficult to ascertain a precise timeline for Joe's earliest forays into the film world, but we do know the precise date of one other important event in his life from this time. On 19 June 1938, Joe married the blonde and beautiful Rosalie Harrison in Boston, and she would remain his wife and his anchor until his death.

Joe and Rosalie met in 1937. Prior to their engagement, Rosalie had been a singer in Rudy Vallée's backing band. Vallée was one of the most popular crooners and teen idols of the 1930s, and his fame reflected on Rosalie, who was more famous in Boston than Joe at this point. Their wedding earned them a front-page banner headline in the *Boston Times*, declaring "Rosalie Gives Up Career for Joie!"[32] Presumably, the last word is a pun on "Joe" and the word *joie*—French for "joy."

When they met, Joe was still at the Wonderbar but making inroads into the movie world. Rosalie felt it unseemly that her future husband be in the nightclub trade—"she didn't want me in cafes,"[33] Joe later explained—so he sold his stake in the Wonderbar. In 1938, he founded Embassy—the company he would helm for the next four decades. Shortly after their marriage, Joe took out a loan and bought his first movie house, the Little Theatre on Lincoln Street—also known as the Lincoln Theatre—in New Haven, Connecticut. In a foretaste of future juxtapositions, Joe opened the theater with a French art film, *Un Carnet de bal* (1937) by Julien Duvivier, and an exploitation short, *How to Undress in Front of Your Husband* (1937). *Un Carnet de bal* was well received by students from nearby Yale University. The latter film was not. A pseudoeducational documentary, it shows an elegant lady (Ethel Barrie, recently divorced from John Barrymore) delicately disrobing, intercut, for comic effect, with scenes of a larger lady gracelessly taking her clothes off. It was, according to Joe, "a bomb. In the Lincoln Theatre the kids had eggs. When they didn't like something they threw them."[34]

Joe's time at the Little Theatre on Lincoln Street was brief. In 1939, he sold out to the New York movie exhibitor Gilbert Josephson. By that time, Joe had already made further inroads as a small-time movie distributor, and the boy who grew up barefoot in Boston was in the movie business.

2

Investing, Exploiting, Saturating

Even the toughest movie critic had never suggested torching our movies.
—*Sam Arkoff*

In the early 1940s, Joe met Max Rosenberg, and the pair formed a company, in addition to Joe's own Embassy, called Motion Picture Ventures. Their first project was *Gaslight Follies* (1945). Rosenberg had somehow come into possession of a small quantity of silent-film footage and had set about repurposing the scavenged scraps into a full-length feature with added voiceovers for nostalgia value. The footage is scratched and degraded, frames are missing, and some parts are played at the wrong speed. *Gaslight Follies* contains very little material that would have been readily recognizable to an audience in the 1940s, and as a compilation film it is a rather sloppy affair. But it is put together with some wit and flair as an exercise in nostalgia.

The film has five sections: the "Stars of Yesteryear" parade is narrated by Ben Grauer; "Time Marches Back" shows silent newsreel footage and is narrated by John B. Kennedy; "For the Ladies" is a selection of women's fashions from 1905; *The Drunkard* is a 1935 film of Al Martin's stage play and the only section with synchronized sound; and finally *East Lynn*, a twenty-minute 1915 adaptation of Mrs. Henry Wood's hugely successful 1861 novel, which is accompanied by a mocking narration by Milton Cross and Ethel Owen.

One factor that arouses curiosity here is the fame of the voice-over artists. Milton Cross and Ben Grauer had hosted the popular and influential radio variety show *The Magic Key of RCA* in the 1930s; Cross was also well known as the host of the Metropolitan Opera's radio broadcasts, and

Grauer's pedigree in covering domestic and world current events for radio audiences was exceptional. John B. Kennedy was a regular contributor to *The Magic Key of RCA* and many other radio shows, and Ethel Owen, who would later become famous as Mrs. Gibson in *The Honeymooners* TV show, was an accomplished and popular radio performer. Quite how such radio luminaries came to lend their distinguished voices to this hastily cobbled together compilation of scavenged footage for a couple of tyro showmen is something of a mystery. According to Rosenberg's daughter, Elizabeth, Milton Cross in particular "was a very big name in New York broadcasting. Much too big, I think, for my father to approach."[1]

One possible but by no means certain explanation for their involvement in such an unlikely confection is Rosalie Levine. As a singer in Rudy Vallée's band, Rosalie would have had at least some contact with Cross, Grauer, and Kennedy when the band performed on *The Magic Key of RCA*. It should be said that this explanation presumes that Rosalie had extensive influence over the radio stars of the day. Even if this were the case, that such figures should lend their names and voices to a low-rent cash-in such as *Gaslight Follies* is an early incongruity in Joe's career, which would be defined by odd contradictions.

Very little has been written about *Gaslight Follies,* and Joe rarely mentioned it in interviews. Research problems are compounded by the facts that it is sometimes referred to by an alternative title, *The Good Old Days,* and that Rosenberg used the pseudonym "Max Finn" for the production. Some reports suggest that *The Good Old Days* was released in 1943, but there is no contemporary evidence for this. *Gaslight Follies,* however, was certainly released in 1945, shortly after the end of the Second World War. It is possible that *The Good Old Days* was released in 1943 and re-released with a new title in 1945, which would make some sense. If *The Good Old Days* had already been made and released earlier, that would explain its speedy appearance in cinemas following the war's end, with its obvious appeal to cinemagoers nostalgic for the simpler times of the prewar era. Although it is possible that Joe and Rosenberg, with opportunistic eyes on a demob-happy nation, began throwing *Gaslight Follies* together on hearing of Japan's surrender, that option becomes less likely when one considers the participating performers' star status and the fact that the war's end would have filled up their schedules considerably.

The end of the Second World War brought both relief and uncertainty, and audiences were nostalgic for earlier times. Although the victory over

Japan was welcome, the manner of the final victory provoked anxieties as the atomic explosions that destroyed the cities of Hiroshima and Nagasaki ushered in the Atomic Age. "Newly discovered force may lead to world brotherhood or obliterate civilization," wrote Hanson W. Baldwin in the *Los Angeles Times* following the carnage in Nagasaki.[2] Joe and Rosenberg, meanwhile, capitalized on current events: "*Gaslight Follies* is the Greatest Atomic Laugh-Bomb to Hit a Movie Theatre!" was their topical slogan for the movie, neatly combining the apocalyptic with the humorous. Indeed, using the deaths of more than two hundred thousand people to advertise a comedy film so soon after the explosions themselves was gallows humor at its darkest. Joe was a witty man, but Rosenberg had a particularly mordant sense of humor, and it is most likely he who came up with the slogan: "The *Gaslight Follies* poster absolutely sounds like my father," says his daughter.[3]

Alongside this audaciously irreverent pitch, other accompanying ballyhoo placed the emphasis firmly on nostalgia. *Gaslight Follies* was advertised as "the funniest screen show in years. 110 giddy glowing golden minutes of the lush old gaslight days!" Audiences were assured, "You'll wake up in the middle of the night chuckling at the fun of it all," and promised, "It's the funniest-corniest thing you've seen on film." Joe toured the provinces telling reporters, "We're intrigued by the fact that old films, made 30 to 40 years ago, stand up to the test of time so they can be shown over and over again, and still give the viewer pleasure."[4] Reporters seemed to warm to Joe, and his promotional tour provides one of the earliest summations of his approach: the *Hartford Daily Courant* commented, "Joe says funny things. But his mind never leaves his work. He's a smart boy who watches the marbles."[5]

Gaslight Follies was warmly received by critics and praised for its inventiveness. The *Portland Evening Express* welcomed the "definite departure from the usual type film,"[6] and the *Hartford Daily Courant* expressed admiration along similar lines.[7] The *Chicago Times* proffered the unlikely suggestion that "Hollywood is fearing a revival of old silents (with sound added) because of the fortune being reaped in the East by *Gaslight Follies*."[8] In the West, the *Los Angeles Times* critic was also impressed, advising, "If you're so old that nostalgia involuntarily mingles with laughter at viewing the screen stars of your grandma's day, or so young that your film education needs completing by seeing them, you shouldn't miss the show called *Gaslight Follies*."[9]

Gaslight Follies was no blockbuster, just a small-scale miscellany from a newly formed outfit that toured the provinces, but there was an appetite for the nostalgia that Joe and Rosenberg were selling. The months preceding the film's release and the months that it spent on tour saw not only the devastations of Hiroshima and Nagasaki but also the emerging truth about the horror of the Nazi death camps and the barbarism of Japanese prisoner-of-war camps. Relief at the war's end was tempered by tales involving all manner of human degradation, much of which had been made possible by technological progress. By contrast, the world prior to the Great War, as manipulated and presented in *Gaslight Follies,* represented a primitive life light years away from the Teutonic efficiency of the Holocaust and the scientific virtuosity that produced the atomic bomb. *Gaslight Follies* toured the provinces in 1945 and 1946, and its modest success must have pleased Joe. But 1947 was on its way—the year Joe would call "the worst year of my life."[10]

It was not poverty, hunger, or violence that created the worst year of Joe's life, but rather Admiral Richard E. Byrd. Famous as an aviator, explorer, and adventurer, the dashing Admiral Byrd had been a childhood hero to Rosalie Levine. He was also a Bostonite, and Joe had by this time made significant contacts in the upper echelons of Boston society, so it is unsurprising that Byrd's path should cross with Joe's. But Byrd was, in Joe's words, "a difficult man to like."[11]

Between 1928 and 1947, Byrd had led a number of expeditions to Antarctica and had amassed a healthy cache of footage from the expeditions, which he wanted turned into a documentary. The prospect appealed to Joe, so he agreed to invest $20,000 in the project and set about finding the right people to piece the footage together into a film. The film, *Discovery*, was released in 1947 through a deal Joe struck with a company called Film Classics. Although Admiral Byrd promised Joe that he would give him the space to oversee the film project, he interfered every step of the way, leaving Joe exasperated with his demands and imperious manner: "He treated me like I was one of his sailors. He wore his uniform and his medals all the time."[12]

Joe finished the film and set about exploiting it, contending with bizarre interventions by his lofty and eccentric business partner along the way: "Byrd brought up some penguins and said we could use three of them for exploitation in a window of Filene's Department Store in Boston, on the street where I sold papers. I asked Byrd what we were supposed to feed them. He said striped bass. And I had to chase all over town getting striped bass for those penguins!"[13]

Byrd was a huge celebrity at this time. He had recently returned to the United States from his most ambitious Antarctic mission, Operation Highjump, and had gained a reputation as America's greatest living adventurer. With the ballyhoo in place, the premier of *Discovery* took place in Connecticut, as Joe recalls: "I'll say this: when we went to New Haven to open the picture, we had the biggest build-up of all time. We got off the train and there were 22 troops of Boy Scouts, the Yale band, the mayor, the city council and the fire department out to greet the admiral. What do you think happened to the picture? The picture flopped!"[14]

"It's tough trying to substitute penguins for sex"[15] was Joe's assessment of his travails in promoting *Discovery.* But what he fails to mention in his later Byrd-related fulminations and what Byrd may have neglected to tell Joe is that although Joe had access to plenty of black-and-white footage of Byrd's early expeditions to Antarctica, Byrd had provided MGM with Technicolor footage of Operation Highjump, footage that became *The Secret Land* (1948). Following the release of *Discovery,* Byrd came clean in a telegram to *Variety:* "Am informed that there is an impression in southern California that moving picture called *Discovery* last story of last expedition which I led to Antarctic. I greatly regret this mistake. . . . The moving picture of my last expedition to Antarctic is *Secret Land,* being produced by Metro, and is only picture of that expedition so far as I know that is going to be distributed throughout the country."[16]

The Secret Land was in color, with high production values and narration from top stars Robert Montgomery, Robert Taylor, and Van Heflin. It made a tidy profit and was well reviewed. For *Washington Post* reviewer Richard Coe, it was a "completely fascinating record, in Technicolor, of Admiral Byrd's most recent trip to the South Pole . . . a fabulous journey."[17] Bosley Crowther of the *New York Times* concurred: "A vivid and fascinating film record, all in color, of the Navy's expedition which was made to Antarctica 1946–47."[18] Joe, in sad contrast, had to make do with black-and-white shots of expeditions that had been superseded by Operation Highjump.

The Secret Land was not released until a few months after *Discovery,* but it was reported on in the trade press around the time of *Discovery*'s release and had a strong publicity machine behind it. *Discovery* was a small-scale hodge-podge compared to the Technicolor wonder of *The Secret Land.* When *The Secret Land* was released, *Variety* jokingly called it "the one in color."[19] MGM's film could be summed up by its strapline: "One of the World's Most Daring Adventures into the Unknown." Joe's experience, perhaps, could be summed up by *Discovery*'s strapline: "It's Cataclysmic Entertainment."

"I wasn't a businessman," said Joe of the affair, "but Byrd made me one."[20] And indeed he did. Faced with the prospect of losing $20,000, it occurred to Joe that *Discovery* could be seen as educational, so he ordered a bunch of 16-mm prints to be made of the film and sold them to colleges.

Alongside his attempts in film production, Joe was keeping busy as a distributor in New England with his partner, Max Rosenberg. It was a lively time to be working as a local film distributor, and Joe and Rosenberg peddled whatever exploitation films they could get their hands on while also distributing arthouse product. European cinema, in particular Italian neorealist films, were popular in the postwar years with both arthouse and exploitation audiences. European films were considered racy compared to Hollywood films and were advertised as such. Even films with no sexual content whatever would feature an alluring lady in a state of partial undress on the publicity material. "The line between art cinema and exploitation," says exploitation historian Eric Schaeffer, "was often a thin one."[21]

Motion Picture Ventures' main supplier of arthouse cinema was Mayer-Burstyn, the company formed by Arthur Mayer and Joseph Burstyn in 1937 and one of the most important distributors of the era. It provided Joe and Rosenberg with Italian neorealist films such as *Open City* (1945), *The Bicycle Thief* (1948), and *Paisan* (1946)—films that were neither critically nor commercially successful in Italy but quickly became considered masterpieces in America. Though Joe was only a distributor for Mayer-Burstyn in New England, later in his career he would routinely take credit for importing these films—and was given credit for doing so by those who should have known better. On one occasion, Mayer was moved to write to the *Los Angeles Times* on behalf of his late partner to take issue with a piece written by Charles Champlin: "Burstyn was a marvelous little man who, more than anyone else, was responsible for bringing foreign films into American Theatres, and I am indignant that his services should not only be belittled but actually ignored."[22]

Nonetheless, Joe and Rosenberg's reputation as distributors in New England was growing, and one important development for postwar movie entrepreneurs came with the U.S. Supreme Court decision on *United States v. Paramount Pictures, Inc.* (334 U.S. 131), which ruled that for studios to control the production, distribution, and exhibition of films constituted an unfair practice. The major studios were ordered to divest themselves of their theater chains, and block-booking (whereby exhibitors were obliged to rent up to a whole season of films from a studio in order to gain access to the handful that might be profitable) was outlawed, thus opening up opportunities for smaller companies to cater for the emptying screens.[23]

In the early 1950s, when the ramifications of the *Paramount* decision were still being felt, Joe split with Rosenberg. According to Elizabeth Rosenberg, "The split with Levine was over an agreement not honored, but by whom and over what specifically I don't know."[24] According to Max Rosenberg, "Our partnership ended with a whimper, not a bang, largely because Joe owed me $30,000," adding, with his customary wit, "Joe's biggest contribution to the film industry was the 28-course meal."[25] Following his split with Joe, Rosenberg teamed up with Milton Subotsky to produce the rock-and-roll classic *Rock Rock Rock!* (1956) before he and Subotsky moved their operations to Great Britain to set up the horror studio Amicus.

Also around this time, in 1952, Mayer split with Burstyn because Burstyn wanted to concentrate on his own distribution company, Joseph Burstyn Inc. When Burstyn died in 1953, it was rumored that Joe would be taking over the company.[26] Joe certainly distributed the Burstyn import *Little Fugitive* in New England in 1953, and Joe Burstyn Inc. distributed a few other films after Burstyn's death, but the extent of Joe's involvement is not known.

Joe continued distributing films in New England and learning the exploitation trade. One genre of exploitation film that was particularly popular after the war was the atrocity picture. These films purported to show war crimes being committed by the Nazis or the Japanese—more often the latter—to appeal to the American audience's sense of postvictory righteousness. One film in this genre that found its way into Joe's hands was *Ravaged Earth* (c. mid-1940s), a film of Japanese atrocities in China made, according to some reports, by a Shanghai businessman. Some years later Joe excitedly recounted the hyperbolic copy he wrote for the billboards: "'*See it!*' I wrote, '*It will make you fighting mad! Jap Rats Stop at Nothing! See the Rape of China!*'"[27]

Joe wanted a classy place to show his latest acquisition, but he got ripped off again. He went to see a famous theater impresario in Boston, Lee Shubert (whose family had established the Broadway district in New York City), and struck a deal. "I shook hands with Lee Shubert! That was like shaking hands with Khrushchev. Nobody told me that I got a standby stage crew with the theatre and a standby orchestra and even a standby treasurer and I had to pay them all every day."[28] *Ravaged Earth* bombed, but salvation came in the form of an unscrupulous exploitation man: "After we'd run ten days a fellow came in to see me and he said 'I've got a picture called *Scorched Earth.* I might open it in Boston.' I said, 'Are you trying to blackmail me?' He said 'Yes.' So we moved his picture in and mine out, changed one word of the advertising on *Ravaged Earth* and nobody knew the difference. We had a big run."[29]

Joe was often on the very brink of disaster at this time, but something always came along to save him—be it luck, fate, or his own street smarts. Nonetheless, he made ever bigger gambles. In the early 1950s, Joe, who by now owned a handful of cinemas, decided to set up a drive-in. Convinced, rightly, that drive-ins were the future, he rashly spent $90,000 on a plot of real estate in Springfield, Massachusetts, to turn into a drive-in theater, replete with two hundred thousand tons of gravel that had to be shifted.

> The contractor and his men kept disappearing on other jobs. Bad weather would have ruined us. I got a printer to make me one engraved invitation to a grand opening and sent it to him. The next day he was on the phone screaming, "This says you're opening in three weeks!" He worked day and night and we made it. Opening night the place was jammed. The fellow with the concessions had put in $15,000 worth of freezing equipment, but he got so rattled he forgot the ice-cream. RCA had given me a screen and electronic equipment on credit—but 10 minutes before we were due to run all the fuses blew on account of the freezers. I walked outside in the dark and sat down and cried. The lights came back on with a minute to go. I blew my top and told the ice-cream man to start tearing out the damned freezers or I'd tear them out and shove them down his throat. But it all worked out all right. The ice-cream man and I made up, the lights stayed on, and it's one of the best drive ins in the country.[30]

The big gamble, the huge amount of expended energy, the enterprise about to end in disaster, and the "lights" coming back on at the last minute would be a recurrent theme in Joe's career. But he was not just lucky, and he did not bet blind. If there was one sector of movie exhibition that was booming in the America of the 1950s, it was the drive-in. They were so popular that not only did they have their own nickname, "ozoners," but traditional movie theaters also acquired a new nickname in the trade press, "hardtops," to distinguish them from their open-air counterparts.

Because of battles with the film industry, drive-ins were rarely used for first runs. In their heyday in the 1950s, drive-ins would feature sideshows, beauty contests, circus acts, playgrounds, launderettes, and funfairs as well as the food-and-drink concession stands. "More and more drive-ins turned to selling an evening of fun," writes ozoner historian Kerry Segrave, "in which the film being screened was only a part—and not necessarily the most important one."[31] The drive-in was an ideal place for Joe to develop his multifarious talents as he learned the different ways to accommodate the different audiences that frequented ozoners. One rule he developed was to banish all clowns from the park after 4:30 p.m. "Kids love clowns, especially if the clowns give them candy, but teenagers hate clowns and wouldn't be caught dead near one."[32]

At his drive-in, Joe experimented with double bills. Noticing that one bad film would leave the place empty, but two bad films would pack the place, he began to work on ways to attract crowds. To be sure, double bills were nothing new, having become popular in the 1930s, but Joe was looking for an alchemy beyond the standard supporting-plus-main-feature formula. The crowds would not come for one Abbott and Costello movie, but they would for two Abbott and Costellos; they wouldn't come for *Black Cat* (1934), but they would come for *Black Cat* and *Black Friday* (1940). Rosalie called these experiments "Double Awfuls."[33]

A man of like mind was Sam Arkoff of American Releasing Corporation (ARP), the company that would morph into American International Pictures (AIP) in 1954. His company became the foremost producer and provider of low-budget weirdies aimed at teenagers and often sold films as a double-bill package to drive-in operators. ARP and subsequently AIP were probably more famous for their exploitation campaigns than for the films themselves: "Why don't you put sprocket holes in the posters and throw the movies away?" one exhibitor is said to have asked Arkoff.[34] Because of a lack of first-run features with decent production values to fill the schedules, drive-ins became synonymous with knock-offs, rip-offs, copies, cash-ins, and weirdies from the likes of AIP and other low-budget producers.

Arkoff, like Joe, was quick to recognize the importance of ozoners.

They did most of their business in the summer, for obvious reasons, which had traditionally been a slow time for movie exhibitors because patrons preferred to indulge in other pursuits in the sunshine and because few hard-tops had air-conditioning. There was, then, a gap in the summer market. The drive-in crowd also had their own tastes, which were shaped by their surroundings. They liked movies in color because it showed up better on the outdoor screen. They were not looking for films with critical acclaim, either. They liked, according to one operator, "any picture with action that fits into the holiday mood."[35] Typical drive-in fare, according to Arkoff, was "pictures intended to be watched on forty-foot-high, drive-in screens through steamed up windshields, and heard through tinny car speakers over the sound of crunching, buttered popcorn."[36]

Joe struck up a relationship with Arkoff in the early 1950s and distributed Arkoff's films in New England. In his memoirs, Arkoff remembers Joe being particularly taken with an early film, *The Beast with 1,000,000 Eyes* (1955). Although Joe had not yet seen this film, he was so enticed by the title and exploitation material that he promised Arkoff that he could sell the picture to a big Los Angeles distributor. Upon seeing the film, however, he reportedly offered Arkoff $100,000 for the title and publicity on the condition that the film be burned so that Joe could make his own version. Arkoff demurred: "Even the toughest movie critic had never suggested torching our movies. I politely told Levine that we were 'flattered' by his offer, but we still thought the picture might find an audience."[37]

Joe was an exploitation man, and he would remain an exploitation man until the day he died. But it was not small-time hustling that brought him to international prominence—it was saturation, and he learned the tools of this particular trade in New England with *Duel in the Sun* in 1954. *Duel in the Sun* had been a pioneering saturation release on its original appearance in 1946. Prior to that release, the film had suffered from negative word of mouth as reports of cost overruns and production problems appeared in the press. As a way of countering this negative publicity, producer David O. Selznick engaged the services of an expert distribution man, Neil Agnew, formed his own distribution company, Selznick Releasing Organization (SRO, letters that also stood for "standing room only"), and opened the film in a saturation pattern that was novel at the time.

Saturation openings in 1946 were markedly different from what they are today, where a single film can open worldwide on the same day. In the mid–twentieth century, a saturation pattern would consist of around four hundred prints, opening in two or three territories simultaneously, often beginning in big cities before moving around the country from territory to territory, accompanied by a trumpeting publicity blitz that covered local press, radio, store promotions, and poster campaigns. When done correctly, such campaigns could create a sense of anticipation rooted in eventism—an urgent and inclusive pitch: "Coming Soon to a Theater Near You!" The reviews of *Duel in the Sun* on its initial release were mixed, but the promotional campaign emphasized the exploitable elements—the film was based on a popular novel, and it had a big budget, big stars, and sex appeal. The saturation technique was successful at bringing in the crowds, but not so successful at bringing in profits. The film was expensive, as was the saturation promotion, so *Duel in the Sun* did little more than break even at that time.

MGM copied *Duel in the Sun*'s saturation technique in 1947 with another big-budget starry vehicle, *The Hucksters*—and with similar box-office disappointment. But Joe saw that if an already-made film could be acquired at a reasonable price, the saturation technique could be profitable. So in 1954 he acquired the New England rights for *Duel in the Sun* and set about promoting it bombastically with 120 prints in what he later wistfully remembered as "my first big saturation."[38] The state-of-the-art production, stars, and sex appeal had already been paid for; they just had to be sold again. Selznick's asking price was $35,000. Joe agreed:

> I went to see a banker I didn't even know. His name is Alan Sturges and he lives just outside of Boston. He runs a country bank, and after office hours he sits outside on the porch and greets friends who come to see him. He's an old-time banker, and the kind you seldom see these days. Sturges loaned me the $35,000 and I bought *Duel in the Sun.* I showed it in New England in indoor and outdoor theatres. I'm a great believer in outdoor theatres. I made half a million dollars on the picture and then looked around to see what other motion pictures were for sale.[39]

Joe's 120 prints toured the thousand-plus cinemas of the six states that make up New England, with Joe trying to get his film into as many theaters as possible. It played on 250 screens in the first twenty-one days of release. New England was, by this time, home to more than 150 drive-ins, and *Duel in the Sun* fit the remit. It was an action picture in color for operators starved of product, and the saturation ballyhoo further supplemented the holiday mood that drive-in operators sought to create in their parks. Joe was making a gamble, but it paid off and made him a small fortune. With his eye on much bigger fortunes, he took all the lessons he had learned, and the talents he had developed and looked for an opportunity to apply them on a much bigger stage.

3

Monsters and Man-Gods

> It had a good title . . . I mean, whoever heard of Ben-Hur? But you go out in the street and lift up a manhole cover and ask, "Who was Hercules?" You'll get an answer.
>
> —*Joseph E. Levine*

The *Paramount* decision of 1948 may have created opportunities for independent operators like Joe to gain a stronger foothold in the movie business, but it had other keenly felt repercussions within the traditional movie industry. The dismantling of studio monopolies was compounded by the threat to the movie business from television, and in such a fearful climate much of Hollywood was looking to play it safe. Though no longer beholden to studio diktats, the exhibitors ironically suffered the most following the *Paramount* case. Lincoln Freeman explained the ramifications of the law of unintended consequences to *Fortune* readers in 1955: "Delivered of the 'ruinous' obligation to buy an entire program of pictures (block-booking), the theatre man suddenly discovered that he had lost his inventory. Then he complained that not only was he unable to forecast what picture he would be showing next April; in order to have one to show at all, he had to enter into 'ruinous' competitive bidding for a commodity that, he was convinced, was produced in minimum quantities so a higher film rental could be squeezed out of him."[1]

Whether producers were deliberately reducing supply to increase demand is debatable. Diminishing audiences made film production riskier, and caution led to fewer productions, which, as in a self-fulfilling prophecy, led to diminishing audiences. Such caution was bad news for exhibitors. In 1953, Leonard H. Goldenston, president of American Broadcasting–Paramount Theatres, warned the Theatre Owners of America that high rental prices and film shortages represented greater threats to the film industry than television and then delivered the doomladed prediction of "less patrons, less money, less theatres, and so less production and therefore, self-destruction."[2]

One way in which the studios fought back against the threat from television was to invest in lavish spectaculars, or "supercolossals": epic cinematic experiences that gave the audiences something they could not get for free at home on blurry back-and-white television sets. In terms of publicity, high-end, high-budget films were well catered for. Colossals such as *Quo Vadis* (1951), *The Robe* (1953), and *Ben Hur* (1959) were well publicized and benefited from a range of innovative exploitation techniques such as "roadshowing"—opening in big cities in a limited release and aping the more prestigious legitimate theater with conceits such as intermissions, seat reservations, and souvenir programs before being released nationally.[3] This consolidation of investment only led to further frustration for the exhibitor. In addition to the high rental prices these expensive and prestigious productions commanded, their publicity budgets focused on metropolitan areas and first-run theaters, while subsequent-run theaters became increasingly overlooked by distributors. The nonmetropolitan, provincial exhibitors, hungry for product, had little choice but to take such offerings despite not being able to capitalize on the initial barrage of publicity, which had all but petered out by the time a movie reached the provinces. The midbudget films and B pictures that had been the studios' bread and butter and the lifeblood of the provincial exhibitor diminished in number throughout the 1950s and were often not well publicized.

Extravagant promotion for grand epics aside, many Hollywood studios sought to cut corners by bureaucratizing the publicity process because eschewing across-board exploitation in favor of identifying and targeting niche audiences brought advertising costs down. But contracting polling and market-research firms to identify niches and demographics followed the model of "spend a dollar to save a cent," indicative of an almost superstitious belief in the efficacy of social science and its application to movie promotion. Again, this development placed yet more pressure on exhibitors, who either had to adapt niche marketing to appeal to the local audience or come up with their own selling techniques. But exhibitors, as one industry watcher observed, "are *businessmen* not *showmen*."[4]

In the late 1930s and 1940s, most exhibitors had operated as vendors for studio product and therefore lacked the necessary entrepreneurial flair for movie promotion. This was significant turnaround. In the 1920s and early 1930s, "showmen" is precisely what many exhibitors considered themselves to be as they integrated films into a fuller evening's entertainment.[5] The emergence of block-booking in the 1930s, wherein an exhibitor was obliged to buy a whole program of films from his studio supplier, diminished the exhibitors' showmanship skills as the showman-exhibitor became a product programmer. Joe was not *telling* everybody this is a circus business; he was "*reminding* everybody this is a circus business."[6]

America's exhibitor anxiety was assuaged to a certain extent in the 1950s by America's atomic anxiety and the monster movies that followed in its wake. These saturation openers provided exhibitors with the product they craved, and the blunderbuss publicity provided the showmanship that exhibitors were now ill equipped to devise.

In 1956, *Godzilla: King of the Monsters* was Joe's first nationwide saturation success. It was fashioned from a film titled *Gojira* produced by Japan's Toho Studios in 1954, which tells the story of the eponymous fire-breathing lizard who, awakened from slumber by atomic testing, wreaks havoc on Tokyo. The inspiration for this film came from producer Tomoyuki Tanaka, who had read a trade-publication synopsis of an American movie called *The Beast from 20,000 Fathoms* (1953), which tells the story of the titular fire-breathing lizard who, awakened from slumber by atomic testing, wreaks havoc on San Francisco. Though its low budget is evident on-screen, *The Beast from 20,000 Fathoms* contains some wonderful stop-motion animation designed by Ray Harryhausen. *Godzilla,* meanwhile, features a man wearing a dinosaur costume. For its American release, *Gojira* was retitled, truncated, and reedited to include inserts featuring an American reporter, Steve Martin (Raymond Burr), who explains the goings-on in English for the benefit of the American audience.

Attempting to unpick who did what during *Gojira*'s transformation into *Godzilla* is notoriously difficult; the story of its journey is complicated by countless contradictory reports. Many people, including Joe, have claimed credit for buying the American distribution rights to *Gojira* from Toho, but the safest bet is Edmund Goldman of Manson International, given his close ties with Toho at the time. Goldman bought the rights in late 1955 and then sold them to Dick Kay and Harry Ross (a.k.a. Harry Rybnick) of Jewell Enterprises, a company specializing in the production and distribution of exploitation movies, most of which were fashioned from existing movies with newly filmed inserts. Kay and Ross reedited and retitled *Gojira* and hired Terry Morse to direct the inserts featuring Raymond Burr.

It is difficult to know precisely when Joe became involved with *Godzilla.* Given his maverick reputation and his habit of overclaiming credit, many modern accounts give him a little too much credit for bringing *Godzilla* to the American public, but *Godzilla*'s success should more correctly be ascribed to group endeavor. It is also important to remember that prior to *Godzilla* Joe was not much more that a New England distributor, although he had had some nationwide distribution experience. His success thus far notwithstanding, he did not leap on to the national stage in a single bound. Contemporary sources attribute *Godzilla*'s distribution to a collaboration between Embassy and Jewell. This collaboration took the form of a new company, Transworld, set up in February 1956 by Joe and Edward Barison, a producer at Jewell who would later work for Joe at Embassy. That same month, Joe screened *Godzilla* for the industry's overlooked exhibitors, who were presented with an oversize seventeen-by-eleven-inch promotional press book promising saturation TV and radio publicity.

Another hugely important figure in the success of *Godzilla* is Terry Turner. In his mid-sixties by the time of *Godzilla*'s release, Turner was a seasoned promoter, exploitation man, and motor-mouth raconteur. He had made his name in the 1920s as a promoter of human attractions for Loews Theaters. He hyped two sets of conjoined twins (then known as Siamese twins) in quick succession: first the Hilton Sisters, then, once that partnership had come to an acrimonious end, their rivals, the Gibb sisters. He achieved more fame and notoriety for promoting the so-called Ubangi Tribe (or "Saucer Lipped People") from the Belgian Congo, initially at a burlesque house and then at circuses in the United States. These and other lurid successes led to him being hired by RKO as an exploitation executive, where he became a pioneer in the adoption of a rival medium, radio, in movie promotion.

In 1943, while promoting *Hitler's Children*, a low-budget RKO propagandistic film about the Hitler Youth, Turner suspected that radio publicity for the film was having a positive effect on box-office takings. The film is based on the book *Education for Death* by Gregor Ziemer, and Ziemer was a notable radio personality in the Midwest. Speculating that there was a causative correlation between Ziemer's radio presence and the film's success in that region, Turner opted to spend 40 percent of his promotional budget on radio announcements, prepared by Orson Welles's Mercury Players, when he opened the film in other territories. The strategy worked, and *Hitler's Children* made more than $3 million from a production budget of around $165,000.[7]

The following decade Turner would be among the first to utilize another rival medium, television, for movie promotion. As had been the case with radio, much of Hollywood was in fearful retreat from this new rival and unwilling to have prestigious product sullied by engagement with an upstart medium. Once again Turner was an early adopter and embraced multimedia publicity involving television, radio, and newspapers to great success. He experimented with television promotion for RKO's re-release of Disney's *Snow White and the Seven Dwarfs* (1937) in 1952 before masterminding RKO's hugely successful re-release of another of *Godzilla*'s antecedents, *King Kong* (1933), that same year: "Television, the ogre of Hollywood, will become the golden goose of the film industry," predicted Turner in 1952.[8] As the 1950s wore on, and with television sales steadily increasing, Turner wrote in *Variety*, "I am more convinced than ever that television (as a solid sales instrument and not as an exploitation gimmick) is here to stay."[9] Throughout his career, Joe was a staunch supporter of using television in exploitation campaigns, and Turner may well have been the initial source of his enthusiasm.

On leaving RKO in 1952, Turner was employed by Joe and worked on various projects, including *Gangbusters* (1955, four episodes of the TV show spliced together for a cinema release), *Wiretapper* (1955, a low-budget thriller), and *Walk into Hell* (1956, an Australian film titled *Walk into Paradise* until Joe decided that *Walk into Hell* would be better box office). Away from Embassy, Turner was the driving force behind the exploitation campaign for *The Beast from 20,000 Fathoms.* Inspired in no small part by *King Kong*'s re-release in 1952, the following year's *The Beast from 20,000 Fathoms* was produced by Mutual Pictures of California and, proving that not *all* Hollywood was consumed with cautiousness regarding promotion and distribution, released by a major studio, the "once violently anti-TV" Warner Bros.,[10] in a saturation pattern amid a blaze of publicity. Following *Beast*'s box-office success, Warner Bros. produced its own monster shocker, *Them!,* about killer ants giganticized by radiation, to further success in another saturation pattern in 1954, just as Joe was refining his own saturation techniques with *Duel in the Sun* in New England. Warner would later distribute *Hercules.*

The saturation openers of the 1950s were of a different stripe from those of the 1940s, such as *Duel in the Sun* and *The Hucksters.* The 1950s saturationers were not star-filled and big budget, or even midbudget. They were quick, cheap, star-free creature features that sought to profit from the atomic anxiety of the age, as Joe had done a decade earlier with *Gaslight Follies*. The public appetite for monster movies had been whetted by the re-release of *King Kong* and the heavy rotation on television of Universal horrors from the 1930s, such as *Dracula* (1931) and *Frankenstein* (1931). The cheapness of the 1950s monster movies meant more money could be invested in promotion and distribution to maximize profit rather than merely breaking even, as Selznick's *Duel in the Sun* had done. Also, America's growing media presented opportunities for greater penetration of promotion. A greater diversity in print media, such as pulp publications, kids' comics, and youth magazines, provided varied and focused advertising opportunities, while the burgeoning popularity of radio and television saw the airwaves contributing to saturation promotion alongside poster and print.

Three weeks before *Godzilla*'s release, a full-page ad in *Variety* boasted, "When it comes to Monsters—we got 'em!" and bragged about the four hundred theaters scheduled to screen the film. Subsequent reports emphasized the film's frantic campaign of ballyhoo. A fortnight after its New York premier in April, *Variety* reported that *Godzilla* was playing in first-run houses throughout America.[11] The promotional campaign was full of the hyperbole and wit that would bring Joe fame. Godzilla was the "Incredible! Unstoppable! Titan of Terror!!" *King Kong*, now an American icon thanks to its re-release and television airing, was back in theaters again in 1956, so *Godzilla*'s posters took a sly swipe: "*Godzilla* makes *King Kong* Look Like a Midget!"

With enthusiastic reportage in the trade press and exhibitors ready to count receipts, Bosley Crowther, the *New York Times* film critic, was more depressed than impressed. Reporting on *Godzilla*'s premier at Loew's State Theatre in New York City on 26 April, Crowther damned *Godzilla* as "incredibly awful," adding, "it is too bad that a respectable theatre has to lure children and gullible grown-ups with such fare."[12] This review provides a taste of things to come. Although Crowther did not yet know the name "Joseph E. Levine," he would become one of Joe's most vocal and bitter critics, and the theme of the disreputable clashing with the respectable would become a feature of Joe's career, as it is of *Godzilla*'s afterlife.

In the years and decades following *Godzilla*'s release, it achieved the status of a cult camp classic in the "so bad it's good" vein. Subsequently, the swinging pendulum of cultural values and a dash of purist revisionism have afforded another reevaluation of the fire-breathing monster, making *Godzilla* a target of some ire from those who believe that it is a bastardization of a classic of allegorical cinema—the original *Gojira*. But the argument that *Godzilla* jettisoned the subtextual allusions to the atomic attacks on Hiroshima and Nagasaki so as not to offend an American audience is overstated; even Crowther grudgingly acknowledged the allegorical resonances in his scathing review. The counterargument is that where *Gojira* is ponderous, *Godzilla* is pacy, and while the Steve Martin inserts may appear clumsy, the on-the-spot reporter conceit was an innovative way of bypassing a protracted and expensive dubbing process. One must also acknowledge that only those gifted with truly outstanding precognitive abilities regarding the capriciousness of cultural values could have predicted that a creature feature starring a guy in a lizard outfit would one day be hailed as a masterpiece. As Jewell's Dick Kay attested, "It was a matter of bucks, not art."[13]

Context is all important when it comes to *Godzilla*. Joe and company capitalized on cultural and industrial trends—namely, atomic anxiety, the creature-feature craze, and the nascent innovations in saturation promotion and distribution. For Joe, it was an important learning experience and a dry run for his *Hercules* campaign. He learned not only how to mount a huge national campaign but also how to get the industry on his side—especially the exhibitors. He also learned the importance of timeliness, opportunism, and the importance of spotting and taking advantage of emerging cultural and industrial trends.

Godzilla's success started its own trend with a craze for Japanese monster movies in America. Distributors Corporation of America distributed *Rodan* (1956) with successful saturation and promotion in 1957, and Warner Bros. distributed the *Godzilla* sequel, *Godzilla Raids Again* (1955) in 1959, attempting to pass the eponymous lizard off as an entirely new creature by retitling it *Gigantis: The Fire Monster*. Joe acquired the rights to *The Mysterians* (1957) and claimed he did so by impressing Toho's owner, Ichizo Kobayashi, with a card trick. *The Mysterians* was distributed by MGM with saturation tactics but without success as the market became crowded with Japanese monsters and the novelty began to wear off.

As the paying public's appetite for Japanese monsters waned, Joe looked to Italy for the Next Big Thing. *Attila* (1954) was a cheap Italian peplum movie about Attila the Hun, played by Anthony Quinn, and was distributed amid the din of a tremendous promotional campaign by

Embassy in 1958. *Attila* was put together by a group of people with whom Joe would remain associated, to varying degrees, for the years to come. It was directed by Pietro Francisci, who would go on to direct the *Hercules* movies; its female lead is Sophia Loren, and it was produced by her husband, Carlo Ponti—both of whom would engage in fruitful relationships with Joe throughout the 1960s.[14] Producing alongside Ponti was another future superproducer, Dino De Laurentiis, who would also have dealings with Joe in the coming years. Prior to Joe's success with *Attila,* both Ponti and De Laurentiis had dismissed it as "a dog."[15]

Retaining the services of Terry Turner and employing a couple more exploitation men along the way, Joe cranked up the promotional intensity for *Attila.* He bought the distribution rights for $80,000 and blew more than half a million on exploitation, leading to a gross of more than $2 million. Importantly, *Attila*'s posters were the first to bear the legend "Joseph E. Levine Presents," words that would grace the promotional materials for hundreds of films over the next thirty years. Joe's giant campaigns and the impressive numbers associated with them attracted the attention of the trade press as Joe's name featured with increasing regularity in the pages of *Variety,* which in April 1959 sought to explain who this fifty-three-year-old new kid on the block was as he prepared the *Hercules* campaign that would make his name: "The picture of Levine is a hazy one at best. About all that is generally known about him is that he is a Johnny-come-lately who has made his pile by his extremely immoderate gambling on the distribution and exploitation of such screen fare as *Godzilla, Attila* and, now, *Hercules.*"[16] The story is perhaps the earliest profile of Joe that we have. It was also a plant, written by one of Joe's press agents, Bill Doll, and appropriately published on April Fools' Day.

As if embodying his own personal saturation pattern, within a few months this little-known minimogul would become the most famous and recognizable showman in America and would remain so until his death. As Joe became more and more familiar to the trade press, the more the trade press warmed to him. As the *Hercules* campaign gathered pace, his name became ubiquitous in the trades; and as the industry welcomed a new showman in its midst, a gentle rewriting of history was taking place in the pages of *Variety.* The exploitation campaigns for *Godzilla* and *Attila,* which, like the campaigns for *Wiretapper* and *Walk into Hell,* had hitherto been attributed to Terry Turner, were now attributed to Joe, as was the initial acquisition of the distribution rights for *Godzilla.*

That Joe received credit where it was perhaps undeserved or should have been shared is not just a testament to his gift for self-promotion, habit of credit stealing, and ease with bullshit; it also reflected the fact that his ascent from nowhere onto the national stage was a good story. Joe gave the trade and national popular press good copy. Also, as Joe was rising to prominence, a ghoulish gap opened up in the market. In 1958, Mike Todd, the great theater impresario and movie producer, was killed in a plane crash and left a showman-shaped hole to be filled. A great flim-flam man and movie legend Elizabeth Taylor's third husband, Todd and his antics were well known and well loved throughout the United States. In the movie world, he is best remembered for his production of *Around the World in Eighty Days* in 1956, a film that boasted cameo appearances by some forty-odd stars for novelty value, ballyhoo, and ticket sales. Todd, having sunk millions of his own dollars in the movie, personally placed "Theater Full" signs outside half-empty theaters in order to generate a buzz among the public. Twelve months after Todd's death, *Film Bulletin* was excitedly welcoming his replacement: "Exhibitors, and anyone else watching the skies for another showman comet to replace the late Mike Todd, might well have blinked their eyes in wonder and anticipation last week. From all celestial indications, it had appeared again—in the person of an affable, dynamic, 53 year old New Englander with the physique of a Notre Dame 'watch charm' guard. His name: Joseph E. Levine."[17]

Joe's massive *Hercules* campaign, orchestrated without Turner, began quietly with stories in local newspapers. In April 1958, the *Boston Daily Record* ran a short interview with Joe. When asked about his next film, he would only say that his newest prospect, like *Attila,* hailed from Italy. When pressed for details, he was tantalizingly cagey: "These things I can't tell you. . . . If I did, I'd have nine competitors on the plane with me. I've got a seven-day option now. I want to make it permanent . . . maybe," before adding presciently, "You never can tell . . . your next million could be lying in a tin can in Europe."[18]

Joe was already a personality in the pages of the Boston press, but tales of him flying to and from Europe bled beyond Boston's borders as many provincial publications carried the curious story of a little-known little man journeying to Italy to acquire, maybe, the rights to a film whose title he would not reveal. But while *Hercules* remained unmentioned, Joe still got his own name into the papers. Right from the get-go, the *Hercules* campaign was not just about promoting *Hercules;* it was about promoting Joseph E. Levine.

Hercules was no *Around the World in Eighty Days.* It was no slick Hollywood production. It was foreign, badly dubbed, and shoddily made, and the closest thing it had to a star was Steve Reeves—a former Mr. Universe who played the titular man-god. Whatever *Hercules* had going for it, it would not have been to everyone's taste. Despite the budget limitations of *The Beast from 20,000 Fathoms, Them!,* and *Godzilla,* these films were imaginative and inventive, and they responded to contemporary anxieties about the atomic age. By contrast, *Hercules* was a fairly crummy cash-in, or by-product, of the Hollywood roadshow spectaculars that became such a feature of American cinema in the 1950s. Supercolossals, such as *Quo Vadis* and *Ben Hur,* were often partly made in Italy because of lower production costs, and *Time* magazine coined the phrase "Hollywood on the Tiber" to describe these "runaway productions." Many of the technicians who gained filmmaking experience working on Hollywood epics would also work on films such as *Attila, Hercules,* and other films of the Italian peplum boom.

As if to underscore the flagrant opportunism of the cash-in on the Hollywood colossals, Joe joked that he considered retitling *Hercules* as *Ben Hur-cules* but recognized the power of the film's immediately recognizable eponym: "It had a good title. . . . I mean, whoever heard of Ben-Hur? But you go out in the street and lift up a manhole cover and ask, 'Who was Hercules?' You'll get an answer."[19] Riding in the slipstream of Hollywood's spectaculars also applied to promotional slogans. *Hercules*'s bombastic pronouncements were tongue-in-cheek apings of the earnest entreaties of Hollywood's more prestigious epics. If *Quo Vadis* was the "Most Colossal Film Ever" and *Ben Hur* the "Greatest Spectacle Ever Filmed," then *Hercules* was "Produced on a Scale so Lavish, so Spectacular, Only the Huge Motion Picture Screen Can Do It Justice!" Joe's instinct to oversell placed *Hercules* at the center of a carnivalesque entertainment experience wherein the ballyhoo was just as important as the movie, if not more so.

Joe was not just selling a movie, he was selling himself, and with *Hercules* the film's very badness would serve as testament to his skills as a showman when box office success came. "When I was told about *Hercules,*" he told Louella Parsons, "I flew over to look at it. The picture broke down when we were showing it, but there was something about it that made me realize there was a potential fortune in it."[20] Joe spent $120,000 on distribution rights and an additional $120,000 on dubbing and reediting it to render the thing palatable. Then he rammed it down the nation's throats with a $1 million exploitation campaign that ran relentlessly for nearly a month before a saturation release of 635 prints—the largest order Kodak had ever had and a record for the number of prints of a single film in simultaneous circulation. Following Todd's death, Joe took heed of one of Todd's cherished maxims: "People are impressed by *bigness,* regardless of content."[21]

If the content of *Hercules* was thin, the bigness of the campaign would compensate, so Joe began selling *Hercules* and himself to the industry, particularly to the hard-done-by exhibitors. In response to complaints about a lack of forewarning about upcoming product,[22] Joe began courting exhibitors four months before the *Hercules* release date. On 20 March 1959, he hosted a massive "Explodation" luncheon for exhibitors at the Waldorf Astoria in New York City, in the process coining a portmanteau word inspired by Samuel Rosen, executive vice president of Stanley Warner Theatres, who had told Joe, "You're not going to *launch* this picture, you're going to *explode* it!"[23] The luncheon was attended by twelve hundred exhibitors and other guests. Those who were not able to attend received a missive from Joe to "Friend Exhibitor," detailing the plan of action for the ten-day "explodation" that was to happen in July, including information on print runs, listings of the magazines that would contain full-page ads for the film, as well as a prediction of the "Greatest TV Saturation in Every Local Market."

Those who did attend the luncheon were treated to an extravagant affair costing $15,000.[24] Exhibitors were given a taste of the promotional material that would feature in the campaign, such as trailers for television and cinemas, as well as information on magazine sponsorship. Pretty models in togas presented attendees with giant press books measuring thirty by forty inches, more than twice the size of a standard press book. Entertainment came from Vaughn Munroe, who sang the *Hercules* theme song—which was soon to be made available as a single through RCA. Joe, the star of the show, made a speech hammering home the vastness of the campaign and its success so far: more than two thousand bookings had already been taken from exhibitors before the luncheon had even begun, after only one week of selling.[25]

Hawking a movie unlikely to receive positive notices from critics, Joe's promotional strategy was to become the news, and heavy press attendance at the explodation luncheon meant that coverage was littered with soundbites from the pampered attendees. One giddy exhibitor exclaimed gratefully, "Levine didn't ask us to put over this picture. He went out and did it himself!"[26] Samuel Rosen remarked, "We need more men like Joe. . . . I hope he sets an example."[27] Charles Boasberg, general sales manager for Warner Bros., also appeared pleased: "This luncheon is in itself one of the greatest showmanship jobs I've ever seen . . . and it's the easiest picture to sell we've ever had. . . . This industry needs more Joe Levines."[28] Reporters covering the event also succumbed to Joe's charm offensive and the offerings at the luncheon. Charles A. Aaronson of *Motion Picture Herald*, wrote: "Exhibition leaders were unanimous in their tributes to the Levine genius for doing something in a big way. 'We need more of this kind of showmanship,' was the basic thought behind their words. . . . The whole affair was one to inspire the use of adjectives, big ones, and to lead to the prediction that this film is indeed likely to rack up a pile of records when it gets into release."[29]

Barring the title and some barbed asides, scant mention is made of the movie itself in reports about the luncheon. One exhibitor recalled Paramount's lackluster campaign for its runaway peplum production *Ulysses* (1954), noting "it was a helluva lot better picture than Levine's";[30] and Charles Aaronson, comparing the explodation luncheon with *Hercules*'s dubious claim to colossal status, wrote that Joe "nearly made the word 'colossal' accurate, for once."[31]

The notion of "exploding" *Hercules* may well be overenthusiastic hyperbole, but it is also a useful metaphor. With a record number of prints in circulation and massive concentrated saturation promotion, the film's release resembled a series of controlled, sometimes simultaneous explosions as it crept around America. Nationwide promotion served as a relentless reminder that if the *Hercules* circus had not yet come to your town, it would be coming soon. "Wherever You Are, You Are Never Far from *HERCULES!*" screamed the ads in a rare instance of truthfulness. The release was set for summer—a summer blockbuster. With summer being a slow time for movie exhibitors, *Hercules* would have little competition, and it could capitalize on the school holidays. Also, more and more theaters were installing air-conditioning and advertised their "Scientifically Air Conditioned" theaters to patrons keen to escape the summer heat.

Hercules was a children's film, "one for the small fry,"[32] and its natural home was the kiddie matinee. But it also had a spiritual home, and that was the drive-in. Like the kids at the matinees, the ozoner audience could be counted on to cast a less-critical eye over offerings cinematic. As a former drive-in operator, Joe knew that world. Also, the drive-in strategy of nestling a movie into a wider array of attractions and distractions mirrored the promotional tactics of *Hercules* as well as Joe's pedigree in promoting exploitation films. *Godzilla* and the re-releases of *King Kong* had been very successful at drive-ins, where they occasionally cropped up together on double bills, but *Hercules* was in color. It was ideal ozoner fare. It had a summer release, which was when drive-ins did most of their business, and drive-in operators could get *Hercules* on its first run and take advantage of the concurrent publicity blitz. It had action, it certainly had no critical acclaim, and Joe had created a holiday mood with his unprecedented campaign. Also, it was a kids' film, and the drive-in, with its myriad amusements, was the ideal place for the disgruntled father cajoled into taking his offspring to the movies. Dad could check out the lovely legs competition while Junior enjoyed *Hercules* with a hot dog.

The saturation campaign for *Hercules,* then, was not as scattergun as it may first appear. It initially targeted areas of the industry that were in distress or overlooked. When the campaign was unleashed on the American public, it sought to appeal to audiences beyond the "small fry" who constituted the most obvious target. In Joe's idiosyncratic assessment, "*Hercules* . . . had something for everybody. It had a dragon for kids, musclemen for growing boys, a shipwreck scene for waiters and clerks. Who doesn't dream of getting stuck on an island with some broads? And the picture had Steve Reeves. He appealed to women."[33]

Over a decade later, Joe delivered this particular piece of salesman's patter, word for word, to another reporter, adding that Reeves not only appealed to women but also to "some men."[34] This is an oblique reference to the extent of the campaign, which included placing ads in under-the-counter beefcake magazines to entice the gay market. Promotional slogans, too, emphasized overt sexuality, promising "Lusty and Licentious Adventure with Hercules!"—"Gifted with a God's Body! A God's Wrath! And a Man's Desires. . . ." These titillating promises may have bewildered the kiddy contingent but attracted teenage boys, reluctant dads, and other patrons keen on cinematic flesh. There were also tie-ins, cash-ins, and merchandise. There were coloring books, comic books, novelizations, toys, and a *Hercules* chocolate bar: "The Strongest Chocolate in the World—If It Breaks, You Can Eat It!"

With its easily understood and massively ballyhooed man-god eponym, the star of *Hercules* was Hercules, not Steve Reeves: "it wouldn't matter who played Hercules," said Joe, "as long as it was a man with a tremendous body."[35] Indeed, Joe may have admired Reeves's muscular frame, but he deemed Reeves's voice too high pitched for the powerful man-god and so had it dubbed over by George Gonneau—an electrical engineer. "Stars," declared Joe, "they're not important. It's the story and the title that count."[36] This comment may be surprising coming from the man who would later pay Robert Redford $2 million for four weeks' work on *A Bridge Too Far,* but, for the time being, the decision to sell the hero and not the star was working, as Berne Schneyer of *Film Bulletin* attested: "'Who's in it?' is a thing of the past. Proper promotion will overcome the lack of star names almost every time—and exhibitors can be convinced of that fact when showmanship is offered as a substitute for stars."[37] The *Hercules* campaign was one of vulgar excess and extravagance, but this did not stop Joe from economizing on star power and employing Steve Reeves stand-ins to be *Hercules* for the day at publicity junkets. If there was to be a star of the *Hercules* show, it would be Joe.

Joe was selling two products to two audiences. He was selling *Hercules* and Joseph E. Levine to the industry and the public. Potential punters could take one or the other. Despite the ever-present fretfulness about the state of the movie business, Joe achieved prominence with optimism in an industry that was feeling sorry for itself. What *Hercules* had that *Godzilla* and *Attila* did not was a focal point for the publicity blitz. Joe acted as circus ringmaster and harbinger of hope for movie lovers and industry watchers. Behind the scenes, he had various exploitation and press men on his books, and Mike Todd's death meant that he could snap up two of Todd's press agents, Bill Doll (who had planted the *Variety* profile) and Bill Watters, to keep the name "Joseph E. Levine" in the papers. With 635 prints touring America's 16,000-plus screens, *Hercules* was shown on more than 11,000 of them.

Joe's entrance onto America's national stage was met with if not quite a hero's welcome, then certainly a great deal of enthusiasm and affection. Joe may not have single-handedly revitalized the American film industry, but his exuberant showmanship did at least hint to doom-mongers that the industry *could* be revitalized, and many commentators positioned Joe as a man from a more positive past. For Sol Schwartz, president of the RKO Theatre chain, the explodation luncheon was "reminiscent of the big selling days" of the 1930s.[38] For Philip K. Scheuer of the *Los Angeles Times,* meanwhile, Joe inspired wistful memories of boyhood:

> In one respect the movie business never changes: When all else fails, you can still import an Italian Spectacle and clean up.
>
> This has been going on as far back as the 1910s. As a boy I remember being impressed by such Roman super-dupers as *Quo Vadis?, Cabiria* and *The Last Days of Pompeii.* In fact, *Quo Vadis* was the first film ever to play two-a-day in this country. *Cabiria* featured a giant muscleman named Maciste who snapped chains, cracked bones and toppled columns, all without apparent effort.
>
> Today, nearly half a century later, we have *Hercules* and Steve Reeves.
>
> And Joe Levine. Mr. Levine, who has big write-ups in *Variety* and *Time,* is being called the new Mike Todd.[39]

And as if to prove that one could admire the objectification but not the object, a few days after his admiring assessment of Joe's career to date appeared, Scheuer published an entertainingly withering review of the movie Joe was peddling: "This Hercules Just Tarzan in a Tunic."[40]

4

The Flim-Flam Man

> All the sachems of Hollywood, who had hitherto been rather condescending to Mr. Levine, now began to wonder how he did it.
>
> —*Gay Talese*

Along with the monsters and man-gods that arrived on American cinema screens in the 1950s came various creatures of the night. The showing of classic Universal horrors of the 1930s on rotation on television in the 1950s introduced a new generation to the spooky delights of *Dracula* and *Frankenstein,* a generation that was keen to see these demons and monstrous creations resurrected and in color. Britain's Hammer Films was ready to oblige. Hammer's first foray into the world of gothic horror with which it would become synonymous was *The Curse of Frankenstein* (1957), which was guided by the hand of Joe's erstwhile partner, Max Rosenberg, who had provided an early script draft for the project and shares the producer credit with Anthony Hinds. It was, like *Hercules* and many of the 1950s creature features, distributed by Warner Bros. to considerable success. Hammer followed up its *Frankenstein* reworking with *The Horror of Dracula* (1958), again to considerable success in the United States, where it was distributed by Universal.

Hammer's early gothic horror movies were influential in the United States, just as *Godzilla* and *Hercules* had been, and Joe also looked to cash in. He did so with a low-budget British horror that was itself a cash-in. *Jack the Ripper* was produced in 1959 by Tempean Films, a company that specialized in low-budget fare. Inspired by the success of Hammer's horrors, Tempean had followed suit with *Blood of the Vampire* (1958), which was scripted by Jimmy Sangster, scribe of Hammer's horrors, and shot in four weeks. Like *The Horror of Dracula, Blood of the Vampire* was distributed in America by Universal. It lacked the Hammer dream team of Christopher Lee and Peter Cushing, but it did have stage legend Donald Wolfit, and it was filmed in color. *Jack the Ripper* could boast no real thespian charge and was filmed in black and white. Nonetheless, Joe paid $50,000 for the distribution rights and set to work selling the world's favorite serial killer. The film was furnished with new sound effects and music, and a dash of color was added with some red blood toward the end. Then *Jack the Ripper* was set loose to frighten America with a blockbuster advertising campaign and a saturation release of more than seven hundred prints—another record for the number of prints in simultaneous circulation. It bombed. Joseph E. Levine, however, did not.

The hyperbole, showmanship, exhibitors' luncheons, and advertising blitz may not have brought the crowds into the theaters, but it kept Joe's name in the papers, fortifying his position—even though few people bought the film he was selling. Joe had announced that he was going to spend $1 million on promoting *Jack the Ripper,* and at an exhibitors' luncheon at the Plaza Hotel in New York City prior to the film's release he performed the show-stopping trick of literally unveiling the advertising budget in cash borrowed from a bank in Boston and transported under armed guard: "Adolph Zukor was standing next to the showcase where I had the money, and, you know, he has millions. 'Is that real, Levine?' he asked. 'Yeah it's real,' I said. 'You know,' he said, 'I never saw a million dollars in cash before.' Well that was the whole point. It cost me $3,000 dollars to borrow, but I got $100,000 worth of publicity out of it. It even made the papers in Australia!"[1]

In these few lines, Joe captured the essence of his showmanship. First, there is self-promotion: Joe's "I" being as important as the movie, or even more so. Second, there is a healthy name-drop: Adolph Zukor was a legendary movie mogul who at the time was chairman emeritus of Paramount Pictures, the studio he had built and the company that was distributing *Jack the Ripper.* Third, there are big numbers and big profit margins: $3,000 bought $100,000—that the amount spent was ineffective is neither here nor there. And, last, there is the tall tale: Joe was associated with the grand gesture, but he also thrived in intimate settings, being a gifted raconteur and collector of anecdotes, with a particular fondness for those involving himself.

Joe's million-dollar stunt received wide press attention at the time, and the tale of it was repeated in subsequent years, with Joe's name featuring much more prominently than the forgotten movie the stunt was meant to promote. Joe himself was fond of the tale and, recalling his exploits for the

Saturday Evening Post in 1967, he adjusted his memories for inflation: "You know the value of the publicity I got? I would estimate that to be at least a million."[2] As for the movie, Joe thought it was "a piece of shit."[3]

In his work on Alfred Hitchcock, Robert E. Kapsis observes that one of Hitchcock's strategies for staying in the public eye during the 1940s and 1950s was to lecture the public, through various media, on the art of suspense.[4] Hitchcock lectured his audience on his own area of expertise, his own peculiar talent, and the "master of suspense" was born. Joe's strategy was similar. Throughout his career, he littered the press with "how I did it" stories, imperiously offering insights into his own peculiar talent and disparaging his imitators: "Other people start out to do what I do, and they get all set up for a Joe Levine campaign. But in Hollywood too many people have to make a decision. They chicken out."[5]

Unlike his showman contemporaries in the 1950s, however, Joe was a pure flim-flam man. Although he would become a producer of note, he had little to nothing to do with the films that initially brought him fame. By contrast, Hitchcock was one of the great directors; Mike Todd was a notable technician who had been a driving force in the development of widescreen processes in the 1950s with Cinerama and, subsequently, Todd-AO; and William Castle, the febrile mind behind so many gimmicks devised to promote movies such as *Macabre* (1958) and *The Tingler* (1959), was a writer, director, producer, and all-around movie maker. Joe was just the public face for overseas product of questionable quality.

With *Jack the Ripper,* Joe was opportunistically following a trend, and he did so without much success. But with *Hercules,* as with *Godzilla,* he had begun a trend that turned into a craze that turned into a minifrenzy. It is a little difficult nowadays to fully appreciate how quickly cinematic crazes erupted in America of the 1950s, but *Hercules*'s success bust the dam for countless Italian peplum movies to flood drive-in and neighborhood hard-top theaters. Sam Arkoff quickly got in on the act with movies such as *Goliath and the Barbarians* (1959) and *Goliath and the Dragon* (1960). Hollywood sex bomb Jayne Mansfield journeyed to Italy to make *The Loves of Hercules* (1960), and as sword-and-sandal movie production went into overdrive in Italy, exhibitors and audiences were soon awash with Goliaths, Samsons, Macistes, Herculeses, and other muscle-bound men accompanied by leggy, busty beauties. Many were successful and, despite having nothing to do with these films, Joe got the credit—albeit tangentially. Only a couple of months after *Hercules*'s release, Richard

Nason of the *New York Times* reported on the hullaballoo and positioned Joe as pioneer. "*Hercules* has set a new high water mark in mass response for a comparatively cheap film of its kind," wrote Nason. "It has forced American and Italian companies to launch crash programs for the production of legendary and Biblical spectacles, and it has sent American distributors scurrying to Italy to buy up gimmick films that can be adapted to the hard sell that Mr. Levine has revived with a vengeance."[6]

Once the peplum boom had subsided, Joe delivered what can be seen as either a measured assessment of his influence or an exercise in what is now known as the "humblebrag": "When I released *Hercules,* it was like an explosion, a torrent. People began to make spear and sandal pictures by the hundreds. So I figure I did a little to hurt as well as help the Hollywood film industry. Because of me business was good and because of me business was bad."[7]

Whether impressed, dismayed, or unconcerned by the phenomenon, reporters would always place Joe's name prominently in stories about the peplum craze. If Joe's strategy had been to promote himself as well as his wares with *Hercules,* by the time *Hercules Unchained* was released in 1960, the press were happy to publish Joe Levine–related stories unbidden, and *Variety* had begun to call him the "Boston Barnum."

As Joe's publicity blitzes became news stories in themselves, subsequent publicity blitzes afforded reporters the chance to recap on previous publicity blitzes. The vastness of the *Hercules* campaign in 1959 gave Robert Alden of the *New York Times* a contextualizing touchstone for his reports on the vastness of the *Hercules Unchained* campaign the following year: "It is important to remember that at the center of this maelstrom of promotion, publicity, advertising and box office receipts was the movie *Hercules,* a film that even Mr. Levine calls 'this little picture.'"[8] Alden does not explain precisely *why* the film is important, and the report is dominantly about the ballyhoo and Joe. But *Hercules Unchained* receives a healthy plug in the form of a large illustration of its promotional poster, taglines and all, stretching across a full page.

Joe's twenty or so years in the film business notwithstanding, in early 1959 few people had heard the name "Joseph E. Levine." By the close of 1960, however, he was famous—unusual, to say the least, for a film importer. In 1960, Joe broke the record for the number of prints of a single film in simultaneous circulation in the United States once more, with *Hercules Unchained* creeping around the country with more than one thousand prints. Shortly thereafter, he broke another record, this time for the number of prints of a single film in simultaneous circulation in the United Kingdom, with more than five hundred prints of *Hercules Unchained* stalking the British cinemas and taking Joe's fame overseas. In a couple of years, he had gone from being an unknown to notable creature-feature dealer, thence from being a trade-paper oddity to become the "Boston Barnum." As the trade-press items begat stories in the mainstream media, so the write-ups in the *New York Times* begat interest from the popular media, and subsequent months would see Joe profiled in *Time, Esquire,* and *Life;* he was also lampooned in *Mad* magazine[9] and made the subject of documentary treatment by the Maysles brothers in *Showman.*

In August 1960, in what *Variety* called "a surprise move," Joe was named the winner of the Motion Picture Pioneer of the Year Award.[10] The November ceremony saw Joe criticizing his critics in rambunctious mood: "What the public wants is what the critics call 'corny.' I say I like it or I don't like it. But I'm in business. People from 8 to 80 who like those pictures are the ones who support the movies—not the intellectuals."[11] Defending corny crowd pleasers against a supposed critical onslaught led by the bugaboo of intellectual culture has been a hallmark of the showman from P. T. Barnum to Alfred Hitchcock to Simon Cowell, but in the early 1960s many prominent writers and intellectuals were equally eager to stand in opposition to a so-called elite culture, and one of them was Gay Talese.

Talese was to become famously associated with the emerging school of New Journalism, which Tom Wolfe, its most prominent practitioner, described as a rebellion against the "aristocratic aesthetic [of] the educated classes."[12] The postwar years had seen an explosion in pop culture aimed, like Joe's wares, at children and teenagers. Comic books, kiddie matinees, teen magazines, exploitation weirdies in the cinema, and rock and roll on the television constituted for many a threat to traditional American tastes and values but for others a lively new culture to be interrogated and explored free from old prejudices. Whether these moments represented the first salvoes in what would become the culture wars or a preening display of intellectual posturing between rival media elites or just a bun fight between demographics, Joe stood to benefit. As America's foremost purveyor of low culture, a position accentuated by his apparent materialization from nowhere, Joe was ideally placed to be revered or reviled by the opposing factions. Either way, his name would get in the press.

In 1960, Clay Felker, editor of *Esquire*—a popular lifestyle magazine for fashionable American men—assigned Gay Talese to interview Joe. Talese was an apt choice, and the resultant article, "Joe Levine Unchained: A Candid Portrait of a Spectacular Showman," is fascinating both for Joe's tall tales and Talese's own analysis. It appeared in the January 1961 issue of *Esquire* and is illustrated with a caricature of Joe as a circus strongman covered from head to toe in tattoos featuring the names of his recent and upcoming movies. Much of the information in the article was appearing in the press for the first time. Joe tells of his poverty-blighted childhood in the West End of Boston, speaks movingly about his adopted son, and tells some anecdotes about the various jobs he had while growing up, and Talese fills in the blanks with extra biographical information. Importantly, Talese gives Joe the space to speak for himself and to deliver his apparently commonsense view of the failures of modern movie promotion and justifications for his own heavy-guns approach: "When I lay out all this money for advertising, it's because I want people to know my picture is playing. Too many films drop dead because people don't know they're playing. Some films are advertised when they reach Broadway, but by the time they get out to the neighborhoods people have forgotten them. Would the Palmolive Soap people spend millions on advertising soap and then not have soap in all the stores?"[13]

Talese's piece is peppered with Joe's witty one-liners and distinctive observations about the film business. As was his wont, Joe aligns himself and his output with the needs and tastes of America's overlooked ordinary folk: "My audience are people who need escape. They are waiters, truck drivers and little guys who work all day. When they go to the movies, they want escape. They want to see guys fighting dragons."[14] The feature is also full of figures—lists of dollar amounts of what was spent on what and how much was made from the amount invested. This is the kind of business data that was usually found only in industry publications, but it formed an integral part of Joe's raconteurial braggadocio, and as his fame grew, it was increasingly fetishized in articles and profiles.

The postproduction dubbing process is another aspect of the movie business that formed the basis of many interview anecdotes: "There was lots of work to do before we could get the films ready for America. Some of the dubbed-in voices in *Hercules Unchained* sounded like fags. So we had to do it twice. Also, after the mast of the ship came crashing down in *Hercules,* the Italians who made the film forgot to make noise. So we dubbed in noise."[15] Joe's unfortunate use of the pejorative *fag* aside, the postproduction dubbing process was, like his revelations about monetary ins and outs of the company accounts, hitherto the kind of procedural ephemera that would have been of interest only to industry specialists and technicians. But with the incorporation of this kind of trivia into his anecdotes, it achieves the status of insider information as Joe appears to offer his audience a glimpse behind the scenes. If Joe's "trick" had been to fool the American public into seeing a tenth-rate supercolossal, he would now reveal his conjuring secrets. Like a placebo that still works on a patient who has been told he has been given a placebo, or like Hitchcock keeping his audience in suspense even as he lectured on how he did it, Joe's outlaw, wise-guy persona and ability as a flim-flam man were only fortified by his revelations of trade secrets.

Talese was charmed by Joe: "He sought to amuse me with such tricks as sticking a quarter to his forehead, and having it stick there . . . without falling off." Joe introduced Talese to Rosalie and took him to favorite restaurants, flaunting his wealth. "He liked dining well in very expensive restaurants," remembers Talese about their meeting, " a few of which he took me to, and what impressed me (in those days) was that he never allowed himself to receive a check from the waiter. He just finished his meal, got up, and left the restaurant. I remarked on that on one occasion when I was with him at the Four Seasons Restaurant, and he explained that he had an arrangement with restaurants to have a regular account, and all his charges (including tips) were taken care of privately by the restaurant's accountant."[16]

Talese liked Joe and recalls, "I found him agreeable, funny, knowledgeable, and very decent to be around,"[17] and this feeling is reflected in the article. Mixed in with Joe's own appealing ebullience is Talese's editorializing, wherein Talese himself appears to be an acolyte. Talese contrasts public perceptions of Joe the motor-mouth showman with Joe the "quiet, peaceful man when away from his work." He also uses New Journalistic affectations to pit the "leather jacket set" that constituted Joe's audience against the "smart, sophisticated fifteen per-cent of America" that constituted the cultural elite who were supposedly offended by Joe's movies and hard-sell techniques. Like others before him, Talese exalts Joe by decrying his wares and writes admiringly of his ability to turn vast profits from "some of the worst films in captivity." Talese also abandons journalistic disinterest by misleadingly writing how "all the sachems of Hollywood, who had hitherto been rather condescending to Mr. Levine, now began to wonder how he did it," neglecting to mention that it was the "sachems" at major Hollywood studios that had distributed *Attila, Hercules,* and *Hercules Unchained.*[18]

If Talese presented Joe much as Joe presented himself, the same can also be said of *Mad* magazine's Levine lampoon, "*Mad* Visits Joe LeVenal: Hollywood's Latest Producing Genius," by Mort Drucker and Larry Siegal. *Mad* was founded by Harvey Kurtzman and William Gaines and began as a comic book in 1952, converting into a magazine in 1955. It was hugely successful throughout the 1950s and 1960s and beyond, and to be lampooned in *Mad* was to be *recognized,* even honored; perhaps today's equivalent would be a guest spot on *The Simpsons.* In the October 1961 issue, Joe LeVenal introduces himself: "Hello, I'm Joe LeVenal, the Hollywood genius who's responsible for all the *Hercules* and other wonderful, cheap film extravaganzas that are so popular today. Unlike mercenary producers who are out to rope *everybody* into seeing their films, I cater to a *select* audience—that part of the population which still isn't intelligent enough to understand *television!*"[19]

LeVenal acts as the readers' host and guide as he takes them on a tour of his filmmaking process. The process begins with a budget meeting with LeVenal and his board of executives, at which LeVenal announces that his new project will have a budget of $10 million—$9,999,500 of which is allocated for advertising and promotion, leaving $500 to buy the film from the "movie supermarkets" of Italy. Once in Italy, LeVenal declines an offer to buy *Hercules in the Land of the Amazon Idiots* on the grounds that it is "a little too 'egghead' and 'message-y' for my audience,"[20] and he settles instead for *Hercules and the Chicken-Fat People.* Back in America, LeVenal reworks the film with extensive postproduction and promotes it with parties of Bacchanalian excess and a maddeningly incessant advertising campaign.

There is little if anything about Joe LeVenal that would have upset Joe Levine. *Mad* magazine satirized the Levine phenomenon by simply exaggerating Joe's own exaggerations. As much as it lampoons, it also consolidates the public image Joe had created for himself. The strip highlights his constant bragging about money, the enormous and expensive promotion campaigns, the cheapness of the initial purchase price for *Hercules,* and the subsequent vast profits, and there are playful digs at Joe's apparent faith in the panacean promises of the postproduction dubbing process.

The success of *Hercules* and Joe's tireless self-promotion ensured that he became an ideal target for *Mad,* a mainstream, satirical magazine whose political lampoons were accompanied by potshots at the various figures and mores of pop culture. This kind of communications culture barely existed before the Second World War. The rise of mass communications after the war meant that politicians became pop-culture figures, so political satire, which was an elite or minority affair in earlier times, became mainstream. The fact that much of the satire in *Mad* was political lent gravitas to the publication and therefore tangential gravitas to its objects of ridicule. After all, to be lampooned alongside President Kennedy is rather more becoming than being lampooned alongside, say, Fabian. *Mad* magazine both satirized and enforced Joe's public image and gave him a wide audience, so his fans *and* detractors could easily find plenty in "Joe LeVenal" to confirm their sympathies or prejudices.

Joe certainly had his fans in the media. By the early 1960s, Embassy was spending significant sums for big publicity splashes in *Variety* that advertised the recently released and the future forthcomers, as well as reminding readers of past successes and, of course, Joseph E. Levine. Joe would later become good friends with Abel Green, *Variety* editor from 1931 to 1973. No doubt that friendship was at least partly responsible for *Variety*'s kindness to Joe and his antics through these years, as were the huge sums Joe spent on publicity features in its pages.

In 1960, Joe hired Edward Feldman as a publicity man to "put him on the map," as Feldman put it later.[21] Feldman had been a publicity man for Fox and subsequently for producer Ray Stark on his production of *The World of Suzie Wong* (1960). A fallout with Stark freed him up to work for Joe at Embassy, and he stayed with Joe for two years, beginning with the launch of *Hercules Unchained.* "He wanted to be famous and he wanted to be considered a big-time movie producer," says Feldman. "In short, he wanted to be a big shot in films. And I must say, he was pretty damn successful with it. And considering the B movies he was churning out, he was almost scarily successful. . . . I had essentially two jobs: to promote Embassy's slate of pictures and promote Joseph E. Levine. Because of this second responsibility, Levine gave me carte blanche to spend what I wanted."[22]

Though Feldman worked for Joe for only two years, they were two significant years. The period between 1960 and 1962 was the time when Joe became nationally famous—in the true sense of famous. His name was known far beyond the industry and the trade press; his name was known and featured in the popular press and, consequently, known by the man in the street. In a short time, Joe achieved a level of fame within the United States that was unprecedented for a film importer and promoter.

It would have been difficult if not impossible to achieve such prominence so quickly without attracting detractors. In fact, Joe needed detractors; enemies, real or imagined, were integral to his public persona. One cannot truly cast oneself as a maverick outsider unless one has enemies who can be associated with an intolerant "establishment." For Joe, *New York Times* film critic Bosley Crowther perfectly fit the role of the voice of outraged conservatism.

Having expressed dismay at *Godzilla,* Crowther was rather more optimistic when writing about the initial rumblings of the *Hercules* campaign. Though he could easily be characterized as a voice of the conservative establishment in cinema, there is little doubt that he truly loved the movie industry and cared about the state of it. Reporting on the *Hercules* explodation luncheon, which he did not attend, he wrote approvingly because "it indicated a rampant urge to sell."[23] Two years later, America now awash with *Hercules* imitators, Crowther's optimism turned to foreboding: "As much as it can spank anybody, the American motion-picture industry can spank Joseph E. Levine for Judas goating it down a path of commerce that may take it—or elements of it—to the brink of ruin. For it was he, a former drive-in manager, who ran the cheap Italian picture, *Hercules,* into a fabulous money-maker in the American market by promoting it five times as much as it was worth and thereby led the sheep in the business to go gambling for similar cheap adventure films."[24]

One might argue, of course, that the path of commerce that had Joe as its figurehead in fact *saved* elements of the motion-picture industry from the brink of ruin. It is ironic, too, that Crowther's doom-laden predictions echoed the doom-laden predictions of the exhibitors in the pre-saturation, pre-creature-feature days. But what is also important is that Joe now had a prominent adversary.

Gay Talese had already name-checked Crowther in his profile of Joe: "He admits that he does not care what the *New York Times*' film critic, Bosley Crowther, says about him. Critics cannot hurt Levine's films. Levine's customers do not read Crowther."[25] Now Crowther returned in kind. As a critic, Crowther often turned his attention to emergent trends in the industry, in particular those he felt were damaging it. In the case of *Hercules* and the subsequent peplum boom, he was able to direct his ire toward a specific person. Thanks to his newly won conspicuousness in the industry, Joe was an ideal target. And Crowther's snooty irrelevance about Joe being a "former drive-in manager" merely strengthened Joe's own public persona as a maverick outsider.

Crowther spent a good deal of the 1960s being angry with Joe. As a general rule of thumb, if Crowther admired a film with which Joe was involved—for example, the Embassy imports *8½* or *Two Women* (1960)—Joe's name would not appear in the body of Crowther's review. However, if Joe was involved with a film that Crowther did not like, Joe's name would feature prominently, usually accompanied by moralizing about the nature of the film in question. Crowther may have disapproved of Joe, but Joe needed opposition to authenticate his persona, and Crowther obligingly became, in Lenin's phrase, something of a "useful idiot."

Across the Atlantic, too, Joe was facing criticism from the more discerning movie commentators. After he unleashed the biggest saturation campaign that the United Kingdom had ever seen, the British bastion of scholarly film analysis, *Film and Filming*, expressed concern: "In our opinion the commercial triumph of *Hercules* [*Unchained*] was attained because the producers spent more money on promotional advertising than for any film ever previously released in Britain. We believe that this is a classic example of the public being forced to like what it gets and being powerless to get what it likes."[26]

But in the United Kingdom, too, Joe had his supporters, and David Nathan of the *Daily Herald* dismissed *Film and Filming*'s claims as "nonsense," adding, "The public has its choice alright . . . but it was blinded by the ballyhoo, stunned by the sales talk and pummelled by the propaganda until it was led up to the box-office of *Hercules Unchained*. It was like that in Barnum's day. It is like that in Mr. Levine's day."[27]

As Joe became more and more famous, more and more people felt compelled to have opinions about him, and these opinions came not just from the professional opinion-havers in the media but from the general public, too. When *Life* magazine published a profile of Joe in July 1962, the following month saw responses in the letters pages. Mrs. N. I. Klien sarcastically praised *Life* for "exposing this sort of thing," adding, "I for one will be sure to stay away from the advertised colossals and keep my children away from them."[28] Another letter writer, Skirmante Makaitis, wrote, "It is only fitting that Mr. Joe Levine should be such a smashing success. All those who sat through the agonizingly dull and incredibly pointless hours of eye-tiring, ear shattering and brain numbing 'super colossal' can gaze upon him and admire this living monument to their own poor taste and gullibility."[29] Later, *Variety* published something approaching a fan letter in its personals pages. In "Open Letter to Joseph E. Levine," the correspondent wrote, "I want to work for *YOU* . . . the most dynamic man in the movie industry today. I am an ambitious, aggressive, creative, imaginative, resourceful, capable young man. Can we get together?"[30]

That Joe was a divisive, even polarizing figure did him no harm whatsoever. He was also fortunate that his quest to become famous coincided with journalistic and media trends that sought to challenge cultural elitism. But far from weakening barriers between high and low culture, these trends saw cultural barriers reinforced as commentators positioned themselves along political lines in the culture skirmish. Joe, so closely identified with the low end of movie culture, profited greatly from these debates as both beneficent caterer to the tastes of the hardworking little guy and opportunistic menace to cinematic decency. But Joe was about to take his persona, tactics, and ballyhoo into enemy territory and to enter the hallowed world of art cinema.

5

The Showman in the Art House

> The most intolerable thing for those who regard themselves as the possessors of legitimate culture is the sacrilegious reuniting of tastes which taste dictates shall be separated.
>
> —*Pierre Bourdieu*

Mike Todd knew well that critics and commentators did not welcome the sacrilegious, as Pierre Bourdieu would have it,[1] mixing of lowbrow showmanship with highbrow pedigree. In 1939, Todd produced and directed *The Hot Mikado* on Broadway. Desirous of a positive critical response and fearful that the show's image would be tarnished by his huckster reputation, he omitted his own name from the billboards and hired a respected director, Hassard Short, as a "front" in order to sway the critics.[2] In contradistinction to his hero, Joe beat out a different path. During an interview in 1966, the following exchange took place:

> JOE: We just finished *Romeo and Juliet* with Nureyev and Fontayne. It's a ballet and it will be a gas. And probably we'll do *Faustus* with Taylor and Burton. We make many an egghead picture. Also, we just finished *Santa Claus Conquers the Martians.*
>
> DICK GRIFFIN: How do you reconcile *Santa Claus Conquers the Martians* with *Romeo and Juliet*?
>
> JOE: Don't reconcile them! Don't reconcile them! I make movies.[3]

Despite his disingenuous protestations, Joe reveled in being involved in high art and low culture simultaneously, and he particularly enjoyed the confusion and upset his wide-ranging dealings caused among those who could not reconcile this "sacrilegious reuniting of tastes."[4] In this exchange with Griffin, Joe is once again exaggerating for effect. *Santa Claus Conquers the Martians* (1964) had not just been finished; it had been completed, released, and forgotten more than eighteen months earlier. Joe simply chose that title to provide an artful juxtaposition—the highbrow clashing with the lowbrow.

The postwar exploitation man had no compunctions about dealing in art cinema and exploitation cinema simultaneously. Movies now considered arthouse classics, such as Italian neorealist films, were more likely to be found on the exploitation circuit than anywhere else. By the 1950s, European films featuring female flesh were particularly popular with exploiteers. *One Summer of Happiness* (1951), for example, is a Swedish coming-of-age drama that features the young and enticing Ulla Jacobsson, who appears in nude-bathing scenes. The success of this film begat *Monika: Story of a Bad Girl* (1955). Distributed and ballyhooed by Kroger Babb, *Monika* is a bowdlerized and rescored version of *Summer with Monika* (1953), which was directed by Ingmar Bergman prior to his embrace by the American arthouse scene. Like *One Summer of Happiness,* it is a coming-of-age drama that contains nude bathing scenes featuring another young and enticing beauty, this time Harriet Andersson.

Up until the mid-1950s, art houses were known as "sure-seaters." So niche was their appeal, so small was their demographic that the prevailing wisdom was that if you popped along to your nearest art house, you would be sure to get a seat. By the mid-1950s, however, arthouse cinema began to acquire its own distinctiveness, thanks in no small part to the distinctiveness of the exhibition spaces, the arthouses. The gray areas that existed in the art/exploitation overlap were now beginning to be fortified into borders. Films such as *The Seven Samurai* (1954) by Akira Kurosawa and *The Seventh Seal* (1957) by Ingmar Bergman saw the beginnings of an arthouse star system of directors, laying the groundwork for the cult of the auteur that concurrently emerged. The huge success of the Brigitte Bardot starrer *And God Created Woman* (1956), meanwhile, suggests that arthouse tastes were not so different from exploitation tastes and gives the impression of images of sex and sensation being commandeered from the exploitation clientele and appropriated by an arthouse audience, who considered themselves more thoughtful. For exploitation historian Eric Schaeffer, it is no coincidence that the rise of the art house coincided with the fall of the classical exploitation film.[5]

In her study of the rise of the art house, Barbara Wilinsky describes the kinds of "extras" that allowed art houses to claim distinction: "theatres featured art galleries in the lobbies, served coffee, and offered specialized 'intelligent' films to a discriminating audience that paid higher admission prices for such distinctions. And many of the people attending art houses did want distinction from their filmgoing experiences."[6] The provision of distinguishing features at art houses, commercial imperatives to enhance the film-going experience, was not so different from the extras provided by drive-in operators or, indeed, by the exploiteers, and these apparent distinctions contributed to art houses' fashionableness and popularity.

The boom in art houses was also fueled by the American intellectual embrace of the auteur theory. Formulated in France by, among others, Andre Bazin and developed by François Truffaut and other auteurist critics in the pages of *Cahiers du Cinema,* then proselytized with evangelical zeal by American critics such as Andrew Sarris, the auteur theory positioned the visionary director as the sole author of a film in a manner similar to the credit accorded to a novelist or painter.

As the discrete arthouse demographic expanded, so inevitably did the market. Joe sought to capitalize in three ways. First, with the arthouse audience being largely self-identifying and keen to consume foreign films of a certain quality, Joe knew the audience and set about catering to them. Second, he sought to use arthouse success and critical acclaim as a springboard to take arthouse films beyond the art house to a more mainstream audience. And, third, with Joe so closely associated with schlocky ballyhoo, he used his apparent inappropriateness for dealing in art cinema to enhance his public image as antagonist to the nation's eggheads. He began his quest with *The Law* (1959).

The Law is based on Roger Valliand's best-selling, Goncourt Prize–winning novel of the same title and directed by Jules Dassin. A versatile director, Dassin made his name with hard-boiled crime and noir thrillers such as *Thieves' Highway* (1949) and *Night and the City* (1950), but during the production of the latter he was blacklisted in Hollywood for his left-wing politics. Exiled to Europe, Dassin made his most famous film in France in 1955, the influential and much imitated *Rififi* (1955). With arthouse cinemas flourishing in the United States, *The Law*'s stars were already familiar to American audiences. Yves Montand was an established actor, crooner, and Lothario; Marcello Mastroianni had starred in *La Dolce vita* (1960), the arthouse hit from Federico Fellini; and Gina Lollobrigida was emerging as one of a group of Italian actresses who were known collectively as *maggiorata fisica,* or buxom beauties. Lollobrigida came to prominence in the 1950s in European films such as *Woman of Rome* (1954) and *Fanfan de Tulip* (1952) and then in Hollywood movies such as *Beat the Devil* (1953) and *Trapeze* (1956).

The combination of directorial panache, arthouse pedigree, and Euro-sex must have been an appealing package for MGM, which bought the worldwide distribution rights to *The Law* in 1960. Through a deal with MGM, Joe handled the promotion in Canada and the United States. He changed the movie's jejune title to the racier *Where the Hot Wind Blows* and dubbed it into English. It told a story of sex, power, and ritual humiliation in a sweaty village in southern Italy and featured sexy Euro-stars, so Joe opened it widely, accompanied, said *Variety,* "by the kind of razzle-dazzle campaign for which Levine has become noted"[7] and by the tagline "Get Set for the Kind of Male–Female Explosion of Excitement You Haven't Seen in Years with Lollobrigida and Montand!" Exploitable elements and a blockbuster campaign aside, *Where the Hot Wind Blows* failed to find an audience and incurred a box-office loss.

With few people aware of Joe's prior experience as a distributor of Italian neorealist cinema in New England, his sudden-seeming switch from the lowbrow to the highbrow, from the drive-in to the art house, raised a few eyebrows among commentators. Even Gay Talese, Joe's apparent acolyte, had doubts. Citing the pedigree of the film's director and stars as well as the original novel's prize-winning author, Talese commented that *Where the Hot Wind Blows* "is not the sort of film one would expect Levine to be involved with" and speculated that if it were to fail, Joe's future would be forever bound to the "leather jacket set."[8] But *Where the Hot Wind Blows* was not Joe's first failure, and the art house was not alien territory.

Howard Thompson of the *New York Times* lavishly praised *Where the Hot Wind Blows,*[9] but Philip K. Scheuer of the *Los Angeles Times* was circumspect. For Scheuer, *Where the Hot Wind Blows,* with its arthouse themes alongside box-office temptations, was a "hybrid film . . . [that] may pose a vexing corollary problem: Is it 'art-house' or is it 'commercial'? Are there, indeed, any longer 'two' audiences?"[10] The answer to Scheuer's questions may appear to be yes: there was an arthouse audience and a commercial audience with different tastes and sensibilities. But Joe knew from his exploitation days that the barriers between art and commerce were considerably more porous than metropolitan critics realized. *Where the Hot Wind Blows* may have failed financially, but it established a template that Joe would capitalize on with *Two Women*, his first national arthouse success. *Two Women*, like *Where the Hot Wind Blows*, was an arthouse film and had been released in Italy in 1960. It, too, was based on a well-regarded novel from an esteemed author, came from an important director, and featured a European beauty: Alberto Moravia, Vittorio de Sica, and Sophia Loren, respectively.

Two Women was produced by Carlo Ponti and was widely considered a return to form for the neorealist pioneer director Vittorio de Sica. Set during the Second World War, it is stark, harrowing, and moving and tells the story of Cesira (Sophia Loren) trying to protect her daughter, Rosetta (Eleonora Brown), from the horrors of war-torn Italy. Its investigation of a mother–daughter relationship is reminiscent of the exploration of a father–son relationship in *The Bicycle Thief*, also directed by de Sica, but the dominance of the female perspective in the movie also acted as a necessary corrective to the overwhelmingly male-dominated war dramas and adventure movies of the time.

Two Women was originally set to be an Italian-American coproduction directed by George Cukor. It was to star Anna Magnani as Cesira, with Loren as the daughter. Magnani did not feel that the casting was appropriate and wrote to her agent, Irving "Swifty" Lazar, "I believe role of mother in book is perfect for me but I should not play it in picture if Sophia plays daughter . . . I honestly feel that she is physically too strong and self sufficient looking to make mother daughter relationship convincing."[11] With Magnani intractable, Cukor dropped out. When de Sica took over the project, he also tried and failed to convince Magnani to take the role, but she would not do so with Loren cast as Rosetta. He then turned to Loren and convinced the twenty-five-year-old actress to play the thirty-five-year-old Cesira. She agreed, and Eleonora Brown, only fourteen years Loren's junior, was cast as her daughter.

According to Edward Feldman, Ponti had some trouble selling the American and Canadian rights to *Two Women* because of the combination of the film's distressing story and Loren's pedigree as a sex symbol in the United States: nobody in America will pay to see a foreign-language movie featuring Sophia Loren "looking like that," were the thoughts of one MGM executive.[12] Joe saw only part of *Two Women* on one of his many trips to Italy, including a particularly brutal scene in which Cesira and her daughter are gang-raped by Moroccan troops in a bombed-out church. Feeling that Loren's performance was worthy of an Oscar, he paid $350,000 for the

American and Canadian distribution rights—a huge amount for an art film at the time. It should be noted that this unprecedented amount, along with Joe's gift for striking a bargain, does rather undermine Feldman's claim that Ponti was having difficulty shifting the film. Nonetheless, *Two Woman* found favor in the United States. Critical and commercial success followed, as did the Golden Globe for Best Foreign Language Film and the Best Actress Academy Award for Loren.

Writing in 1959, film scholar Arthur Knight observed the influence that metropolitan movie critics could have on the success or failure of an arthouse picture: "For good or ill, it is in the field of the art film that the critical confraternity swings the most appreciable weight. And the distributors and exhibitors of such films, unfortunately, seem to ponder their reviews with a far greater intensity than the audience for which they were written. A favorable notice from Bosley Crowther or John McCarten, they know, will bring in the crowds; if the notices are unfavorable, they realize that they might as well just bring in another picture."[13]

A bad review from a respectable source could indeed destroy a movie's chances at the art house, but a positive recommendation was, to contradict Knight, certainly no guarantee of a healthy box-office return, as the case of *Where the Hot Wind Blows* attests. *Two Women* was universally praised, but Joe was not about to let the fate of this movie and his huge investment be dependent on the critics' opinions. In promoting *Two Women,* he sought to combine critical approval with prestige and promotion, initially seeking arthouse distinction for *Two Women* and lobbying hard for Loren's Oscar. *Two Women* opened in a subtitled version, playing in select arthouse theaters; that these theaters were concentrated in the metropolitan areas where the voting members of the Academy of Motion Picture Arts and Sciences lived was certainly no coincidence. Following Loren's Oscar win, which was especially newsworthy because she was the first actress to win the award for a non-English-speaking role, Joe took *Two Women* nationwide, dubbed into English, in a small-scale saturation pattern. "I nursed that picture like it was a baby," said Joe shortly after the Oscars. "When Sophia won the Academy Award last April it had been running for six months but the public was still waiting. It made money before the Award dinner but it's grossed a million more since."[14]

In late 1961, Joe told *Variety,* "I'm going heavy on the art-type stuff,"[15] and heavy he went. Arthur Knight's observations notwithstanding, by the early

1960s the critical fraternity's stranglehold over the art scene was loosening thanks to the increasing popularity of arthouse movies and arthouse cinemas. Popular connoisseurship had led to an arthouse star system of actors and directors—Brigitte Bardot and Jean-Paul Belmondo were as important to American arthouses as Ingmar Bergman and François Truffaut. With a booming arthouse scene in the United States, art houses were, like provincial exhibitors and ozoner operators before them, hungry for product. But although America's art houses contained the core audience for much of Joe's product in the early 1960s, Joe was looking to take arthouse movies to nonarthouse audiences, and *The Sky Above, the Mud Below* (1961) provides an interesting example.

Directed by Pierre Dominique-Gaisseau and produced by Carlo Ponti's occasional partner Arthur Cohn, *The Sky Above, the Mud Below* is a travelogue that documents a grueling seven-month expedition through unmapped territory in what was then Dutch New Guinea. It was well received by critics, and *Variety* spotted its potential, suggesting that it could be successful in art houses if backed by tasteful promotion: "This needs careful handling. But has the essentials for good arty theatre."[16] Its Oscar win for best documentary in 1962 increased the prestige of the product, and so Joe acquired the distribution rights. He released it in art houses, backed by the kind of tasteful advertising suggested by *Variety,* but he also concurrently released it in grind houses and on the exploitation circuit, backed by taste-free exploitationist ballyhoo, its posters proclaiming,

> They lived with guru CANNIBALS!
> They filmed actual fertility rites.
> They witnessed the secret orgies of the cult of the severed head.
> They were forced into intimacies with their savage hosts!

With *The Sky Above, the Mud Below,* Joe was looking back to the arthouse/exploitation crossovers of his early career and the development of his peculiar talent for movie exploitation. He spent $350,000 on promotion—an amount unheard of for a documentary.[17] He also, perhaps unwittingly, kick-started another cinematic trend and secured the movie's reputation as a proto-*Mondo* movie among grindhouse fans and historians.

The success of *The Sky Above, the Mud Below* in grind houses whetted the public's appetite for ethnographic documentaries with a sensationalist bent. This kind of film, replete with bombastic advertising and faked footage, had been a staple of the exploitation trade before the Second World War, when they were known as "exotics." The exotics of the Depression era offered the aggrandization of white Western culture by showcasing the eccentricities and deviances of assumedly primitive cultures. In the 1960s, the genre returned with a vengeance. *The Sky Above, the Mud Below* paved the way for *Mondo Cane* (1962) and a slew of sequels and imitators, compendiums of odd behavior and supposed cultural backwardness from around the world.

Having helped to create the conditions for the success of these films, Joe rather missed the boat on the *Mondo* craze. He once told a reporter that he did not buy the rights to *Mondo Cane* because he did not think it was any good,[18] but the documentary *Showman* clearly shows Joe attempting to acquire the rights to the film at the Cannes Film Festival. Embassy did, however, acquire and distribute one of *Mondo*'s many sequels, *Women of the World* (1963), which was made up of footage left over from *Mondo Cane* and which Joe described as "a great film."[19]

One arthouse genre in which Joe invested heavily was the multidirector portmanteau film. These multistory films were a showman's dream because they provided three, four, or more trendy directors in one movie. The tales they contained were often linked by themes of sex, sin, and crime. One of these films, *Boccaccio 70* (1963), produced by Carlo Ponti, prompted the observation by the *Hollywood Reporter* that "Joseph E. Levine has found a just about perfect synthesis of art and commerce."[20] The Catholic Legion of Decency was much less impressed by this "grossly suggestive concentration upon indecent costuming, situation and dialogue" and condemned it.[21]

Joe felt that *Boccaccio 70* was too long, clocking in at a whopping 208 minutes, so one of the four segments was removed. The remaining segments were directed by de Sica, Federico Fellini, and Luchino Visconti, directors who were well known among discerning and voguish American cinemagoers, and starred arthouse icons Sophia Loren, Anita Ekberg, and Romy Schneider, respectively. The director of the deleted segment, Mario Monicelli, and its star, Marisa Solinas, were less well known in the United States, even though Monicelli had already been nominated for two Oscars.

There was to be a sequel, *Boccaccio 71,* with segments directed by Charlie Chaplin, Jacques Tati, and de Sica, but it never came to fruition. Also at this time, Joe sought to further capitalize on the pedigree of arthouse star directors when he bought the rights to two of Ingmar Bergman's lesser-known early movies, *The Devil's Wanton* (a.k.a. *Prison*, 1949) and *Night Is My Future* (a.k.a. *Music in Darkness*, 1948), which Embassy released in 1962 and 1963, respectively, cheekily branding them "vintage Bergmans."[22]

As Joe sought to woo the arthouse crowd, his arthouse investments brought him to the attention of Dwight Macdonald, one of postwar America's most influential and truly maverick intellectuals. In his *Esquire* column, which he reserved mostly for demolishing all that he found unpalatable about American movie culture, he took aim at Joe. Having quickly rubbished *Hercules*, along with Joe's "cynical" saturation tactics and the movie's drive-in audiences in the "hinterlands," Macdonald questioned Joe's arthouse ambitions: "Mr. Levine aspires to more than just profits; he wants to make the art scene too. His ambitions, nourished by the millions he made out of *Hercules*–Reeves, are now flowering like some exotic plant, say the Venus Fly Trap. Among the films that his Embassy now has in hand are: *Seven Capitol Sins* (episodes directed by Godard, De Broca, Chabrol, among others); *Love at Twenty* (Truffaut and Wajda among others); *Boccaccio 70* (Fellini, Visconti, De Sica)."[23]

Like Bosley Crowther, Macdonald cared deeply about movie culture and culture in general. His writing was often incisive and infused with coruscating wit. He was unabashedly elitist, and snobbish affectations were as important to his public image as vulgar bombast was to Joe's. Macdonald's most famous essay, "Masscult and Midcult" (1959),[24] is a lengthy and furious denunciation of what he viewed as the unacceptable compromises of middlebrow culture and the deleterious mesmerizations of mass culture, whose effects he compared to totalitarian propaganda. But mass culture provided Macdonald with the enemies he sought across the cultural landscape. During his tenure as America's foremost cultural snob, he attacked New Journalism and auteur theory, accused Bosley Crowther of liking *La Notte* (1961) and *Last Year in Marienbad* (1961) in an effort to appear fashionable (even though Macdonald himself admired both films), and resigned in disgust from *Film Quarterly* upon its appointment of auteurist critic Andrew Sarris. When Joe started trampling over the carefully constructed cultural borders that Macdonald had appointed himself to guard, Macdonald was, like Crowther, an ideal enemy for Joe.

Macdonald's characterizing of Joe as an interloper in the rarefied world of the art house and his highlighting of Joe's supposedly pretentious ambitions read as familiar snobbish posturing. But Macdonald took his role as cultural guardian and gatekeeper very seriously and held his views sincerely, so his concerns cannot be dismissed entirely. In his piece about Joe, Macdonald's principal gripe concerns Joe's announcement that an hour was to be cut from his production of *Long Day's Journey into Night* (1962) for distribution in the provinces and the sacrilegious clashing of art and commerce. With his truncation of *Boccaccio 70,* Joe perhaps did have an artistically felonious past, but Macdonald was unaware of it, and the facts surrounding the bowdlerization of *Long Day's Journey into Night* were a little more complex than the simple removal of its least commercially appealing aspects.

Playwright Eugene O'Neill wrote the claustrophobic and explosive family drama *Long Day's Journey into Night* in 1940, but feeling that it was too painfully autobiographical he kept its existence a secret until his death in 1951, with instructions that it should not be produced for twenty-five years after that event. Despite these instructions, the play was first produced in 1956. So not only was the play regarded as a masterpiece, but it also carried a special cultural resonance as an undiscovered treasure from a dead legend of American literature. The film of *Long Day's Journey into Night* was produced by Ely Landau using his own money, directed by Sidney Lumet, starkly photographed by Boris Kaufman, and starred Katharine Hepburn, Ralph Richardson, Jason Robards, and Dean Stockwell. Embassy handled the distribution, and Joe received an executive-producer credit.

For Macdonald, O'Neill's masterpiece was "probably our greatest play," and the original three-hour cut of the film "not unworthy of the original, and I can think of no higher praise."[25] His horror, then, that the film should be cut is understandable, but there were pressing practical concerns that affected Joe's handling of *Long Day's Journey into Night.* Macdonald was not the only critic to admire the film. Many others did, too, but their voices were lost when the movie's opening in New York coincided with the longest newspaper strike in that city's history. Exhibitors were unwilling to accept a movie that ran for almost three hours that had no critical support behind it. According to Sidney Lumet, Joe had been fully supportive of the original version but sought permission from Ely Landau to abridge the movie, and around forty minutes were excised. Lumet also said that Joe fought hard to promote the movie and lobbied to secure an Oscar for

Hepburn, whose Academy Award nomination followed award wins for all four principal actors at the Cannes Film Festival. Truncated or not, *Long Day's Journey into Night* failed at the box office, and it was Joe who took the financial hit, having reimbursed Landau the full production budget in return for the rights.[26] "Levine was a vulgar vulgarian," Lumet recalled, "but he wrote a check for the entire cost of *Long Day's Journey* without even blinking."[27]

To be sure, there is no way that Macdonald could have known the ins and outs of such distribution problems in detail, though much of his film writings indicate that he was well informed about the financial and industrial aspects of filmmaking. But Joe reveled in being a provocateur, and there is every chance that Macdonald may have been goaded into an ad hominem sideswipe, his sensitivities tickled after reading a typically provocative interview with Joe: "The O'Neill devotees are screaming their heads off . . . but wouldn't it be a greater crime if this classic were not commercially successful? It's a great picture in its entirety. It will be greater with an hour cut."[28] The foregrounding of commercial intent and belittling of highbrow sentimentality were tactics that Joe the oppositionist favored, and on a practical level he was still trying to sell a difficult movie. He could not really say he had made the film worse by cutting it.

Joe was adept at baiting the cultural elite and reeling them in by capitalizing on the cultural prejudices of the time. Macdonald may have been a staunch critic of auteurism, but he was still affected by modish thinking that privileged the text at the expense of production contexts. He had also long been a critic of the industrial nature of the studio system and compared Joe to Louis B. Mayer, whom he had elsewhere described as "the great symbol of all that was vulgar, mindless, the old Hollywood."[29] But Macdonald's withering characterization of Joe as craving entry into the rarefied "art-scene" clashes with Joe's clear ambitions to take art cinema out of its designated domain of exclusivity in order to find a bigger audience.

Joe's ostentatious positioning of himself between the highbrow critic and the critic's object of desire bothered not only Macdonald but also many others. Joe appeared as a nuisance. The response was snooty and revealed a reversal of the dictum "shoot the messenger." In legend, a messenger bringing bad news would be ritually killed to appease superstitious beliefs. By contrast, Joe was criticized for the goodness of the message, for the quality of his output. As Bourdieu observes, cultural choices "always owe part of their value to the value of the chooser."[30] With Joe flagrantly casting himself in the role of cultural chooser, he and his peplum pedigree tainted the artefacts he offered.

In late 1961, one illustrative review by Eugene Archer in the *New York Times* concerned Joe's Christmas offering, *The Wonders of Aladdin,* and his perceived besmirching of eminent reputations: "Who would have thought, when Italian neo-realism was in full crescendo, that Vittorio de Sica, the dour director of *The Bicycle Thief,* and Aldo Fabrizi, the tragic priest of *Open City,* would one day be playing second fiddle in one of the hackneyed costume fantasies from the dubbing chambers of Joseph E. Levine? . . . Signor de Sica, as a genie with invisible feet, dangles awkwardly in outer space, looking for all the world as if Mr. Levine had hung him out to dry."[31] Archer's review is willfully misleading, first in its implication that, prior to Joe's intervention, Fabrizi and former matinee idol de Sica were exclusively associated with critic-friendly arthouse fare and second for not mentioning Joe's connection to de Sica via *Two Women,* which had been released in the United States the previous March.

Archer's tactic of condemnation by selective inclusion and omission was most notably deployed by his *New York Times* colleague Bosley Crowther. Crowther's review of *Two Women* also neglects to mention Joe's role in bringing the movie to America.[32] It is doubtful that Crowther was unaware of the connection because Joe was so well defined on Crowther's radar. For Crowther, the arthouse boom of the 1960s compromised the prestige of arthouse cinema because of the apparently indiscriminate and undiscerning appetites of arthouse distributors, exhibitors, and patrons. He also cited "Joe Levine's Embassy" as an unwelcome intruder into the art scene for snapping up the cream of foreign-made arthouse fare with promises of big promotion.[33] But this seemingly unholy marriage of prestige and populism had provided arthouse cinema with a visibility and accessibility that it had hitherto lacked.

Lavish promotion had served to undermine, to some extent, the sometimes destructive influence that critics such as Crowther and Macdonald had over arthouse cinema, and many of Joe's films were winners at the box office and with Oscar. Following Loren's Oscar win for *Two Women,* Joe himself picked up the Best Foreign Film statuette on behalf of de Sica and Ponti for *Yesterday, Today, and Tomorrow* (1964) at the ceremony in 1965. The Best Foreign Film Oscar for the previous year had gone to Federico Fellini's *8½,* one of the most iconic masterpieces of the 1960s art house and a great success at the U.S. box office, backed by Joe's heavy-guns promotion—or "big coin ballyhoo," as *Variety* had it.[34]

Fellini's *8½* is his seventh feature; factor in as halves his two vignettes for omnibus films and a shared director credit on *Variety Lights,* and you get *8½,* the film's title. It is an avant-garde, semiautobiographical study that sees Guido, a director played by Marcello Mastroianni, lost in reverie and fantasy as he experiences creative ennui while shooting a science fiction movie. It is variously a visionary memoir, self-indulgent autohagiography, paean to creativity, and smug auteurist diatribe. Alberto Moravia compared *8½* to James Joyce's novel *Ulysses,*[35] and it is an apt comparison, both works being by turns sublime and infuriating. Fellini's film was also an arthouse event movie.

Fellini's early work, such as *La Strada* (1954), had established him as one of Italian cinema's most exciting directors. Subsequently, *La Dolce vita* was an arthouse sensation, its success fueled by controversies and condemnations from the Vatican and America's Catholic Legion of Decency. Joe missed out on *La Dolce vita.* On returning from one of his many excursions to Rome, he reported his "handshake deal"[36] for the American rights to Fellini's film, but it was eventually distributed by Astor Pictures, which paid "in excess of $500,000,"[37] and ballyhooed by Joe's former press agent, Bill Doll. *La Dolce vita* made Fellini an arthouse superstar, and *8½,* following an entertaining vignette to *Boccaccio 70,* was the next full feature from the Italian master, whose motif-ridden meditations on life and the world's shortcomings were catnip to critics.

Joe acquired the rights to distribute *8½* in the United States and Canada through a distribution deal he made with Columbia before he had even seen the film. According to a story planted in *Variety* by a publicity company on Joe's payroll, the $400,000 fee he paid for the rights was less than what competitors had offered, but Fellini was prepared to accept the initial deal in anticipation of the greater returns expected from Joe's showmanship. "*8½*'s success in America is assured because if there's one thing Joe Levine knows how to do, it's how to sell a good film," ran the plug.[38]

Joe set about making *8½* into a cultural event not entirely dissimilar to *Hercules.* A sense of anticipation, a building up of expectation, and a ratcheting up of excitement were all tricks he had used to lure the drive-in crowd to *Hercules:* "Wherever You Are, You Are Never Far from *HERCULES!*" Distant rumblings of an impending and approaching marvel were also a key feature of Joe's *8½* promotion: "The Raves Have Started!" exhorted one trade ad, alongside choice excerpts from the trickle of rave reviews that would become a flood. Just as *Hercules*'s enticements aped the breathless boasts of the roadshow epics, so *8½*'s promotion cut and pasted superlatives from reverential reviews to create a mosaic of hyperbole.

Crowther and Macdonald were two notables whose positive reviews helped to bolster the critical reception of *8½*. True to form, Crowther omitted Joe's name from his review, but he did mention Joe's involvement with *8½* in his worried account of big-money interlopers in the art scene.[39] Macdonald limited his comments about Joe to a characteristically sarcastic aside regarding what he saw as gratuitous budgetary information and sloppy copyediting in Embassy's press book for the film.[40]

Nesting in a bed of almost universal critical acclaim—Pauline Kael was a notable detractor—*8½*'s promotion foregrounded intellectual mystery and sex appeal. The posters feature elliptical invitations: smaller posters promised "a motion picture that goes beyond what men think about—because no man ever thought about it quite this way"; larger posters featured a cryptic entreaty from the director:

> This film talks about you . . . about your life . . . about your family . . . about your work . . . about your doubts . . . about your dreams . . . You will see yourself in the leading role as though you were looking in a mirror . . . This is your film.
>
> —Federico Fellini

Alongside these appeals to intellectualism and creative engagement appears the no less appealing figure of Claudia Cardinale, depicted from behind descending a staircase, sashaying hips accentuated. All publicity material, of course, bore the legend "Joseph E. Levine Presents."

Joseph E. Levine Presents the audience with an invitation to step into an alien world of strangeness and sights of the like you never before have seen, baited with the siren sex appeal of exotic beauties. The drive-in and the art house may have contained different audiences with different tastes. The former may have wolfed down hot dogs, while the latter sipped freshly ground coffee, but both were seduced by eventist ballyhoo. And if it seems counterintuitive to compare Joe's *Hercules* campaign with his *8½* campaign, it seems doubly counterintuitive to note significant differences. *Hercules* and its campaign featured no stars. *8½*, by contrast, relied heavily on the celebrity and star systems of the American art house, the kind of ephemeral appeal more commonly associated with the vacuities of pop culture. Marcello Mastroianni, Claudia Cardinale, Anouk Aimee, and, of course, Federico Fellini were all reliable brand names for the less-discerning viewer who wished to appear cultured.

Of his success in promoting *8½,* Joe recalled to Peter Dunn in 1978: "I made it into a hit. I made it into a cocktail picture. You know what a cocktail picture is? That's a picture people talk about at cocktail parties. Nobody understood it. They just talked about it."[41] Elsewhere he said that "the eggheads ate it up. Every egghead found something *different*—like looking at a painting. Now it's become a picture you teach from. A fuckin' *classic.*"[42] He also called Fellini "phoney as a glass eye,"[43] but there was more fondness than feuding between Fellini and Joe. A mutual acquaintance described their relationship as "a great love affair between two conmen."[44]

Joe's apparent disdain for "eggheads" indicates a striking difference in his public attitude toward the *Hercules* audience and the *8½* audience. Joe was fiercely defensive of the *Hercules* audience, "the little guys that need escape," but throughout his career he was also wont to lampoon the eggheads in the art house and to ridicule the snootiness of his own audience. The British writer Wyndham Lewis observed through the character of Horace Zagreus in his gargantuan satire *The Apes of God* (1932) that "people feel themselves under the special protection of the author when they read a satire on their circle."[45] Perhaps Joe knew that he could mock eggheaded pretentions with impunity, confident in the knowledge that each pretentious egghead would know that Joe was not talking about *him,* but about the other fellow, the pretentious egghead who went to see *8½* simply so he could discuss it loudly at cocktail parties. Or perhaps Joe was simply posing as the great vulgar mogul, capitalizing on the sacrilegious incongruity of selling both *Hercules* and *8½,* and maintaining his public profile as the bugbear of cultural elites. But one should also recognize Joe's mischievousness, and his words should be read as a gentle taunt, a good-natured jibe at the pretentions of the age. Joe may have disparaged critics, but he never expressed any real contempt for his audience, be it drive-in, grind house, or art house.

In 1965, critic Stephen Taylor published the article "After the Nouvelle Vague" in *Film Quarterly,* one of the more serious movie publications of the time, and made a curious aside about Joe: "Joseph E. Levine, who, as everyone knows, is Lorenzo the Magnificent of a cinema whose products are tailored to the distributor's measurements."[46] Taylor is not specific about which products he was referring to. He could have been referring to Joe's overtly commercial ventures, from *Hercules* to *The Carpetbaggers;* he could equally have meant Joe's alterations to and bowdlerizations of *Boccaccio 70, Long Day's Journey into Night,* and *Contempt* or, at a push, even *Gaslight Follies* or *Godzilla: King of the Monsters.* Despite the non-specificity of Taylor's disparaging aside, it is an interesting one nonetheless and emblematic of the cultural milieu from whence it came.

Lorenzo the Magnificent (Lorenzo de Medici) is the best known of the powerful Medici banking dynasty. Grandson of Cosimo de Medici and son of Piero the Gouty, Lorenzo was de facto ruler over the Republic of Florence in the latter half of the fifteenth century. In addition to their banking interests, the Medicis were prominent patrons of the arts—none more so than Lorenzo. The most cultured and versatile of the Medicis, Lorenzo supported and helped to develop such divergent and varied talents as Michelangelo, Botticelli, and Leonardo da Vinci. His position, then, as a major figure of Italian Renaissance art was secure and remained unchallenged for centuries—that is, until the 1960s, the time of Taylor's article.

Medici scholar F. W. Kent observes that from the 1960s on academics and historians sought to obliterate Lorenzo's reputation in a modish display of sacred-cow poking. Lorenzo's reputation subsequently became that of an overrated dilettante, a view bolstered by snobbish associations with his family of "parvenu bankers."[47] Taylor's "as everyone knows" gambit indicates how well known this scholarly volte-face was in intellectual circles.

Parallels can also be drawn between the intellectual culture of the 1960s and that of Renaissance Florence. The Italian Renaissance was the period that saw the veneration of the individual artist in the West. In earlier times, artists, from painters to troubadours, were associated with the lower classes; they were largely anonymous and undertook manual labor. Similarly, with the arrival on American shores of the auteur theory, so began the veneration of the movie director, which occurred in part as a reaction against the industrial and mass-entertainment strategies of Hollywood's now crumbling studio system.

As the author-director was increasingly sanctified, so the patron of the arts—the moneyed backer—was viewed with suspicion and disdain. Many powerful intellectual voices haughtily belittled Joe as a pretentious interloper who, despite his unsuitability, sought entry into a rarefied world, just as the Medici clan had sought to gain entry into the kingdom of heaven by building monuments to God to atone for their usury. In ascribing status-chasing intentionality to Joe, his critics were indulging in the kind of received wisdom that would become, and remains, a critical cliché—the assumption that what any successful person in the arts truly craves is acceptance and acclaim from critics: "OK. So this fellow may be a millionaire, but what he *really* wants is *my* approval." Like most clichés, there is probably a kernel of truth in this one, but there is far too much evidence to the contrary for this particular bromide to apply to Joe.

Although Joe capitalized on critical acclaim for many of his films, he never sought critical acceptance for himself. Quite the reverse. His public image was that of a combative gate crasher. His relentless teasing of the critical fraternity, his incorrigibly jolly and repeated use of the epithet *egghead* to describe its inhabitants, and many other contrivances in his public persona confirm this. It would not have done that image any good for him to be accepted as an insider; he had to be an outsider. His showman's status and therefore his livelihood depended on it. Rather than craving acceptance, Joe reveled in the fact that he was selling movies to the same people who could not stand his presence in *their* domain.

But there was a seriousness to this oppositional relationship, too. Critics may have chosen to ignore, resent, or even be repelled by the industrial and commercial pressures of cinema; Joe could not. He was not, as the saying goes, running a charity. Of his arthouse investments, he told Murray Schumach of the *New York Times*, "You take an art picture. It opens in big cities. It may do great. But it doesn't get bookings anywhere else in the United States. The exhibitors will not get behind a foreign film. They have not learned to accept them. The United States and England are the only countries in which foreign films are classified as art films. . . . You cannot stay in business by making O'Neill pictures. I will never get my money out of *Long Day's Journey into Night*."[48]

Nonetheless, as Sidney Lumet told Mark Harris, Joe "really stuck by [*Long's Day's Journey into Night*] when it was doing no business."[49] To see Joe as a mercenary or cynic, then, is wrong-headed. Despite his concerns, he never quite left the art house behind until later in his career. Through the 1960s, he maintained contracts with Marcello Mastroianni, Sophia Loren, and Vittorio de Sica and brought many more curios and oddities from overseas to American screens. He was motivated by a love of movies as much as by profit, and the two are not mutually exclusive. Joe loved movies and the movie business. He also sought to loosen the stranglehold critics had over the art house, a pursuit that again undermines the notion that he craved critical acceptance. In 1967, he stated his case, both echoing Arthur Knight's assessment from the previous decade and hinting at the Sophoclean irony that territorial critics were helping to destroy that which they were trying to protect: "I think my company brought more art house films here than any other company," he told the *Film Daily*, "You don't bring them here and be at the mercy of a couple of critics in New York. If they don't like an art film you're dead. If a commercial film is panned by the critics nobody pays any attention."[50]

Joe certainly had a point. With few people paying attention to reviews of commercial cinema, critics did have a tendency to make their point more forcefully with arthouse movies, jealously guarding their area of expertise. But questions of authority and public image are important here, too. Joe needed the egghead critic as his straw man, just as the critical expert needed the pretentious interloper. Critics' tendency to privilege the film text and director was complemented by a sentimental opposition to commercial forces, even though the commerciality of the art house raised these films' profile and status. Joe, meanwhile, capitalized on the arthouse boom that he helped to shape. In doing so, even if he attempted to circumvent critical influences with ballyhoo, he still relied on critical acclaim and prestige to promote his films, but his own public image demanded that he provoke and relish the critical opprobrium heaped upon his person.

6

The Showman on the Screen

> Jean Luc Fuck! I could have made that frog cocksucker another Fellini.
>
> —*Joseph E. Levine*

Two films, both from 1963, provide insights into Joe's public image and posthumous reputation. *Showman* is a documentary about Joe made by the brothers Albert and David Maysles, and *Contempt* is a film from Jean-Luc Godard that is widely perceived to be an attack by the French auteur on Joe, its producer. Joe was deeply ambivalent about *Showman* and sought to suppress it. He also said that *Contempt* was "the worst film anybody ever made."[1]

Showman is the little-seen first feature from the Maysles brothers, American pioneers of "direct cinema," a form of documentary filmmaking developed in the late 1950s by filmmakers such as Michel Brault and Gilles Groulx in Canada and then by other documentarists in France and the United States. Direct cinema sought to capture objective truth by utilizing the kind of unobtrusive filming style made possible by relatively lightweight portable cameras. Following *Showman,* the Maysles would produce ground-breaking documentaries such as *What's Happening! The Beatles in the USA* (1964), *Salesman* (1968), *Gimme Shelter* (1970), and *Grey Gardens* (1976). For Peter Rosen, filmmaker and friend of Joe, *Showman* is "a better story than any book [about Joe] could be, and by far the Maysles Bros best film."[2] It is perhaps the most interesting document about Joe that we have, but it is rarely screened—thanks largely to Joe's suppressive interventions following its production.

Showman was controversial from its inception. A friend of David Maysles had pitched the idea of making a film about Joe for a television series of portraits of American leaders. "We already have too many films about Jews" was the response, a comment that prefigured some later controversies. This rejection made the Maysles, themselves Boston Jews, determined to make the film anyway—"out of spite," remembered Albert Maysles in 2007.[3] Filmed over a period of two weeks, *Showman* follows Joe from New York to Boston to Cannes. There are no interviews to camera. The Maysles instead follow Joe going about his business, making deals, meeting Sophia Loren and Kim Novak, overseeing promotion for various films, and pontificating about upcoming projects. Money is a key obsession. *Showman* is littered with the fetishistic twitterings of Joe and his underlings about figures, sales, and deals; the first audible words we hear from Joe are "fifty thousand dollars," followed by a handshake. The film is startling in its intimacy. According to David Maysles, "Levine thought we were just a couple of nuts from Greenwich Village,"[4] so the Joe they show is unguarded. Joe thought *Showman* could be a good promotional tool, but once he saw it, his lawyers intervened, and even now it is difficult to see.

"Thank God he doesn't have a Jewish voice," Rosalie commented when the Maysles privately screened *Showman* for Joe and his wife.[5] Jews were not absent from American screens in the early 1960s, but as the United States and its media sought to portray an assimilationist democracy in the postwar era, ethnic differences and characteristics were toned down and homogenized. The screen Jew in mid-twentieth-century America was, from biblical epics to war dramas, associated with victimhood. Race-related archetypes, stereotypes, associations, and eccentricities were consigned to earlier, supposedly less-sophisticated times. In a period of what Steven Alan Carr has termed "ethnic absence" on-screen,[6] Joe's appearance as a loudmouth, boisterous, bossy Jew in *Showman* must have been alarming, if not shocking—a resurrection of both the vaudeville archetype of the Jewish huckster impresario and the power-hungry, money-motivated controller of culture in anti-Semitic literature. When *Showman* was submitted for Oscar consideration, the committee universally judged it anti-Semitic, and the screening was stopped after five minutes. When the Maysles screened *Showman* privately for Otto Preminger, the great director declared, "Hitler couldn't have made anything more anti-Semitic."[7]

Albert Maysles commented many years later that the associations of the film with anti-Semitism were at the core of Joe's ambivalence about it. Growing up in Boston in the era of Father Coughlin's nasty broadcasts, Maysles himself was no stranger to anti-Semitism, and he believed that the situation was even worse during Joe's Boston childhood. But these things had not passed, and at least one contemporary example can be found in Edward Feldman's memoir, wherein he writes about anti-Semitic remarks directed at Joe from executives of Britain's Rank Organisation during a rough-cut screening of *The Last Days of Sodom and Gomorrah* in 1961.[8] The Maysles brothers were sympathetic to Joe's misgivings: "His attitude is very understandable," said David Maysles of Joe's reaction. "We're all very sympathetic with him. When Levine was growing up our parents were in the same location in the West End, at a time when anti-Semitism was at fever heat. He felt this enormously so that a kind of fear has led to a misconception of other people's attitudes."[9]

That we now see Albert Maysles, the recently deceased brother, as a grandee of factual cinema is testament to his influence on the medium. But to see him as the affable godfather of American documentary is to forget how revolutionary his films were in the early 1960s. If Joe wanted *Showman* to go unseen, then America's cultural gatekeepers indirectly aided him. It was excluded from consideration for the Robert Flaherty Award for Documentary, presented by the Film Institute of City College. It was also later rejected by National Education Television for the selection of American documentaries submitted to the Cannes Film Festival. Both decisions left filmmaker, critic, and Robert Flaherty Award juror Jonas Mekas "boiling mad." For Mekas, *Showman* was "a powerful portrait of a businessman; the world and the personality of one of the film moguls is nakedly presented. The film will become a lasting document of a unique kind, a source of study and talk for years to come."[10]

Mekas's fellow jurors for the Flaherty Award included both Dwight Macdonald and Arthur Mayer, Joe's erstwhile colleague from his New England days, and it would be interesting to know what they thought of the film, if they even saw it, but it was weeded out in the prescreening process. Mekas felt that the Cannes decision "complete[d] the fiasco" of institutions failing to recognize that which was new and innovative in documentary cinema.[11]

Unfounded accusations of anti-Semitism, a resistance to the innovative and new, and Joe's own legal actions combined to keep *Showman* out of the public eye in the early 1960s. However, many years later Joe was still complaining about it:

> Those Maysles Brothers, those guys put one over on me. What they started out with was a good idea. It would have advertised all

> my pictures. I thought it would make a good promotion to show at exhibitors' conventions. Everywhere they took pictures of Sophia and all the stars, whoever the hell was working for me at that time. Then they cut everything away and there was a couple of nasty things in there I didn't know they had. They'd interviewed people in my office. They interviewed a guy I'd fired and what he said was in the movie. It's been haunting me for years. I've tried to buy the negative from them . . . they can't show it for money but they've shown it to every sonofabitch in the world. I don't know what they get out of this film.[12]

Certainly, Joe's guard was down when the Maysles were following him, and for Joe the Great Showman to have two unknowns "put one over" on him was not conducive to his public image as a street-smart film promoter. Although *Showman* could well have compromised Joe's public image, there is little in it that is truly negative—quite the opposite in fact.

Showman shows Joe as a fast-talking, fast-moving, hardworking showman who is dedicated to his job and fueled by incorrigibility and enthusiasm. His raconteurial gifts are amply demonstrated, as is his adamant refusal to glamorize his poverty-stricken past when he makes a visit to the West End of Boston. He is bumptiously entertaining when in full flow around underlings, but schoolboy shy around Sophia Loren. Most entertaining is his Olympian castigation of David Susskind during a radio interview in response to Susskind's criticism of *Hercules*. Susskind, a multifaceted producer and talk-show host, laughs along at Joe's upbraiding, putting his head in his hands in mock exasperation as he becomes incapable of getting a word through Joe's finger-wagging upbraid. Only a couple of years later, Joe would lose a quarter of a million dollars investing in Susskind's legendary Broadway failure *Kelly* (1965), which closed after only one night.

Showman, however, is not a puff piece. Joe is shown weakened by tiredness, and there is criticism of his propensity for stealing ideas from his staff, who are filmed in conversation on the street. If Joe genuinely thought he was agreeing to an admiring tribute, such as that by Talese, he was being naive. New Journalism sought to place popular culture on the intellectual map as a cultural corrective; direct cinema sought to offer a disinterested critique by unobtrusive regard. "Our intention was to represent Levine as close to his real self as possible," Albert Maysles explained many years later. "As Orson Welles put it, 'In a fiction film the director is

God; in a non-fiction film God is the director.' In that way we were in good company, ourselves going into it without prior judgments and in the process an open-minded observational approach."[13] By contrast, what written work there is about *Showman* is riddled with prior judgments and willful misreadings, with praise for the film pervaded by priggish disparagements of its subject.

For Gerald Peary, this film about "the overweight, crude Levine" presents an either/or question: "Is Joe E. Levine a barbarian, philistine jerk? Or is he a shrewd, all-American entrepreneur?"[14] Stephen Mamber is also reductively dichotic: "If one were to take sides, one could conclude that Levine is either a monster destroying public taste or just a very ambitious guy who has won out over other ambitious guys."[15] Simon Plant embraces cliché in his assessment of "a dark portrait of power which probes Machiavellian movie producer Joseph E. Levine."[16] And Jonathan B. Vogels detects ad hominem mischievousness in a film that "memorably illuminates [Joe Levine's] adamant regard for profit before artistic merit." He further complains, "Levine might as well be selling soap or breakfast cereal. . . . [He] refuses to distinguish between or among the various films he has produced, even though *Hercules,* a frothy epic . . . and *Two Women,* a dark contemplation of life in post-war Italy, are markedly different."[17]

Nowhere in writing about *Showman* does a love of cinema in all its forms or even a love of the film industry seem viable motivators for Joe's drive. But *Showman* does indeed show his multifarious appetites, wide-ranging abilities, and versatility. During the two weeks of filming, we see him overseeing the promotional campaigns for *Two Women, Boccaccio 70,* and re-releases of *Hercules* and *Hercules Unchained;* he tries to buy the rights to *Mondo Cane* and brags about "big" upcoming projects, such as *The Carpetbaggers,* as well as about a potential deal with Nobel Prize–winning author Pearl S. Buck. A remarkably varied slate of films and ambitions.

Most written work about *Showman* not only misrepresents Joe but also underestimates the film itself. Thanks to its intimacy and unobtrusiveness, *Showman* provides a far more sympathetic and complex portrait of Joe than can be discerned from the associated literature. It is, as noted, an extremely interesting and revealing document of Joe at a particular moment in his career. But if Joe felt that its release would damage his reputation, then much of the later writing about this film suggests that his much-vaunted gut instinct was unfortunately correct.

Joe was very sensitive about his depiction in *Showman.* He acquired the rights, which are still held by his estate, and though it occasionally pops up at Maysles retrospectives at film festivals, there is little chance of a legitimate release though DVD or streaming in the foreseeable future. Joe may have misjudged the Maysles' intentions, but, according to Albert Maysles, it was the depiction of his Jewishness that made him most uncomfortable. As an interesting postscript, some years later Joe invited the Maysles to his office to view a portrait of him by Jamie Wyeth. "He found his own imaginings of stereotypical anti-Semitism in the painting," remembered Albert Maysles. "We quite honestly refuted such false claims," adding, "Interesting how he valued our opinions."[18]

Many commentators also see *Contempt* as an attack on Joe. In this case, they are quite correct because that is what it is. Like *8½,* it is a director's film about the difficulties of being a director. It is also, as Jacques Aumont observes, "a giant *J'accuse . . . !* which portrays [producers] as dealers of death."[19] Critically derided on its initial release, *Contempt* has since been reclaimed as a forgotten masterpiece thanks to a remastering job and re-release in 1997. Much of the film's revised reputation lies in what is seen as Godard's incisive critique of American hegemonization of cinema, which appeals to both the knee-jerk anti-Americanism of cultural elites outside America and the guilt-sodden self-loathing of the cultural elites inside America. Vulgar, philistine, hegemonic Hollywood is personified in the character Jeremy Prokosch (Jack Palance), a vulgar, philistine American movie producer whom Godard supposedly based on Joe. In *Contempt,* Joe is the puppet master of hegemony: at one point, the odious Prokosch obediently scampers off to take a phone call from "Joe Levine calling from New York."

Hollywood's presence on the Tiber caused many frustrations and resentments, and *Contempt* is set against the backdrop of the once bustling Cinecittà studios, which in the film are now deserted, eviscerated by American greed, short-termism, and lack of imagination. Although America's runaway productions had run away to Italy prior to Joe's peplum successes (Paramount's *Ulysses,* for example), *Hercules* and its successors inspired countless production companies to decamp briefly to Italy for the cash-in. Having escalated the trend, Joe and Embassy followed suit. In 1961, *Variety* carried a story planted by Joe's press agent, Edward Feldman: "[Joe Levine is] finding difficulty in purchasing pictures outright for reasonable amounts, [and so] is concentrating on entering into various co-production deals which would provide a continuous flow of product over the next several years. Unable to uncover ready made films which he can tailor to his exploitation technique, he aims to increase the production values of his films and feels that the only way to do this is to actively participate in the making of them."[20] Quite how involved Joe was in the production of films such as *Morgan the Pirate* in 1960 and *The Wonders of Aladdin* in 1961 is open to speculation. Clearly, Feldman's piece sought to emphasize Joe's ambitions to move beyond promotion and into production, but his role in these films was much more likely to be that of investor than that of producer.

When Feldman planted his report in *Variety,* Joe was exec-producing *The Last Days of Sodom and Gomorrah* (1962). Following Joe's much publicized move into the art house, *Time* magazine jokingly sought to placate any readers worried about his low-brow pedigree: "some of his admirers fear that he is going to give up the drum and take up the lute. But with *Sodom and Gomorrah* now shooting in Morocco, Joe seems in no danger."[21] But *The Last Days of Sodom and Gomorrah* was to be Joe's peplum swan song and a case study of the tensions and resentments caused by Hollywood's presence on the Italian scene.

According to some reports, Joe pulled out of *The Last Days of Sodom and Gomorrah* during filming, yet he retained an exec-producer credit and was heavily involved in its promotion. He was, not unusually, enticed by the title and invested $800,000 following entreaties from producer Geoffrey Lombardo: "How can you help but make $800,000 with something called *Sodom and Gomorrah*?" Joe asked. "I think of it as the Las Vegas of 400 years ago."[22] But the production was fraught with problems and resentments. On location in Morocco, temperatures rose higher than 120 degrees Fahrenheit, and extras from the Moroccan army were called away because of the Algerian Putsch—the failed Algerian coup d'état in 1961. Lombardo, assistant director Sergio Leone, and Joe fell out with director Robert Aldrich. According to Christopher Frayling, Lombardo felt that Aldrich was "out of control," and Leone felt that Aldrich "did everything he possibly could to demolish [Lombardo] financially."[23] Indeed, *The Last Days of Sodom and Gomorrah,* along with the financial failure of Luchino Visconti's film *The Leopard* in 1963, caused the collapse of Lombardo's company Titanus Films. For Frayling,

> the longer term legacy of the whole debacle was to confirm certain

> sections of the Italian film community in their deep cynicism about mercenary American film-makers abroad. As Lombardo put it at the time: "They treated us with a certain disdain, as if we were underdogs, from a lower caste. When Italian film culture started to show signs of life, they did all they could to kill it stone dead." . . . "Economic conditions," Leone remembered, "made it virtually impossible to shoot a film in Italy." The sound stages at Cinecittà, he added, were like deserts, surrounded by unemployed technicians and extras.[24]

It was against this backdrop of decline and acrimony that Godard would set *Contempt,* with much of the initial action taking place in the ghost town of Cinecittà. The foregrounding of the deserted studios allowed Godard to capitalize on existing resentments and prejudices and to point the finger of blame at opportunistic American producers—Joe in particular.

The mercenary American producer was, by the time of *Contempt,* a well-worn archetype. F. Scott Fitzgerald had based Munro Stahr, the protagonist of his unfinished novel *The Last Tycoon,* on "Boy Wonder" Irving Thalberg. As head of production at Universal and, later, founding father of MGM, Thalberg was the man who did more than most to make Hollywood movies a producer's medium for its Golden Age before his death at age thirty-seven in 1936. In *The Last Tycoon,* Stahr is a brilliant but lonely high achiever fated to be an outcast. By the 1950s, the ruthless Hollywood producer came close to being a pop-culture cliché in films such as *The Big Knife* (1955) and *In a Lonely Place* (1950). Perhaps the most famous depiction of the Hollywood producer at this time came in 1952 with *The Bad and the Beautiful*, directed by Vincente Minnelli and featuring Kirk Douglas as the brilliant, unscrupulous, and emotionally tormented Jonathan Shields. Ten years later Minnelli and Douglas would reconvene for a quasi-sequel, *Two Weeks in Another Town* (1962), which was also set against the desperate backdrop of Cinecittà and a clear influence on *Contempt.*

By the early 1960s, the age of the auteur, the producer had shifted from archetype to enemy, from stereotype to scapegoat. With a fearful film industry facing the threat from television and an uncertain future, looking to the past to apportion blame for the contemporary state of affairs became popular, so the producer-led studio system was an opportune target for fashionable and simplistic critiques that implied the mutual exclusion of art and commerce. To be sure, although the studio system may have produced some of the greatest popular art of the twentieth century, anecdotes about visionary artists abused and suffocated by studio stricture, from Eric von Stroheim to Buster Keaton to Orson Welles, abounded. That many of the most interesting and critically acclaimed films of the postwar period arrived on American screens via the auteurist approaches of continental Europe provided strong circumstantial evidence for the legitimacy of the growing auteur cult, which privileged the artist-director over the philistine, money-mad producer. For many directors of this era, the auteurist stance was more manifesto-driven affectation than sincerely held conviction—the producer Georges de Beauregard was as much an architect of the nouvelle vague (new wave) as Godard or Truffaut. But Godard, as *Contempt* attests, had his own resentments and, indeed, insecurities.

Contempt, like *Where the Hot Wind Blows* and *Two Women,* follows the formula of respected and bankable director, European beauty, and a source novel by an esteemed author: Godard, Brigitte Bardot, and, once again, Alberto Moravia. Moravia's source novel, *A Ghost at Noon,* was published in 1955 and tells the story of a screenwriter, Riccardo Moltini, who is hired to script an adaptation of Homer's *Odyssey* for a mediocre German director, Rhinegold, and a commercially minded Italian producer, Batista.[25] Largely an interior monologue, the novel shows the sensitive Moltini being forced to confront not only his wife's increasingly contemptuous attitude toward him but also his own failures as he compromises his literary ambitions for money.

To research *A Ghost at Noon,* Moravia spent time observing the making of Paramount's *Ulysses,*[26] precisely the kind of Italian superspectacular envisaged by the producer Batista in the novel. Interestingly, Moltini remarks that the German director Rhinegold is "certainly not in the same class as the Pabsts and Langs,"[27] a notable line because not only does Fritz Lang play the director in *Contempt,* but also the original script for *Ulysses* was written by G. W. Pabst. Having sold the script to Dino De Laurentiis and Carlo Ponti, Pabst was hired to direct, but once Kirk Douglas was cast in the lead role, Paramount came on board and tussles began over the script. Pabst was fired and replaced by Mario Camerini, and the script was reworked by Hugh Gray and that great Hollywood hack Ben Hecht.[28]

A Ghost at Noon is, then, an interrogation of the dilution of art and cinematic culture. Moravia was consistently vocal about what he felt was the compromising of the Italian film industry by external forces, from his critique of peplum films in *A Ghost at Noon* to his criticism of the trend toward spaghetti Westerns in the mid-1960s.[29] As a critique, *A Ghost at Noon* is rather more balanced and incisive than *Contempt,* which is more manifesto driven. Upon making *Contempt,* Godard distanced himself from the source novel by disparaging it with faint praise in the journal *Cahiers du Cinema:*

> Moravia's novel is a nice vulgar read for a train journey, full of classical, old fashioned sentiments in spite of the modernity of the situations. But it is with this kind of novel that you can often make the best films.
>
> I have stuck to the main theme, simply altering a few details, on the principle that something filmed is automatically different from something written, and therefore original.[30]

Godard's words here appear to betray his insecurities. He aggrandizes himself by denigrating the novel. As if worried about being tainted by association, he preemptively dissociates himself from the unfashionable and much disparaged *cinema de qualité*—a style of prewar French cinema that was defined, for the auteurists, by a lack of imagination and an overly reverential treatment of middlebrow source material. That his desperately obvious assertion that words are different from images and the protestation of his own originality should appear in *Cahiers du Cinema,* the auteurist bible, gives the impression of a man fearful of losing credibility.

Contempt had three producers: Georges de Beauregard, Carlo Ponti, and Joe. Prior to production, de Beauregard, the producer of the nouvelle vague, announced that *Contempt* would feature "the sharp, personalized filmmaking concepts of Godard . . . wedded to important box-office values."[31] These important box-office values can best be discerned from the choices made about who would star in the film. Godard had wanted Frank Sinatra and Kim Novak to play the roles of Paul and Camille, the couple whose marriage disintegrates over the course of the movie. Ponti, however, wanted Sophia Loren to play Camille and Marcello Mastroianni to play Paul. When news filtered through that Brigitte Bardot wanted to work with Godard, the deadlock was broken, and her involvement piqued Joe's interest.

Brigitte Bardot became a global icon following her starring role as

Juliette in *And God Created Woman* (1956), directed by her husband at the time, Roger Vadim. Bardot delivers a commanding performance, rendering Juliette's destructive sexuality with extraordinary force. *And God Created Woman* was a hit in American art houses and grind houses but, like Elvis Presley's "Heartbreak Hotel," is better assessed in terms of impact than success, the former being much more profound than the latter was great.

And God Created Woman was not Bardot's first film. Already famous as a model and actress in her native France, she had appeared in more than a dozen movies, mainly comedies, including *Doctor at Sea* (1955), a lightweight British comedy that gave Bardot her first English-speaking role. It was *And God Created Woman,* however, that turned her into a global icon. Her acting talent, extraordinary beauty, and on-screen magnetism led to a flood of interest in the fledgling star. Grindhouse operators and exploitation men snapped up films such as *Plucking the Daisy* (1956), which, after being retitled *Mademoiselle Striptease,* did the rounds in the United States and the United Kingdom. In the arthouse circuit, she starred in Henri-Georges Clouzot's *La Vérité* (a.k.a. *The Truth*, 1960), which was nominated for a Best Foreign Film Oscar, and had a walk-on part as herself in Jean Cocteau's *La Testament d'Orphée* (1960). While highbrows sought to deconstruct the Bardot phenomenon, as Simone de Beauvoir did in her essay *Brigitte Bardot and the Lolita Syndrome,*[32] Bardot was busy being credited with popularizing the bikini, bouffant hair, St. Tropez, and gingham dresses.

Media interest ensured Bardot stayed in the news, and her colorful private life ensured a high level of media intrusion. That she had suffered a nervous breakdown in 1958, along with a suspected suicide attempt, only added to her appeal in gossip columns and among the intelligentsia. Such naked vulnerability inspired a benevolent protectiveness from Bardot's legions of cultured male devotees, who were able to distinguish their noble intentions toward this fragile creature from the baser desires of her more philistine admirers. Like Elvis Presley, James Dean, and Marilyn Monroe, she still commands an enormous affection from her fans, one that transcends her work as an artist, even now, when she is more closely associated with the kookier aspects of animal rights activism and the unsavoriness of France's political right-wing than with cinema.

By 1963, Bardot was both popular and hip. In a rare moment of consonance on a production marked by factionalism, Godard, Ponti, and Joe agreed on Bardot for *Contempt.* Bardot attracted Joe, and Joe brought money, so Embassy's money paid not only for Bardot's star power but also for higher production values, such as Raoul Coutard's justly celebrated lush widescreen color photography. Though increasingly common in American cinema, color and widescreen were not particularly associated with European cinema at the time, notable exceptions being *And God Created Woman* and the films of the peplum cycle—and echoes of both resonate through *Contempt.* Peplum production provides the backdrop, enabling Godard's rendering of the philistine American producer bugaboo in Prokosch; *And God Created Woman* provides an artistic antecedent, with Bardot's dissatisfied Camille appearing as an older version of her frustrated Juliette.

Following Bardot came Michel Piccoli to play Paul, Camille's husband; Jack Palance to play Prokosch; and Fritz Lang to play Fritz Lang. Once production began, Godard was faced with a host of problems and headaches. Impetuous, instinctive, given to improvising on the fly and working quickly, Godard was used to none of the obstacles placed in his way on this fairly big-budget production. The Italian crew were highly unionized, with regulated breaks and working hours; Jack Palance required detailed direction and was continually frustrated by Godard's uncommunicative methods; Brigitte Bardot not only brought her latest boyfriend, actor Sami Frey, whom Godard felt was a distraction, but also attracted a swarm of paparazzi, whose constant presence was an additional source of enervation for the director.

Another source of personal frustration and, no doubt, sadness was the slow and inexorable implosion of Godard's relationship with Anna Karina, his wife, muse, and collaborator. It is certainly more than mere speculation to suggest that the deterioration of Godard's marriage informed the onscreen deterioration of Camille and Paul's marriage. Godard's analysis of marital breakdown is surgical yet tragic, reminiscent of and no doubt influenced by Roberto Rossellini's *Voyage to Italy* (1954). Godard's telling of marital disintegration is boosted by brilliant performances by the two principals, who capture the complexities, contradictions, and impotent hopelessness of being in a failing relationship. Bardot embodies Camille as being at once confused, resentful, flighty, petty, and mournful, while Piccoli's Paul is similarly contradictory, being self-aggrandizing and self-pitying, manipulative and oblivious. The performances, Coutard's ravishing color photography, Georges Delarue's haunting score, and Godard's sensitive approach all combine to make *Contempt* one of the most tragically romantic depictions of a relationship in all cinema. Godard's rendering of movie production contexts, however, is painted with a much broader brush.

Georges de Beauregard had produced many of Godard's features, and, with Beauregard, Ponti had coproduced Godard's *A Woman Is a Woman* (1961) and *The Soldiers* (a.k.a. *Le Petit soldat,* 1963) prior to *Contempt.* So Joe was the new producer on Godard's block, and the relationship rankled, as Raoul Coutard explains: "Since the Americans were involved we had to follow a set work schedule. We had to send a daily telex to Levine to assure him that things were going as planned. That really upset Godard since he couldn't do exactly as he wanted."[33]

Contempt was an expensive production in which Embassy had invested heavily. As befit such a production, Joe required a detailed script that was to be followed, a strict shooting schedule, and regular status updates. Godard was used to none of these requirements and resented the intrusion into his artistic autonomy. For Joe's part, he had recently had his fingers burned by an "out of control" director on *Sodom and Gomorrah,* so his guard was up. While Joe fumed in his New York office, Godard's irritation found its way onto the screen in his merciless lampooning of the producer Prokosch.

The odious caricature of the producer is Godard's most significant departure from Moravia's source novel. In *A Ghost at Noon,* the producer is an Italian named Batista and was based on Moravia's friend Carlo Ponti. For Moltini, the novel's sensitive scribe, "Batista . . . was the kind of man whom his collaborators and dependents, as soon as his back was turned, referred to with charming names such as 'the brute,' 'the big ape,' 'the great beast,' 'the gorilla.' I cannot say that these epithets were undeserved . . . [but] . . . these nicknames erred, in my opinion, in not taking into account one of Batista's highly important qualities—I mean his most unusual artfulness, not to say subtlety, which was always present, though concealed under an apparent brutishness."[34]

In stark contrast, Godard's Prokosch is an irretrievable idiot, a boorish, philistine, vulgar buffoon who believes himself to be a Nietzschean superman but who is, in fact, a moron. Palance, who hated the shoot and repeatedly phoned his agent to help him wriggle out of it, is brilliant. There are some wonderful moments. Prokosch's oafish egotism is bluntly drawn when he is writing a check: lacking a surface to lean on as he writes, he bends his assistant over and uses her back. Later, in one of many outbursts of stupidity, he declares, "I know exactly how Gods feel . . . exactly," as Godard shoots him from a low angle, standing heroically, emphasizing the grandeur of his delusions.

Oftentimes, however, Godard can appear smugly elitist and jarringly petty as he uses Prokosch's outsider status and lack of learning against him. Prokosch is unable to communicate with the other characters without the aid of a translator, whereas Fritz Lang is able to speak at least three languages fluently; Prokosch reads inappropriate quotations from a little book he carries, whereas the cultured Europeans quote Dante and Hölderlein at length and discuss their finer points; Prokosch displays brutish, unfocused energy, whereas Lang exudes sagacious serenity; Lang is regarded by the other Europeans with respectful awe, but Lang regards Prokosch with a superior, resigned, impotent disdain.

In the Internet age, Godard would have fallen afoul of Godwin's Law, a web rule that states that during online debates the first person to draw comparisons to Hitler or the Nazis automatically loses the argument. Throughout *Contempt,* Prokosch's methods are explicitly associated with Nazism—and not just as a humorous allusion to a bossy "little Hitler," but very specifically. The comparisons to Nazism are given a ring of authenticity because they are spoken by Lang, who fled Germany in 1933 rather than head Joseph Goebbels's propaganda machine. When this experience is referred to in the film, Prokosch responds, "This is not 1933, this is 1963, and he will direct what was written." Later, when Prokosch says, "Whenever I hear the word *culture,* I reach for my checkbook," Lang responds, "Some years ago . . . some terrible years ago, the Nazis used to take out a pistol instead of a checkbook," a reference to the line "When I hear the word culture, I release the safety catch on my Browning," which is often misattributed to Goebbels but should be correctly attributed to the playwright Hanns Johst.

Godard's po-faced comparison of an American ignoramus to the monsters of Nazism is both lazy and unconvincing, made worse by the widespread and highly likely belief that Prokosch is a caricature of Joe Levine. For James Verniere, "Palance's producer is a stab in the back of *Contempt*'s legendary vulgarian producer Joseph E. Levine."[35] An item published in the *Observer* in 2000 claims that Godard "sent up Levine as the ignorant Hollywood mogul played by Jack Palance."[36] And a listings article for a festival screening of the restored film in 1997 provides extratextual tittle-tattle for an enhanced viewing strategy: "For those not in the know, Palance's performance as a loathsome producer (based not so loosely on the film's actual producer, Joseph E. Levine) is a delight."[37] In light of such interpretations, Godard's clumsy comparisons become startlingly crass. Joe had suffered greatly and been deeply scarred by the vicious anti-Semitism he experienced during his poverty-stricken youth. For Godard, a privileged child of wealth, to liken Joe, however obliquely, to the Nazis imbues *Contempt* with a damaging fatuousness, and that critics and scholars so gleefully continue to indulge in this particular viewing strategy is testament to an obnoxious snobbery.

Of all the extratextual mythologies that inform understandings of *Contempt,* the most popular concerns Joe's demand that Godard shoot an extra nude scene with Bardot to help make the film more marketable. The basic story of Joe's demand is neither unconvincing nor unsurprising. Joe was, after all, an exploitation man, and in October 1963 *Variety* had reported on Joe's demand for extra scenes. However, even this apparently straightforward example of producer interference has been embellished by willful misreadings and compounded by intermittent bouts of blindness. According to Philip Lopate, "Carlo Ponti and Joseph E. Levine . . . were upset that the rough cut was so chaste. Not a single nude scene with BB—not even a sexy costume!"[38] And Colin MacCabe, Godard's biographer and film scholar, claims, "Joe Levine saw the Bardot vehicle in which he had invested and discovered to his complete consternation that, despite the fact that this was a film of adultery, and sexual betrayal, there was no shot of Bardot nude. But Bardot *was* nudity—that was what Levine had paid for and that was what he was going to get."[39]

On the contrary, Bardot spends large portions of *Contempt* in various states of undress, even before Joe's required inserts. She is shown sunbathing nude, an open book covering her bottom, and during the film's middle segment she spends around twenty minutes either in the bath or wearing nothing but a towel, flashing flesh as she wanders around an apartment arguing with her on-screen husband. It is, then, impossible to take reports that suggest that Joe was responsible for all the nudity in *Contempt* seriously, the eminence of the reporters notwithstanding. In his authoritative biography of Godard, however, MacCabe does concede that, beyond a bare Bardot, Joe demanded extra scenes because he wanted a "psychological explanation" for Camille's behavior.[40]

Ponti had tired of Godard by this stage, and so he took *Contempt* and bowdlerized it. He recut it, added a jazz score, dubbed the entire film into Italian (thereby obliterating the theme of miscommunication occasioned by the multilingual protagonists and rendering redundant the character of Prokosch's translator, Francesca), and dumped the film into Italian cinemas. Joe, at least, sought to make it more coherent and, yes, sellable.

Although MacCabe accuses Joe of the apparent thought-crime of seeking a "pornographic charge" to open *Contempt,* he admits that it "would be a much less beautiful and moving film without the long opening scene."[41] This is true. Joe's intervention resulted in perhaps the most celebrated scene of Godard's career and, indeed, of both Bardot's and Piccoli's. The scene, photographed by Alain Legrand because Coutard was working on another project, is one long take. Paul, in vest and shorts, is lying back on a bed, propped up on an elbow. Camille lies beside him on her stomach, entirely nude, questioning him about which parts of her body appeal to him as the camera pans slowly from her head down to her toes and back. Paul, seemingly distracted, is both indulgent and obsequious. He provides Camille with answers of adoration, patronizingly furnishing her with the responses he thinks she wants to hear, indicating his willingness to acquiesce, his quickness to compromise and gratify, and thus exemplifying the patheticness that Camille comes to hold in contempt.

Despite the fact that the opening scene added the coherence and nudity that Joe wanted, many commentators interpret the scene as an act of sabotage and defiance by Godard, pointing to a lack of eroticism in it and the fact that it is shot through blue, white, and red filters—the French tricolor (and the colors of the American flag). This interpretation runs the risk of underestimating Godard and the film as well as of ascribing a lurid intentionality to Joe, but there still may be some truth in it. Godard's irritation with Joe is there for all to see in the character Prokosch, and even while *Contempt* was still in production, Godard took to the trade press to distance himself from Joe and, by extension, *Contempt* itself. No stranger to the occasional showman's gesture, and with his own publicity machine seemingly in overdrive, Godard railed publicly against Joe for not submitting *Contempt* to the Venice Film Festival,[42] criticized the wastefulness of the American film industry (with specific reference to *Contempt*),[43] and praised himself for making *Contempt* dub proof.[44] All of these stories found their way into *Variety* in the week before the New York premier of Godard's latest film, *Vivre sa vie* (1963). Later, Godard seemed to be predicting and relishing the future commercial failure of *Contempt.* For Godard, Joe was merely a packager of films who "doesn't know what's in the package." He questioned Joe's recent success with *8½:* "he doesn't know why he had success with [*8½*], and he doesn't know why he won't have success with mine."[45]

Contempt was released in the United States in December 1964, nearly a year after it had been released in France, and it was a critical and commercial failure. Reviews were infused with an irritated, knowing weariness, displaying a soggy disdain for both Bardot's body and Godard. The *New Republic* declared sarcastically, "Those interested in Brigitte Bardot's behind in CinemaScope and in Color will find ample rewards in *Contempt.*"[46] The *Motion Picture Herald* claimed that "aside from the spectacle of Miss Bardot seen nude from the rear and often there is little of commercial or artistic value."[47] Most of the critics' ire, however, was directed at Godard. The *New Yorker* spoke of his "stunning self-indulgence";[48] *Time* described the film as "doodling disguised as art";[49] and the *New Republic* railed against the film's now celebrated middle segment, calling it "an archetype of arrant egotism and bankrupt imagination in a director."[50] But Godard chose to overlook the hostile critical reception and pointed the finger of blame at Joe: "[*Contempt*] was very badly produced by a distributor because he had no idea what sort of product he was turning out."[51]

As for Joe, he all but disowned the film. The marketing materials were lackluster, and the usual round of interviews befitting such a big-budget, starry production did not materialize. In fact, Joe rarely mentioned the film, and when he did, it was usually in response to another's praise for it. Joel E. Siegel was fond of telling the tale of how, as a young film critic, he met Joe by chance and told him how much he admired *Contempt.* "You liked that piece of shit?" fumed Joe. "Jean Luc Fuck! I could have made that frog cocksucker another Fellini."[52]

In 1965, Levine donated seven films to New York's Museum of Modern Art, but *Contempt* was not among them. Just as Godard pointed the finger of blame at him, so Joe responded in kind. When a representative of the museum asked him about Godard, Joe replied, "He's what's wrong with the French film industry." When the representative temporized, "Well, he might be a little difficult," Joe responded forcefully, "Difficult? He's crazy. His efforts are studies to show his contempt for people. That's why he called the movie *Contempt.* That's why I didn't give it to you."[53]

In an interview with Calvin Tomkins the following year, Joe denounced the film and Godard further, claiming *Contempt* to be "the worst film we ever made—maybe the worst film *anybody* ever made. We lost a million bucks on that lousy film, because the *great* director Jean-Luc Godard refused to follow the script. . . . He never even answered our cables."[54]

Nowhere else has Joe spoken with such venom about a film he was involved with. But *Contempt* is a great movie, though flawed, and the feud between Joe and Godard should not be allowed to overshadow that fact. It is a shame that the welcome revisionist appraisal of this film is riddled with denigrations of Joe, who in pieces about the film is variously described as "vulgarian producer,"[55] "tacky American producer,"[56] and "distributor of *Hercules* and other schlock."[57] Joe was, among other things, vulgar, tacky, and a distributor of schlock, and there is nothing wrong with any of it; but there was a good deal more to his peculiar talent than that, and such denigrations are reductive and snooty in the context of their purpose—which is to elevate Godard.

The evidence suggests that both Joe and Godard were out of their respective depths on *Contempt.* Joe felt he had the tried and tested triumvirate of trendy director, respectable source novel, and European beauty, but he clearly failed to understand Godard's working methods and the freewheeling approach that produced the exuberance that made Godard such an arthouse darling. If Joe felt he could make such an impetuous and visionary director conform to the strictures of commercial movie making, especially from afar in New York, he was mistaken. Godard, meanwhile, as a director for hire was faced with the organized and regulated world of the international coproduction and responded petulantly to having signed away his independence. The resultant film is a deeply flawed masterpiece. Camille and Paul's marital breakdown is rendered brilliantly, and Godard's critique of production frustrations is often legitimate and funny. But *Contempt* is marred by his airing of petty and specific grievances in the most unimaginative manner as he scurries to the comfort zone of calumny and wheels out the Nazis.

7

Bad Taste in Hollywood

> Don't miss *The Carpetbaggers* because, like the Beatles, it has to be seen to be believed.
>
> —Cosmopolitan

At the Golden Globes ceremony on 11 March 1964, Joe was presented with the Cecil B. DeMille Lifetime Achievement Award. Quite why remains a mystery. Attempting to ascertain why a particular person or project won a particular award at a particular time can be a fool's errand, compounded by the difficulties of attempting to ascertain why a particular person or project *did not* win a particular award at a particular time and further complicated by attempts to fully analyze the temporal mores and the peculiar mixture of groupthink and caprice that informs such judgments. Nonetheless, in 1964 Joe was an odd choice.

In 1963, the Cecil B. DeMille Lifetime Achievement Award had been bestowed on Bob Hope, who had been a high-profile and successful star since the 1930s; the previous year it went to Judy Garland, who, though still only thirty-nine years old, had had a similarly lengthy tenure in the movies. In 1965, it went to veteran actor James Stewart, and in 1966 to John Wayne. Alfred Hitchcock had to wait until 1972 to be similarly honored, and Sam Goldwyn until 1973, when he was ninety. In a career stuffed with incongruities, Joe's inclusion on this list still appears vividly incongruous. Joe had been in the film business since 1938, but he had been a known quantity within the national industry for only about five years—hardly a lifetime. And although it would be pleasing to think that the Hollywood Foreign Press Association was honoring Joe's work as movie exhibitor, drive-in operator, and exploitation distributor, it does seem unlikely. The list of the award's recipients, even as it stands today, is dominated by stars, directors, moguls, and producers. In 1964, Joe had yet to make his name as a producer, and his receipt of the award is the only time in its history that it has been presented to someone ostensibly associated with movie distribution and (self-)promotion. It is unlikely that it was given in anticipation of future achievements, but by 1964 Joe was beginning to make his name as a producer of note and notoriety.

Despite significant arthouse successes in the early 1960s, the aggravations of *The Last Days of Sodom and Gomorrah* and *Contempt* had taken their toll, and although Joe did not abandon international productions, he turned his attention to Hollywood. A tantalizing opportunity presented itself in the form of Robert Aldrich, the troublesome director of *The Last Days of Sodom and Gomorrah.* This film was something of a misfire for Aldrich, who had had a run of great films in the 1950s, including *Vera Cruz* (1954), *Kiss Me Deadly* (1955), and *The Big Knife* (1955). Following the *Sodom and Gomorrah* debacle, Aldrich was to hit another rich creative seam in the 1960s. Films such as *Whatever Happened to Baby Jane?* (1962), *Hush, Hush Sweet Charlotte* (1964), *The Dirty Dozen* (1967), and *The Killing of Sister George* (1968) were ideal projects for Joe's hard-sell exploitation technique, but it was not to be.

Whatever Happened to Baby Jane? was a project Aldrich was keen to make. Based on a novel by Henry Farrell, the film details the resentful, guilt-ridden, and dependent relationship between two aging sisters, both former movie stars, who live lives based on lies and decayed dreams. To play the leads, Aldrich had already secured the services of two Hollywood stars from its Golden Age, Joan Crawford and Bette Davis, whose real-life rivalry was legendary. Edward Feldman, Joe's press agent, was excited about the project. Joe was not, as Feldman recalls:

> Now understand, Levine is very, very difficult to deal with. Things deteriorate quickly until finally Aldrich and [his attorney] come storming out of Levine's office, headed for the front door. . . . Aldrich says to me as he exits, "Forget it Ed. This is not going to happen. Levine's impossible."
>
> So I rush into Levine's office and say to him, "Joe, run after them, apologize, and let's make this movie. We could make a fortune. *Then* never talk to Aldrich again."
>
> Levine says, "I don't give a shit. Let them go."[1]

Joe's temperamental nature had lost him a film that was not only tailor-made for his style of exploitation but also, given its critical and commercial success, an ideal Hollywood calling card. But the situation was still profitable for Joe. Having advanced Aldrich $61,000 to secure the screen rights to the novel, Joe demanded that Aldrich pay him $85,000 for the rights to the novel *and* the screenplay that Lukas Heller and Aldrich himself had already written for the movie.[2] Twenty years later, such capricious cruelty in his business dealings would destroy his friendship with Richard Attenborough when Joe demanded he pay $1 million for the rights to *Gandhi*—Attenborough's labor of love on which he had worked for two decades.

Joe's intractability over *Whatever Happened to Baby Jane?* was also a contributory factor in the dissolution of his relationship with Edward Feldman. Their association had been a stormy one. Feldman had been charged with the task of making Joe's name and photograph ubiquitous features of the trade and popular press, and Joe was given to fits of pique and fury if he felt that the task had not been adequately accomplished. "As I look back on my tenure with Levine," recalls Feldman, "I think I did a really good job for him, probably some of the best publicity work of my career."[3] By the time Feldman left Joe in 1962, Joe was famous, and his star was still ascending. Feldman did indeed do a remarkable job for him. Nonetheless, when Feldman handed in his six weeks' notice, Joe wished him well but then later the same day sent an underling to demand Feldman leave the office by 5:00 p.m. *Whatever Happened to Baby Jane?* was an exploitation man's dream, so Feldman accepted an offer from Seven Arts, which was producing the movie, to oversee its publicity. Later, he would become a successful producer in Hollywood with films such as *Witness* (1985), *The Golden Child* (1986), and *The Truman Show* (1998).

Following Joe's successes with foreign films for drive-ins and art houses, his business was expanding. By 1963, Embassy had more than one hundred employees, and Joe had offices in Boston, London, Rome, and New York; he bought an apartment in New York, too, that being where he conducted most of his business, and he was located in Greenwich, Connecticut, for his domestic life with Rosalie and the children. With an expanding business, Joe needed more product. "I have to have more regular films as well as art films," he told Hazel Flynn of the *Citizen News,* "I can get 5000 more bookings than with an art film."[4] He remained in the art market but felt it was becoming riskier, thanks, in his estimation, to the pernicious influence of critics. "Very few art films are now being made," he told the

Motion Picture Exhibitor in February 1964. "Most of them are being made in Hollywood, and the so-called 'eggheads' choose the ones they like and pay not a bit of attention to the others."[5] Joe wanted product and he wanted commercial product: "sex, violence, and action—just the things that sell."[6] Hollywood was the logical place to go, and Joe spent much of the 1960s working in Hollywood, but he never moved to Los Angeles.

With Hollywood in his sights, Joe looked for a commercial property, and in 1961 he paid $300,000 for the rights to *The Carpetbaggers,* Harold Robbins's blockbusting novel. The sum was sizable, but it is a big book, and it yielded two movies for Joe—*The Carpetbaggers* in 1964 and a prequel, *Nevada Smith* in 1966. Unlike *Godzilla, Hercules,* and, apparently, *Two Women,* there was stiff competition for the rights to Robbins's novel, the prepublication galley proofs of which had been distributed among studio executives to whip up interest. Joe won out over the competition a few months after publication, and, like the other projects mentioned, it was very much the right project at the right time.

The Carpetbaggers is a sexy pot-boiling novel set in the jet-set worlds of Hollywood, high finance, and the aviation industry. It sold in the millions and caused considerable moral outrage for its sexual content. In the opinion of the *New York Times*'s Murray Schumach, "It was not quite proper to have printed *The Carpetbaggers* between the covers of a book. It should have been inscribed on the walls of a public lavatory."[7] Nonetheless, the public was keen to read it, Joe was keen to own it, and Hollywood was keen to make a movie from it.

When *The Carpetbaggers* was published, it provided the American reader with a degree of sexual frankness that had hitherto been absent from the bookshop shelves of America. The year 1959 saw the first U.S. publication of D. H. Lawrence's novel *Lady Chatterley's Lover* (1928), which was immediately banned on the grounds of obscenity. The following year the publishers Grove Press successfully fought to have the ban overturned by the Supreme Court. In 1961, Grove Press also published Henry Miller's long banned novel *The Tropic of Cancer* (1934), sparking a wave of obscenity lawsuits against vendors selling the book. It was in this atmosphere of moral crusading and debates over the crossover constituencies of literature and pornography that Robbins's sexually explicit potboiler appeared in bookshops and bubbled up the best-seller lists. Having secured the rights to *The Carpetbaggers,* Joe then acquired the screen rights to *The Tropic of Cancer* while it was still mired in legal disputes at the state level.

Joe was looking to make bigger-budget pictures, and to do this, he was looking for a Hollywood home. With the rights to two high-profile scandalous novels in his possession, he had useful assets for his negotiations with Paramount, for whom he would work as an independent producer from 1963 to 1966. According to Paramount historian Bernard F. Dick, "Predictably, Levine gave Paramount high gloss trash . . . sex lacquered to a glossy finish, whose shiny veneer concealed a complete lack of substance."[8] This is perhaps an unfair summation of the joyously lurid camp of Joe's adaptations of Robbins's novels and other censor-baiting properties, particularly in the implication that there was any genuine attempt to conceal the superficial delights of these movies.

The Carpetbaggers was only one-third of the initial three-picture deal Joe signed with Paramount in 1963, which indicated his desire to transfer his versatility as a promoter to his production schedule. *Tropic of Cancer,* Miller's impressionistic account of the grubby poverty of his Parisian quest for an artistic rebirth, was widely regarded as a literary masterpiece despite the moral outrage it occasioned; and *Imperial Woman* (1956), a novel detailing the life of the Chinese empress dowager Cixi came from the Pulitzer Prize–winning writer and Sinologist Pearl Buck and had all the ingredients of a prestige picture or roadshow presentation as well as plenty of exploitable elements, given the mythology that surrounded Cixi's sexual appetite. But Paramount produced *Tropic of Cancer* in 1970 without Joe's involvement, and *Imperial Woman* has yet to be made into a film. It was, then, Robbins's adaptations that dominated Joe's initial partnership with Paramount.

Prior to Joe's arrival at Paramount, the once great studio had been beset by problems. In the late 1950s, critics were pointing to a lack of leadership at the studio and hinting that the advanced age of its senior management team was leading the studio toward a damaging artistic conservatism. The studio was in debt and needed a way out. Paramount's then president, Barney Balaban, who had been appointed in 1933 to address the studio's previous problems of overbureaucratization and dearth of showman spice, acknowledged his critics in 1959. Paramount had been relatively slow to react to the ramifications of the *Paramount* decision of 1948, he told reporters before promising an ambitious future for the studio by being more adventurous in its employment of outside talent.[9]

The 1950s had seen the rise of the independent producer in Hollywood, who would present a ready-made "package" of property, story, and personnel to a studio, which could then fund, coinvest in, and/or distribute as it saw fit, thereby alleviating studio pressure to produce in-house. Paramount had independent producers, but it had not capitalized on them to the extent other studios had. Its most successful independent producer at the turn of the decade was probably Hal Wallis. In the 1960s, Paramount also contracted Otto Preminger and Samuel Bronston, the latter filling the supercolossal hole left by the death of Cecil B. DeMille, the studio's previous supplier of spectaculars, in 1959.

Among such illustrious company, Joe appears more than a little out of place. Wallis had been tutored by Darryl F. Zanuck at Warner Bros. and had produced *Casablanca* (1942) and *The Maltese Falcon* (1941)—though his Paramount fare was rather dominated by vehicles for Dean Martin and Jerry Lewis, some of Elvis Presley's best and worst films (though all made money), and the odd "serious" project, such as *Becket* (1964). Preminger was one of Hollywood's most visionary producer-directors who barely put a foot wrong at Columbia and United Artists with films such as *Laura* (1944), *The Man with the Golden Arm* (1955), and *Anatomy of a Murder* (1959). Bronston's epic credentials had been established by movies such as *King of Kings* (1961) and *El Cid* (1961). Joe was relatively untried as a producer. His only real producer credits thus far had been on *Morgan the Pirate* and *Wonders of Aladdin,* cheap European kiddie fare that found neither critical nor commercial favor. But Joe was not just being engaged to package productions for the studio; he was being engaged to further package those productions for the paying public, as reported in the *New York Times:* "A few days ago someone asked George Weltner, the new president of Paramount Pictures, what he thought would be the biggest problem in his new job. 'Packaging,' he shot back. 'That is the toughest job of all.' Having said this, Mr. Weltner promptly handed over a substantial portion of his 'packaging problem' to a man many regard as a 'master packager'—Joseph E. Levine."[10]

The Carpetbaggers was the basis of an ideal package for Joe's talents. The public loved it, the critics hated it, and it was controversial. Joe's deal with Robbins would yield future projects and a firm friendship. In addition to *The Carpetbaggers* and *Nevada Smith,* Joe would also produce adaptations of the Robbins novels *Where Love Has Gone* (1962), *Stiletto* (1960), and *The Adventurers* (1966); Joe also bought the rights to *The Dream Merchants* (1949)—though that became a TV movie in 1980 without his involvement. According to Robbins's biographer, Andrew Wilson,

Robbins undertook script doctoring work for Joe on *Contempt,*[11] but it is unlikely that Godard used any of that material.

Joe and Robbins became rather kindred spirits. Robbins provided popular dramas of sex and money unencumbered by literary pretention and ripe for Joe's exploitation techniques. Robbins, meanwhile, brought Joe's showman flair into the literary world. For Joe, "Harold is the PT Barnum of the book business. He eats up this circus life. Some writers won't lift a finger to help the book, the picture or themselves, but not Harold. I've never asked him to cross a tightrope over Times Square, but he'd do just about anything else I ask."[12]

The Carpetbaggers is a hefty tome that needed licking into shape for filming. Numerous screenplay drafts were written, and whole chunks of the book were hacked out—including material that would later be used to make *Nevada Smith.* With much of Robbins doorstop novel excised, the movie still clocks in at more than two and a half hours. It tells the slimmed-down story of the rise and rise of Jonas Cord, ruthless tycoon, control freak, and serial user and abuser of women as he builds a vast business empire, forever consumed by the fear of being engulfed by the insanity that killed his twin brother.

Cord, played by George Peppard, makes a fortune in the aviation and movie industries, and the parallels between him and the real-life tycoon Howard Hughes are unmistakable and were widely commented on in the press upon the appearance of both book and film. Robbins specialized in peopling his novels with thinly veiled caricatures of real-life persons, and *The Carpetbaggers* contains two other notables: Rina Marlowe, played by Carroll Baker, is reminiscent of Hollywood's original platinum blonde, Jean Harlow; and Nevada Smith, played by Alan Ladd (and by Steve McQueen in the prequel), is a loose amalgam of silent-screen cowboys Tom Mix and Ken Maynard. The movie was directed by a Hollywood veteran, Edward Dmytryk, who had directed *Hitler's Children,* and was later briefly jailed for refusing to name names to the House Un-American Activities Committee during Hollywood's Red Scare, but his eventual capitulation in 1951 ensured his release. It was adapted for the screen by John Michael Hayes, who had scripted four of Alfred Hitchcock's films as well as camp classics *Peyton Place* (1957) and *Butterfield 8* (1960).

In the early 1960s, the deregulation in the literary world was to an extent mirrored in the movie world, thanks in no small part to the

European arthouse imports with which Joe was so heavily involved. The year 1964 was important in terms of American censorship. On 22 June, the Supreme Court overruled states' allegations that *Tropic of Cancer* was obscene. That same day, in the case *Jacobellis v. Ohio* (378 U.S. 184 [1964]), the Supreme Court held that the movie *Les Amants* (1958) was also not obscene, with the decision featuring Justice Potter Stewart's famous declaration on pornography: "I know it when I see it, and the motion picture involved in this case is not that." A couple of months earlier *The Carpetbaggers* arrived on American screens.

Long before *The Carpetbaggers* was released, Joe began baiting the censor. The Motion Picture Association of America (MPAA) Production Code, which had been such a powerful proscriptive force in Hollywood since the 1930s, was losing its relevance and looking anachronistic. Capitalizing on this situation and strengthening his image as a bigmouth provocateur, Joe announced that he would, if necessary, release *The Carpetbaggers* without the MPAA's seal.[13] His threat was designed to catch the mood of the times, but it was pure flim-flam. It is unlikely that Joe would have seriously considered releasing the movie without a seal. With a proposed budget of $5 million, it was an expensive project, and the lack of a seal could damage films at the box office because many exhibitors were reluctant to show them. Later, when Paramount came on board as coproducer, Joe's threat looked even less likely. No major studio had yet released a film without an MPAA seal; MGM would be the first to do so in 1966, with *Blow Up*. *The Carpetbaggers* needed a seal, so Joe and Paramount worked very closely with the MPAA to get one. The delicacy of the protracted negotiations conducted with the MPAA and the Catholic Legion of Decency not only earned official approval for *The Carpetbaggers* but also ensured that the boundaries of what used to be called "decency" could be pushed. The situation was mutually beneficial. The MPAA was keen to avoid obsolescence, and Joe wanted a spicy movie to sell.

With Robbins's novel so well defined on the cultural radar, and most of America well aware of its contents, *The Carpetbaggers* was presold on scandal. Joe took to the press with a strategy of highlighting by denial. Just as movie exploiteers would attract an audience by plastering a town with "warnings" about a film's supposedly shocking content, so Joe repeatedly, relentlessly, and deliberately unconvincingly made claims for the tastefulness of his forthcoming film. "Some say *The Carpetbaggers* is in bad taste," he combatively told one reporter, "I say it isn't."[14] Readers of *Newsweek* were tantalized with an almost puritanical promise of what would *not* be in the film: "The book was filth. Filth and dirt," Joe told them. "We don't have any of that in the picture, but the wonderful thing about the film is that you have the feeling that you are reading the book."[15]

Amid posters and lobby cards depicting torrid bedroom scenes, proclaiming, "It is unlikely that you will see in your life all that you will see in . . . THE CARPETBAGGERS!" there was plenty of media scuttlebutt promising Carroll Baker in the nude. Baker was no stranger to controversy, having shot to fame in 1956 as the eponymous Baby Doll, the lead role in a film whose scenes of sweaty sleaze had caused headaches for the censors and outrage for the Catholic Legion of Decency the previous decade.

Joe had met Baker at a charity ball and said to her, "You're just the girl I want for my next film. It is the best part you've had since *Baby Doll*, but you have to take my word for that. Without any question, you must accept the part and shake my hand to bind the deal."[16] Baker did not know at the time that she had just been chosen for *The Carpetbaggers*, but Joe had a good eye, and she was perfectly cast. A very underrated talent, Baker was blonde, beautiful, and very sexy. Although it is impossible to say how much excitement there was among the general population at the prospect of seeing Baker disrobe, a considerable giddiness was inspired in the popular press. Long before the scene was shot, the MPAA had made it clear that *The Carpetbaggers* would not be granted a seal if it contained Baker's scripted nude scene. "The scene of Rina would be unacceptable as described," wrote Geoffrey Shurlock of the MPAA to Paramount producer Edward Schellhorn; "she should not be sitting naked at her dressing table, she should be properly clothed."[17] Two weeks later Shurlock reiterated his concerns when the script was redrafted: "As we have already informed you, this scene of Rina sitting naked at her dressing table would be unacceptable under the Code."[18] Although there was no real intention of including the scene in the finished film, it was shot anyway; "once the wraps were back on Carroll," reported *Newsweek*, "they were off the press agents, who lost no time in getting the exposure exposed."[19] The scene was, however, restored for the movie's European release, with *Variety* assuring its readers that the much-vaunted nudity was rather tame and "more ballyhooey than actuality."[20]

Questions of taste and allegations of bad taste swirled around the film, just as they had for the book. Writing in *Life* magazine, Thomas Thompson railed against the film, ("degenerated nonsense"), the stars ("not stars enough"), and especially the producer:

> The blame must be placed at the feet of Joseph E. Levine, an ebullient producer who can be counted on to ballyhoo this big budget bomb to a fare-thee-well. He first gained fame importing the Herculanean biceps of Steve Reeves to US movies, later he produced such excellent films as *Two Women* and *Divorce—Italian Style*. If foreign sex sells well in this country, he apparently reasoned, then why not peddle the home-grown variety? Saves dubbing costs too. So he went ahead, thoughtlessly leaving out the one ingredient that lifts such foreign films from the category of voyeurism: good taste.[21]

Bosley Crowther, too, hated the "sickly sour distillation of Harold Robbins's big-selling novel" and was characteristically critical of Joe: "JOSEPH E. LEVINE has completed the circle. He is back peddling *Hercules*, or, at least, a curiously close resemblance to that overblown film. . . . The drums have been beating for it, as they did for *Hercules*. It will probably be seen by millions of people—and that should satisfy Mr. Levine."[22]

In rolling out his bad-taste bandwagon, Joe was catching another zeitgeist: camp. This slippery sensibility was soon to be memorably articulated by Susan Sontag in her famous essay "Notes on Camp," which was published in the *Partisan Review* a few months after *The Carpetbaggers*' April release. "The discovery of the good taste of bad taste can be very liberating," wrote Sontag, "The man who insists on high and serious pleasures is depriving himself of pleasure; he continually restricts what he can enjoy; in the constant exercise of his good taste he will eventually price himself out of the market, so to speak. Here Camp taste supervenes upon good taste as a daring and witty hedonism. It makes the man of good taste cheerful, where before he ran the risk of being chronically frustrated. It is good for the digestion."[23]

Joe had contributed much to the smooth functioning of Sontag's digestive system. Among the camp artefacts she lists are Steve Reeves movies and Japanese creature features. Now there was *The Carpetbaggers*. Most reviews of the film were "bad" but, oddly, not negative. Philip K. Scheuer wrote that the movie was in "bad taste" but conceded that "it has the curiosity pull of a trashy novel. One sits there squirming in the captive presence of its unremitting boldness for two-and-a-half hours."[24] *Cosmopolitan*'s movie reviewer wrote, "Under the assumption that the movie goer has read Robbins' novel, whoever made or cut this film obviously felt it would be OK to leave out great hunks of exposition, fail to define characters and or situations, and just generally horse around, in the hope that bedroom scenes and lots of gamy talk about 'hookers' would save the situation. It probably will." The reviewer concluded with advice apparently at odds with the body of the review: "Don't miss *The Carpetbaggers* because, like the Beatles, it has to be seen to be believed."[25]

Joe did not need Susan Sontag to tell him about the liberating value of discovering bad taste; he had been dealing in "so bad it's good" movies for his entire career, from *How to Undress in Front of Your Husband* to *Gaslight Follies* to *Hercules* and beyond. What Sontag calls a "private code, a badge of identity even, among small urban cliques"[26] had been alive and well for many years—if not centuries or millennia—among the less well heeled. While the debates about high versus low culture trundled along, members of the intelligentsia in their small urban cliques had, via camp, found an archly affected way of seeming to provide cover, an excuse even, as they smuggled the cultural products of the lower end into their lives. Though *The Carpetbaggers* would not qualify as true camp in accordance with Sontag's various sophistications—it is far too knowingly over the top to be considered true camp—many of the reviews for the movie highlight a repellent attractiveness in it that saw metropolitan critics accepting, if not altogether embracing, its gaudy mass-market populism on what appeared to be their own terms.

The critical fraternity's ironic viewing strategies aside, *The Carpetbaggers* became Paramount's most successful nonroadshow film ever, thus ensuring that Joe could rely on, to some extent at least, Paramount's backing for the next few years. *The Carpetbaggers* had also pushed back censorship boundaries in the United States. This shift in boundaries led to much controversy, which led to much good publicity for Joe and his film. But there were simmering resentments toward Joe in Hollywood, just as there were on the art-house circuit. Many felt that the MPAA had dealt too leniently with his censor-baiting film. Voices of protest led to a clampdown by the MPAA, which led to uncharacteristic climb-downs from Joe, which led to *Harlow*, the most compromised film of Joe's career, and yet more allegations that Joe was a bad influence.

8

Hollywood Undermined

He's on that anti-Hollywood kick again.

—*Philip K. Scheuer*

Having proved his worth as a producer-packager with a much-talked-about film based on a much-talked-about novel, Joe was, not unusually, being talked about, and that was the way he liked it. He wasted no time in getting people to say nice things about him and publicizing the nice things they said in the pages of *Variety.* On 22 April 1964, *Variety* featured a gigantic eighty-three-page feature/advertisement for Embassy Pictures, its wares, and its president. Bookending the succession of one- or two-page spreads for Embassy's recently or soon to be released products are pages set aside for the great and the good of world cinema to shower praise on Joe. Joe is presented not only as somebody who is worthy of praise but also, more importantly, as a man who matters, a man of status and stature. Federico Fellini wrote: "You know, for years I used to have this image of the American movie mogul: fast, decisive, magnanimous, maybe a little fat, maybe a little impatient, maybe a little sentimental, but a real human being. Then I came to the States and saw that those men had disappeared. It was a big disappointment, believe me. Now it seems to me that I've found one that meets my image. Thanks, Joe!"[1]

The plaudits that ooze from the pages could have been no more gushing had they flowed from the pen of one of Joe's own publicity men or even Joe himself. Another Italian auteur, Vittorio de Sica, wrote: "From a director's point of view he is a perfect producer. He is understanding and respectful of creative talent and never interferes with artistic concepts."[2] From Hollywood, Edward Dmytryk wrote, "He made it a point, more than once, to let me know that he was only interested in the picture's sales values and the creative end was entirely in my hands. . . . He's a good producer in that he gives a director complete freedom and autonomy and I must say I've never enjoyed directing more."[3]

From England, Stanley Baker, the star and producer of the upcoming Embassy/Paramount production *Zulu*, wrote that he and director Cy Endfield "had several visits and many conferences with Joe Levine. But they were just that: visits and conferences. Constructive helpful suggestions, yes but otherwise a free hand to produce our picture as we had planned, without hindrance—that was what Joe provided us."[4] Perhaps most importantly, Paramount's new president George Weltner confirmed his faith in Joe, whose original three-picture deal had now grown to eight: "It is my feeling that Joe Levine is far from the zenith of his success, popularity and influence. Paramount is so sure of this that it now has commitments with Joe for eight pictures budgeted at over $30,000,000. These eight films . . . represent the largest number of pictures an individual producer has committed to a major company within a 15 month period."[5]

Joe's burgeoning reputation as a producer rather preceded the actual evidence, just as the ballyhoo for his pictures preceded the promised spectacle. But this was not a case of jam tomorrow, as Lewis Carroll's White Queen might have it, because Joe's productions were stacking up. Joe's *Variety* splash invited the U.S. film industry to judge Joe not only by his track record and future prospects but also by the company he kept and the caliber and range of people who felt it in their interest to say nice things about him. More than this, such a marketing broadside, which covered more than half of the issue, provided a strutting exhibition of Joe's and Embassy's confidence, power, success, and wealth. After all, eighty-three pages in *Variety* did not come cheap. Unsurprisingly, *Variety*'s editor, Abel Green, provided his own tribute to Joe in the issue.

Following the hints and intimations of the scandalous lives of real-life figures in *The Carpetbaggers,* Joe would reference scandalous reality more directly in *A House Is Not a Home* (1964), produced and distributed in America by Embassy without Paramount's involvement. Paramount did, however, distribute the movie overseas and provide studio space for filming and the costumer Edith Head. *House* was produced by Clarence Greene, directed by Russell Rouse, and written by the pair. Greene and Rouse were Hollywood journeymen writers who are best remembered for their film noir collaborations—most notably the penning of the taut classic *DOA* (1950)—and for their work on the Oscar-winning screenplay for the Doris Day/Rock Hudson vehicle *Pillow Talk* (1959).

A House Is Not a Home is based on the autobiography of America's most famous madam and provider of prostitutes to America's rich and powerful, Polly Adler, who had died in 1962. It was originally to be made at Columbia, but there was little hope that the film would receive a seal from the MPAA. Geoffrey Shurlock wrote to Sol Schwartz at Columbia saying that it would be "difficult to bring in a picture based on this material within the above quoted code requirements," which read, "The methods and techniques of prostitution and white slavery shall never be presented in detail, nor shall the subjects be presented unless shown in contrast to right standards of behavior. Brothels in any clear identification as such may not be shown."[6]

As with *The Carpetbaggers,* audiences had the prospect of a nude scene dangled in front of them, and the film's star, Shelley Winters, told of how the film would "surprise everybody because it will be in good taste and worthy of a Code Seal if Joseph Levine wants to ask for one."[7] It was eventually released in America without a seal through Embassy.

Following on from the bordello-themed melodramatics of *A House Is Not a Home* came *Where Love Has Gone* (1964), which, like *The Carpetbaggers,* is another ripe reworking of a Harold Robbins tome and, like *The Carpetbaggers* and *A House Is Not a Home,* alluded to real-life scandals among America's jet set. The movie opens with a juvenile girl murdering her mother's lover, and many in the press were quick to notice the similarity between Robbins's tale and the murder in 1958 of Johnny Stompanato, a former marine with Mafia connections who had been in a relationship with Hollywood star Lana Turner. Stompanato was a violent man who had been deported from Britain after pulling a gun on Turner's costar on the British set of *Another Time, Another Place* (1958). In a fortuitous move for future fans of James Bond, Turner's costar, a relatively unknown Sean Connery, disarmed Stompanato and sent him on his way. Once it was discovered Stompanato was traveling on a fake passport, British authorities quickly dispatched him back to America. Shortly thereafter, during a violent argument in Turner's Beverly Hills home, Stompanato was stabbed to death by Turner's fourteen-year-old daughter, Cheryl Crane. She was cleared of murder on the grounds of justifiable homicide because she was protecting her mother from an attack. Robbins denied that the Stompanato case was an inspiration, but he was rather wont to do this, even when the parallels between his sensationalized fiction and sensational fact were all too obvious.

Joe reconvened his *Carpetbaggers* team, Edward Dmytryk and John Michael Hayes, for *Where Love Has Gone.* Susan Hayward plays the nymphomaniacal Valerie Hayden, Bette Davis her controlling mother, Joey Heatherton her killer daughter, and Mike Connors her alcoholic husband. All the characters are hopelessly flawed in some way, and the film drips with technicolored histrionic misery; but this tale of adultery, alcoholism, blackmail, murder, sex addiction, and suffocating matriarchs does not have quite the same brazen charge as *The Carpetbaggers,* having been rushed into production to capitalize on the anticipated success of its predecessor.

Where Love Has Gone did not hit the commercial highs of *The Carpetbaggers,* but it still pulled in a worthwhile return. Meanwhile, Joe was developing, after a fashion, his own auteur reputation as a producer of a particular kind of populist trash. Bosley Crowther helpfully adumbrated Joe's auteur credentials when he wrote of "such obvious compendia of smut as Joseph E. Levine's productions."[8] Scandalous films about scandalous lives were marketable and profitable, and so in August 1964 Joe announced that his next project would be a biopic of Jean Harlow—Hollywood's original platinum-blonde bombshell—to be produced with Paramount. Having announced his project to the assembled guests at the Beverly Hills Hotel, Joe theatrically declared, "This is my star," and a curtain slowly parted to reveal Carroll Baker, "seated in a sleek, yellow Isotta Franchini and wearing a Harlowlike costume," reported Peter Bart of the *New York Times.*[9] During the course of the evening, Joe also confirmed *Harlow*'s director to be Gordon Douglas. Douglas was an accomplished Hollywood hand who held and will always hold the distinction of being the only person to have directed Elvis Presley and Frank Sinatra in feature films (Elvis in *Follow That Dream* [1962] and Sinatra in four movies, including *Young at Heart* [1954] and *Robin and the Seven Hoods* [1964]). Douglas had also helmed the sci-fi classic *Them!* and Paramount's *Sylvia* (1965)—a Carroll Baker vehicle with which Joe was tangentially involved as Baker's Svengali.

In the 1930s, Jean Harlow (Harlean Harlow Carpenter) had been Hollywood's sex symbol for its Golden Age. Coddled as an infant by her overprotective and ambitious mother, she lived a short life marked by success, scandal, and controversy, including three marriages, the second of which ended with the suicide of her husband, Paul Bern. Harlow herself died in 1937 at age twenty-six. Her short, dramatic life was ideal fodder for a film, and Joe was not alone in thinking so. When he announced his project, there were two other proposed productions of Harlow's life in the pipeline. Sidney Skolsky, the famous columnist and occasional screenwriter, was planning to embark on his own production and had been in talks with two stars for his film, but he lost one of them, Baker, to Joe and the other, Marilyn Monroe, to suicide. Twentieth Century Fox was also planning a biopic and was in talks with Kim Novak, but in a protectionist move Paramount quickly acquired the rights to this project. Shortly after Joe's announcement, two more productions of Harlow's story were announced. One was to come from Columbia Studios but, like Skolsky's and Fox's, never came to fruition. The other was to come from Bill Sargent of a company called Electronovision. Sargent's production, much to Joe's chagrin, was scheduled to be released before Joe's. But Joe had a scandalous edge because his production was to be based on Irving Shulman's gossipy and salacious *Harlow: An Intimate Biography* (1964); "We will go as far as we can and stay out of jail,"[10] he told one reporter. But Joe was about to walk into a smutstorm of his own making, one that was exacerbated by the impending release of Sargent's rival production.

Although *The Carpetbaggers* had attracted the crowds and even won over some critics with its smutty appeal, many were not impressed. Crowther decried a lax censor, and in an article portentously entitled "Bad Taste in Films: More Cheapness and Vulgarity Appear" he complained, "Now there is no real proscription against the kind of disgusting bad taste we recently saw in *The Carpetbaggers,* for instance—the kind of dishing of cheap suggestiveness that gives no real insight into human beings but is merely ladling out dirt for dirt's sake. . . . And there is no one to tell a promoter such as Joseph E. Levine to lay off a subject as distasteful as that to be found in *A House Is Not a Home.*"[11]

In the 1950s and 1960s, the MPAA had lost some of its puritanical zeal, but the battle lines between what was considered art and what was not remained. Crowther was not a prude, but his objections to "such obvious compendia of smut as Joseph E. Levine's productions" were heightened by what he saw as anomalies occasioned by the relaxation of the Production Code, in which "deliberate and degenerate corruptors of public taste and morals" such as *The Carpetbaggers* were granted a seal, but "serious, sincere dramatic film[s]" such as *The Pawnbroker* (1964) were denied one.[12]

The Pawnbroker was produced by Ely Landau, directed by Sidney Lumet, and photographed by Boris Kaufman—three members of the team that had collaborated with Joe on *Long Day's Journey into Night*. A character study of a Harlem-based pawnbroker, played by Rod Steiger, who is haunted by memories of the Holocaust, *The Pawnbroker* is mercilessly pessimistic and one of the most powerful American films of the 1960s. It was initially denied a seal because of nudity but was eventually ruled an exception and became the first film featuring bare breasts to be granted a seal of approval from the MPAA.

Ely Landau had complained in interviews, with justification, that *The Pawnbroker* had been denied a seal while *The Carpetbaggers* had been granted one, indicating a double standard. Once *The Pawnbroker* was granted a seal, however, another double standard became apparent. *The Carpetbaggers* had not been allowed to show Carroll Baker's bare back, but *The Pawnbroker* was allowed to show Thelma Oliver's bare breasts. *The Pawnbroker* is, as Crowther rightly observed, a "sincere, dramatic film"; *The Carpetbaggers*, for all its qualities, is perhaps not. The sight of Thelma Oliver's breasts in *The Pawnbroker* prompts a flashback for the pawnbroker to his life in a Nazi concentration camp, so it serves a purpose far removed from any pleasurable context. For the viewer, Oliver's breasts are connected to the ugliest of humanity's worst excesses, so that any beauty is undermined, resulting in their justifiable inclusion in the film. Carroll Baker's bare back, however, in conjuring up no visions of atrocity, was bound for the cutting-room floor. Female flesh should be shown seriously, sincerely, and dramatically or not at all seemed to be the message.

Just as well-regarded masterpieces of literature such as *Lady Chatterley's Lover* and *Ulysses* paved the way for the less well-regarded explicitness of blockbusting airport novels such as *The Carpetbaggers*, so the censor- and critic-baiting smuttiness of *The Carpetbaggers* movie loosened the censor's belt for serious American drama films. Received wisdom is that the Production Code gradually lost its influence throughout the 1960s, but 1965 was rather a blip year that saw the code's last gasp. There is little doubt that a film such as *The Pawnbroker* benefited from *The Carpetbaggers*' particular brand of garish hokum: makers of serious drama could point to it and demand further concessions by claiming artistic seriousness and dramatic intent. Crowther was not alone in condemning *The Carpetbaggers*' receipt of a seal. The MPAA had been heavily criticized for granting it one, and these criticisms were compounded by its overly zealous application of the code in the case of *The Pawnbroker.* With the code losing credibility, the wounded MPAA lashed out. Its vaguely defined enemy was smut, and one culprit was *Harlow.*

When the script for *Harlow* was first submitted to the MPAA, E. G. Dougherty of the MPAA noted that the "basic story seems to be acceptable from the standpoint of the production code,"[13] but there were objections. In a letter to *Harlow*'s story editor Erwin Gelsey, Geoffrey Shurlock wrote, "As you doubtless know, there has been considerable criticism lately of over-emphasis in coarseness and undue bluntness, both in dialogue and in action, and [we] have been asked by the board of directors to do something about it."[14]

The apparently permissive climate created by *The Carpetbaggers* was being reined in, and some of the MPAA correspondence makes for amusing reading. Suggestiveness and innuendo in the *Harlow* script were required to be toned down: "(P. 12) We feel that this emphasis on Jean's non use of bras is overboard. We call your attention to the fact that, in addition to this page, it is referred to again on pages 16, 18 and 37. This suggests an undue emphasis."[15] Some of the fruitier dialogue was also to be excised: "Page 160. the underlined words in the following dialogue are unacceptable and should be eliminated: 'Well, castrate me <u>with a cheese grater!</u>'"[16]

In the censorious atmosphere of 1965, even Joe, ever the courter of controversy, seemed keen to distance himself and his production from allegations of smut. In 1962, he had threatened to release *The Carpetbaggers* without a seal if necessary, but preproduction publicity for *Harlow* saw a far less combative Joe. Upon being reminded at a press conference of his comments regarding jail avoidance, he contended that he was merely being "facetious" at the time,[17] yet the frankness of early script drafts suggests otherwise, and Joe privately expressed worries about the kind of controversy the as yet unmade film was attracting. With a second-draft script by Sydney Boehm in hand by the end of 1964, a story conference was called in February 1965 to begin reworking it.

Boehm had parted company with the project by this time, and the minutes of the meeting show Joe working with another writer—Irene Kamp, a script polisher for Paramount—in the company of Paramount's head of production, Howard Koch; *Harlow*'s director, Gordon Douglas; and other executives. Early on in the meeting, Joe explains his concerns: "We will have to be very careful about sex. Normally we go pretty far. But never has a picture been on a spot like this one. This is the most publicized picture in the business." Later he comments: "One reason for my coming here is to tell you of the tremendous problem we have with this picture. We do not need to get rough. Have just a good picture. Have to tone things down you would normally go for." Joe repeatedly expresses concern about sexual elements, advising that the new script should "play down lesbianism," while Howard Koch worried that "the censors are going to give us trouble" and posits that another "device" was needed to replace Paul Bern's homosexuality, which was made explicit in Shulman's book and the previous script.[18]

Considering Shulman's source biography, Jean Harlow's well-documented sexual appetite, and the reputations of *Harlow*'s star and producer, the finished film is very coy. Bern's homosexuality is alluded to fairly strongly, and there are hints that Harlow's stepfather—Marino Bello—may have attempted a sexual relationship with her, but these are the only hints of scandal in a film that Joe, uncharacteristically keen to avoid controversy, sought to neuter. Ironically, it was the curtailing of the smut factor that led him into another potential source of controversy, this time about writing credits.

Harlow's screenwriting credit goes to John Michael Hayes, whom Joe had recently appointed as Embassy's literary properties executive, but various others worked on the script in its various stages, and one of them was Sydney Boehm. In many ways, Boehm was an ideal choice for *Harlow*'s scribe. In the 1940s and 1950s, he had scripted hard-boiled noirs such as *Union Station* (1950) and *The Big Heat* (1953), so he could bring a rougher edge to the dialogue and story. He was versatile, too, having scripted sci-fi and Westerns, and he had collaborated with Gordon Douglas and Carroll Baker on their previous Paramount movie, *Sylvia*. Having parted company with the *Harlow* project, Boehm grew protective of both his script and reputation and told Paramount's story editor, Erwin Gelsey, that he would publicly dissociate himself from the final film if it was not to his liking. Later, when his name had been removed from the film entirely, a frustrated Boehm wrote to Mary Dorfman of the Writers' Guild of America,

> I told Mr Gelsey that I must insist on reading the material before I left because if the new work was a distortion of mine, I PUBLICLY, IN TRADE ADVERTISING, WOULD EITHER REFUSE ALL

> CREDIT OR INSIST MR HAYES PUT HIS NAME ALONGSIDE MINE.
>
> I should have known better. When it comes to getting box office publicity or manoeuvring to prevent unfavorable publicity, today's reincarnation of PT Barnum, the producer of record, is the master. By giving his vice-president a sole credit, he has forced me to become a non-advertiser.
>
> I charge that these "threats" of adverse publicity, wise or unwise on my part, brought on this sole credit for the writer executive who, despite once waiving credit, has a stake in the profits of the corporation, Embassy. I charge this was producer Levine's way of spiking my guns.
>
> Although I dislike what has been done with the *Harlow* script, I am fighting to prove that we have not returned to the pre-Guild years when the Joseph Levines doled out writing credits to fellow executives, relations, etc.[19]

This particular matter was resolved fairly speedily and—more crucially—quietly. Fairly or not, the Writers' Guild arbitration committee decided unanimously in favor of Hayes being awarded sole credit. However, this particular debacle does show how large-scale productions can be beset by infighting and rancor as well as how Joe's increasing power led prominent figures in Hollywood to treat him with suspicion. But whereas this matter was dealt with in-house, other *Harlow*-related spats were fought in a more public forum.

Irving Shulman's biography of Harlow had been the subject of a good deal of controversy following its publication in 1964. Reviews for the biography ranged from the dismissive to the outraged. Richard G. Hubler of the *Los Angeles Times* wrote, "Schulman's [*sic*] work here is a simple extension of the deft manipulation of the imagination that is next to obscenity, a reworking of the facts for the sake of sensuous titillation alone. . . . On a guess, approximately half the book is concoction, flavored with snideness."[20]

Shulman later faced a "concerted attack" on the *Les Crane Show* in August 1964 by two of Harlow's friends, who disputed his work.[21] By the end of 1964, Shulman was dealing with litigation from Harlow's friend Kay Mulvey[22] and from her father,[23] and another lawsuit would follow from the widow of Harlow's stepfather.[24] Given all the unwelcome attention being generated by Shulman's controversial work of biogossip, Joe took steps to distance himself from the book and its author. But in January 1965 *Variety* ran a story about Shulman's role in the *Harlow* campaign: "Author Irving Shulman . . . admitted he has been on producer Joseph E. Levine's payroll to write controversial remarks geared to plug Levine's forthcoming biopic of Jean Harlow. Shulman confessed . . . 'I was hired to make up stories to create controversy.'"[25] Joe dismissed the claim, telling the *Hollywood Reporter,* "He's a liar. As a matter of fact I have never met Mr. Shulman and I don't care if I never do."[26] And just as Shulman's book was under numerous threats of litigation, so Joe was worried about the same for his film. "This morning there was a letter purporting to be from the brother of Paul Bern," he told colleagues. "This is the second letter like it. Have received thousands of letters which I turn over to the legal department."[27]

Joe had distanced himself from the book that initially had provided the distinction for his production in a market that was briefly crowded with Jean Harlow biopics. He had sought to distance himself from the allegations of smut that, rightly or wrongly, helped to distinguish his work as a producer. Now he and Paramount sought to tone down any similarities between the biopic and the real-life Hollywood in which the real-life action happened. A five-page memo from one of Paramount's producers, Eugene H. Frank, reveals the extent of Paramount's worries regarding the representation of the key players and institutions of Harlow's life. In the film, MGM becomes Monolith Studios; the script had initially presented a trumpeting elephant as the studio's logo, yet this image was deemed too close to MGM's roaring lion and excised. Frank called for script writers to make Monolith's head (named Shelley in the original script but Everett Redman in the final film) as unlike Louis B. Mayer as possible (despite the fact that Mayer had died in 1956) and requested that research be conducted on whether Mayer's given name had ever been prefixed by the words *uncle* or *king* and, if so, that such epithets should be removed from the script (they were). Research was undertaken to ascertain whether Harlow's first husband, Charles McGrew, was still alive, with a view to his character being removed from the script if he were (it was). All references to Mont Clair Carpenter, Harlow's real father, who was at the time in litigation with Shulman, were removed from the script. Changes were required to the character of Richard Manley so that "there will be no resemblance to Howard Hughes." Even minor characters, such as Harlow's doctor and Monolith's secretaries were to be scrutinized for resemblance to the real

Dr. Sugarman or any real MGM secretaries. Paramount was also legally prohibited from portraying actor William Powell, to whom Harlow was once engaged, "by name, appearance, personality or characterization" because of an injunction placed on Fox that transferred to Paramount when it bought the rights to Fox's Harlow project.[28]

Such caution in depicting public and not so public figures was, perhaps, sensible and politic, yet the characters in *Harlow* seem to be products not of mere caution but of timidity bordering on fearfulness. The characters of the domineering Mama Jean (Angela Lansbury) and Harlow's abusive stepfather, Marino Bello (Raf Vallone), were reconstructed, the former becoming a doting parent and the latter a caddish man-child. Paul Bern (Peter Lawford) is love struck by Harlow until their wedding night reveals the impotence (the device used as a euphemism for his homosexuality) that leads to his suicide. Jack Harrison (Mike Conners), who can be broadly read as a Clark Gable/William Powell hybrid, is a ladies' man with a roving eye who is, ultimately, protective and caring of Harlow. Everett Redman (Martin Balsam) is remarkably mild mannered for a studio boss, and Harlow's agent, Arthur Landau (Red Buttons), is presented as her father figure and protector—though his nobleness is understandable given that the real Arthur Landau was the main source for Shulman's biography. The characters in the film are almost uniformly bland; the one exception is the lecherous and manipulative Richard Manley (Leslie Nielson), yet this Howard Hughes surrogate merely serves to accentuate the fictional Harlow's virginal, babe-in-the-woods persona.

The tempering and toning down of *Harlow* and the strategy of avoiding controversy ultimately meant that Joe's film was left without distinction in the marketplace. Whereas *The Carpetbaggers* had been marketed with the confident tagline "It is unlikely you will see in your life all that you will see in . . . THE CARPETBAGGERS!" no such claims could be made of *Harlow.* This lack of distinction was particularly problematic for Joe, given that Bill Sargent was to beat Joe's release date with his own rival production, also entitled *Harlow.*

Bill Sargent represented Electronovision, a moniker that served not only as the name of his company but also the name of a filmmaking process he pioneered, which involved using multiple television cameras to record directly onto film. Sargent had already scored a minor hit with *Hamlet,* a film in which the Electronovision process (though with only a single camera) was used to record the successful Broadway play starring

Richard Burton as the eponymous prince in 1964. Sargent released the film all over America with nine hundred prints and coaxed punters to the box office by promising to burn all the prints following a limited run of only two days.

In January 1965, Sargent announced that his next project was to be a biopic of Jean Harlow, which would be filmed in seven days. Sargent told the *Film Daily* that he had come "under pressure not to make 'The Harlow Picture.'"[29] He was also happy to name his tormentor, the *Hollywood Reporter* telling how at a press conference "Sargent . . . lashed out at Joe Levine who is producing *Harlow* based on a work by Irving Shulman. Sargent said Levine has made moves indirectly effecting [*sic*] his film. He termed 'the pressures' as 'unavailing.'"[30]

In subsequent months, Sargent adopted a more aggressive strategy. He sought to aggravate his foe and succeeded in doing it. Joe had always been prone to outbursts of temper, and on 5 April 1965, the night of the Academy Awards, Sargent crossed a line. Joe was in attendance to receive the statuette awarded to *Yesterday, Today, and Tomorrow* for best foreign film, and the mischievous Sargent flew a blimp over the auditorium advertising his own *Harlow*. Later, as Joe was receiving plaudits and shaking the hands of those congratulating him on his success, he noticed that one of those hands belonged to Sargent. Joe exploded: "You Son of a bitch! Don't shake my hand!" The shaken Sargent responded in kind, replying, "Another crack like that and I'll slap you down right here and now."[31]

Following this incident, Sargent, curiously, took to praising Joe. He told Ronald Gold that he felt "Levine has done the motion picture industry more good than anybody, including Louis B. Mayer."[32] Elsewhere he expressed admiration for Joe "having the guts to go out and do things and put the industry where it belongs," adding that the hoopla surrounding his own *Harlow* could only help Joe's *Harlow:* "The controversy will only stir up interest in the Levine production."[33]

Given the context, it seems that Sargent's praise for Joe also served as taunts. According to Joe, Sargent sent him a telegram offering him the role of Louis B. Mayer in his production. "I would tell you what's on my mind about this man," Joe told radio host Mike Wallace, "but I can't say it. You'd cut me off the air."[34] It is also doubtful that the normally publicity-hungry Joe welcomed the extra publicity. In the course of preparing his *Harlow* project, Joe and Paramount had already bought the screen rights to Fox's proposed production and had secured a guarantee that Fox would not make films featuring a "platinum blonde theme" in a requested time frame.[35]

For Joe, Sargent "violated every rule of fair trade practice . . . he's started a thing that could well end the motion picture business as we know it. That's a strong statement."[36] Not only was Joe annoyed that Sargent had not followed proper procedure by failing to register his title with the MPAA—had Sargent done so, he would not have been able to use the same title—he was also angered by what he saw as the flagrant opportunism of the exploitation. "He has taken the title," complained Joe,

> he has used the coloring that we have used in our ads, he has used the title of the book, copied it exactly—the figures—and he's using it in his ad. Additionally, his ads reads [*sic*]: "The movie that the world has been waiting for." Well, you know, Mike [Wallace] that nobody in the world knows about his film. But I've publicized mine for two years worldwide. . . . This man has come in and taken from me everything . . . only because he isn't a member of our association [MPAA], without which we could not exist.[37]

A week or so earlier Sargent had joked, "They had started out with sex and sensationalism. Now I hear they're going to make a nice clean picture. They're following me!"[38] This comment was uncomfortably close to the truth. Having sought to clean up his production, Joe was left with a film that had little to substantially distinguish it from its rival beyond production values. Joe subsequently placed full-page ads in the trade and popular press, demanding, "LET THERE BE NO CONFUSION!" The advert appeared on 12 May 1965, nearly three months before the release date of Joe's *Harlow* but, significantly, only two days before the release of Sargent's.

Sargent was less reticent about portraying Hollywood's big shots. His *Harlow* features a Louis B. Mayer (Jack Kruschen), a Stan Laurel (Jim Plunkett), an Oliver Hardy (John J. Fox), and an Al Jolson (Buddy Lewis); the film also boasts star appearances from Ginger Rogers (as Mama Jean) and boxer Sonny Liston in a cameo. Nonetheless, Sargent's *Harlow* received few kind words from the critics, who pilloried both the film itself and the Electronovision process.[39] "As bright as Electronovision's *Hamlet* was dark," complained Philip K. Scheuer, "it is so floodlighted . . . as to look washed out. At first it gives the impression of being photographed through water." Nevertheless, Scheuer predicted that the film might be a hit, "particularly with a vast majority confusing it with, or unconcerned about, Joe Levine's *Harlow*."[40]

Sargent's beating Joe to the screen may have served to help Joe's version with the critics. Comparisons were inevitable, and Joe's *Harlow* fared a little better, being cast in a more positive light when juxtaposed to Sargent's earlier effort, as shown in Bosley Crowther's review: "Maybe this one is a little less odious, because it does have a little more class, a little more sumptuous production, a little more feel for Hollywood." The remainder of Crowther's review, however, is dismissive: "Most of Mr. Shulman's shocking story has been glossed over in John Michael Hayes's hackneyed script. . . . But worst of all, Miss Harlow, as played by Miss Baker, is pious and dull. So much for the famous 'sex symbol' of the '30's. She's a nothing on today's unbridled screen."[41]

Given Crowther's regular attacks on Joe's supposedly salacious output, it is a little ironic that this very vocal opponent of Hollywood smut should have been left feeling short-changed; nonetheless, his assessment of Baker's Harlow is fair. It is the eponymous sex bomb who suffers most from the compromises of the production. The finished film presents Harlow as a virginal naïf, and her struggles are presented as irritating obstacles, in the face of which she remains angelically steadfast. In a bid to avoid allegations of smut, the film made Jean Harlow not the Harlow of Shulman's admittedly sensationalist tome, nor the Harlow of the popular imagination, nor even the Harlow that exists in factual, historical record. Joe certainly had concerns regarding the depiction of Harlow, as this exchange in a script meeting shows:

> JOE: Will the people who liked Harlow say that you have done her dirt?
>
> IRENE KAMP: I do not see how they could say that because I have certainly not done her harm compared to the picture they must have of her.
>
> K. EVANS: She is not as vulgar as in the first script. She does love Mama Jean. There is conflict. I think you will get a great deal of sympathy.[42]

Once Joe had left the meeting, Irene Kamp pointed out, "Everyone who knew Harlow knew she had a rough life, and will feel cheated if they don't see some of it," to which Howard Koch replied, "After we have shot it and Mr. Levine says 'No' we will be in trouble."[43] Yet Kamp's comments were prescient. Alongside Crowther, Scheuer was also left feeling "cheated," complaining that the film's makers "have depicted her as more sinned against than sinning. Which must have taken some doing by Levine, who started out, at least, by using the scandalous book by Irving Shulman. . . . Even Levine & Co. chicken out at the finish, as if confessing doubts of the validity of their whole operation."[44]

Given the weight of evidence, Scheuer's observations appear to be correct. Having become involved with one of the most controversial properties in Hollywood, Joe sought to make the film as uncontroversial as possible. Salaciousness in mainstream Hollywood fare, as decried by Crowther and subsequently by the MPAA, led to Joe's strategy of smut avoidance. This strategy, combined with compromises borne by a fearful approach to depicting Hollywood's Golden Age, led to Jean Harlow, of all people, being depicted as unfeasibly angelic, rising to stardom in a Hollywood that was by and large unthreatening. Moreover, for Scheuer, it was not merely the bland portrayal of Harlow that was the problem—Scheuer's "*even* Levine & Co." gambit (emphasis added) suggests a disappointment that contemporary America's most notorious producer should have presided over such anodyne fare.

But Scheuer had other complaints, too, regarding standards of behavior and codes of conduct in Tinseltown: "In the present atmosphere of bad feeling, name calling and recrimination, it is scarcely any wonder that reviewers, themselves put on the spot, have been inclined to take a pox-on-both-your-houses-attitude toward Bill Sargent's *Harlow* and now Joe Levine's *Harlow.*"[45]

The *Harlow* debacle all but destroyed Electronovision, which closed its doors amid a flurry of unpaid bills and legal disputes before Joe's *Harlow* had even opened. In an interview, Sargent said of his financial troubles, "I make this flat, emphatic, undeniable, not possible to misquote statement—that it has all been caused by Joe Levine, not indirectly but directly."[46] Sargent occasionally resurfaced in the motion-picture business, with one notable success—he produced *Richard Pryor: Live in Concert* in 1979—and one notable failure—in 1976, the United Nations stepped in to halt his upcoming production, *Death Match,* which was to be a live, pay-per-view fight to the death between a man and a great white shark, planned to capitalize on the *Jaws* craze of the time. Joe, meanwhile, went on to exec-produce *The Oscar* in 1966 and would be further accused of besmirching Hollywood's name and reputation.

The Oscar tells the tale of washed-up actor Frankie Fane (Stephen Boyd) and the corrupt methods he uses to manipulate influential members of the academy so that he can "win" the coveted statuette. It was directed by Russell Rouse and written by Clarence Greene, the duo that had previously produced *A House Is Not a Home,* and it features a whole host of big-name cameos from the likes of Bob Hope, Merle Oberon, and Hedda Hopper, all playing themselves. It was released in 1966 to almost uniformly bad reviews. Richard Schickel of *Life* wrote, "The vulgarity and stupidity with which the producers approach *The Oscar* is so blatant and moronic that one's initial outrage at the naked corruption of their motives soon turns to helpless laughter";[47] and Richard Davis of *Films and Filming* ascribed a motive of shameless opportunism to the project: "Joseph Levine, mogul of the mediocre, has sought in the most blatant way to cash in on the success of *The Carpetbaggers* and *Harlow* and has combined the basic elements of both into a . . . monumentally bland [film]."[48]

Beyond the bad reviews, others were concerned about how Hollywood was presenting itself in recent movies—Joe's recent movies specifically. Reporting from the set of *The Oscar,* Scheuer pondered what he saw as Joe's Hollywood trilogy: "What with *The Carpetbaggers, Harlow* and *The Oscar* I must ask Joe why he's so preoccupied with a Hollywood he never made."[49] Later, in his not entirely negative review of *The Oscar,* Scheuer wearily notes that Joe is "on that anti-Hollywood kick again."[50] This theme of Joe undermining Hollywood with his recent films would be taken up with much greater zeal by Bosley Crowther in his review of *The Oscar*:

> Another distressing example of Hollywood fouling its nest—professionally, socially, commercially and especially artistically—is provided by a film called *The Oscar.* . . . Obviously the community doesn't need enemies as long as it has itself. . . . The point is that . . . [Bob Hope, Merle Oberon, etc.] and other people in the goldfish community have willingly contributed their services to oblige Joseph E. Levine and Clarence Greene and Russell Rouse in producing this arrantly cheap, synthetic film, which dumps filth and casts aspersions on the whole Hollywood system—a community that may not be perfect but is not so foul as hinted here. And it is

> their candid re-enactment of the ceremony of giving out Academy Awards that encloses this fictitious nonsense in a frame of quasi-reality.[51]

More was to come from Crowther on the matter. The following week he published an article titled "Is Hollywood Killing Itself?" in which he took issue with the recent films that "have given disgustingly bad images of the kinds of people who make pictures." Five films were in his sights: three of them were Joe's, and the other two (*Inside Daisy Clover* [1965] and Sargent's *Harlow*) are mentioned only in passing. For Crowther,

> the disgrace is that none of these pictures—not one of them, I would say—has shown the slightest bit of understanding or desire to understand and reflect the extraordinary business of making films. Not one has shown the faintest recognition of the kinds of toils and tensions involved in the process of making movies, in uncovering and developing stars, in preserving manufactured illusions, in enduring disappointment and defeat. Not one has begun to give an idea of the kinds of triumphs and tragedies that can come from the glowing satisfaction and despairs of being involved with films.[52]

Successes and failures aside, Joe's capacity to exasperate continued unchecked, and Crowther's vituperations would, no doubt, have pleased him. But films such as *Harlow* and *The Oscar* were not as successful as Joe hoped. Beyond his work for Paramount, he was busy producing, funding, importing, and distributing movies through a wide range of associations, but his scattergun approach was not always finding targets.

9

The Scattergun Approach

> It's hard to tell in my business. In 1966 I made seven family films. Nobody—but nobody—went to see them, including my own family.
>
> —*Joseph E. Levine*

The mid-1960s was just about the most frenetic period of Joe's career, years that saw him embarking on a wide variety of projects. Joe did not make Paramount his exclusive home. These years saw him working with more than a dozen companies in a variety of production and distribution deals. Even in the first flush of the Embassy/Paramount marriage, Joe was reticent about the idea of a merger: "I just don't know. If I was sure, neither they nor I would be signing these outside deals. Everything, you see, would be part of the merger. They're too big for me to swallow, even with my big belly. They'd swallow me. It would frighten me. I like complete autonomy to do what I like, which is impossible with a public company. While they're thinking about it, we're doing it."[1]

One of Joe's most significant projects of this period, *Zulu,* for which he was executive producer, provides good evidence of his capacity to make decisions quickly, even impetuously. *Zulu*'s star and producer, Stanley Baker, had appeared in the ill-fated *The Last Days of Sodom and Gomorrah,* and Joe got to know him and took a shine to him. There are various conflicting stories of how Joe became involved in *Zulu,* some of which are presented in Sheldon Hall's study of the film's production, *"Zulu": With Some Guts behind It—the Making of the Epic Movie.* All of the stories involve a quick decision based on the title. Most of the stories suggest that Joe never read the script and put his faith in both the title and Baker. "I don't want to look at the script," were Joe's words, as Baker recounts in one tale. "What's it called?" When Baker told Joe that the movie was called *Zulu,* he replied, "Fine. You got a deal."[2]

Zulu tells the story of the Battle of Rorke's Drift in 1879, when around

150 British soldiers successfully defended a British mission station in South Africa from an attack by more than 4,000 Zulu warriors. It is a thrilling tale of derring-do and a staple of many a British Bank Holiday television matinee—its undeserved reputation for jingoistic racism notwithstanding. Alongside Baker, it stars Michael Caine, Jack Hawkins, James Booth, and many more faces familiar to British audiences. It was directed by Cy Endfield, an American director who had moved to the United Kingdom to escape the Hollywood blacklist when he was named a Communist during the Red Scare in the 1950s. Baker and Endfield had collaborated previously on the less well-known but no less well-regarded *Hell Drivers* (1957), a superbly tense edge-of-the-seat yarn featuring an even more remarkable roll call of British character actors.

Zulu's preproduction predated Joe's Paramount deal, but Paramount would come on board later. Two years before the film was released, Joe was promoting it with his own idiosyncratic hyperbole, telling Paul O'Neil of *Life*,

> I think of it as a cowboys and Indians picture. They used to make hundreds of them but nobody makes them anymore. The public wants one. Ten thousand frenzied savages charging all at once—actually we're only having two thousand of them but with three cameras it's easy to multiply. They tell me them fellows drink some kind of grass whisky—how would you like to be the cameraman filming THEM? I feel there's a need for this picture—no psychiatrists in it, no nuts in it, no dope peddlers in it. It's the real thing. . . . I think we've got ourselves a post office picture here. With some pictures you have to worry about the weather . . . but with a post office picture, if you get the advertising right, neither snow, nor rain, nor heat, nor gloom at night will keep the customers from tearing the box office right off the front of the building. Saturation![3]

Zulu's spectacularization of blood-and-guts heroics has little in common with the arthouse stylings of *Contempt*, but both were shot on location around the same time, both were difficult projects, and both were helmed by temperamental directors. Reports of Joe's effectiveness as a producer from production personnel on these two projects are, however, very different. Whereas Godard and his faithful Godardian followers lampoon

Joe for his ignorance and philistinism, Cy Endfield's widow said of Joe, "Cy always said that *Zulu* was the only film where he'd been left to get on and do what he wanted. . . . Joe Levine was a very good producer in that respect."[4] Stanley Baker also praised Joe for his hands-off approach.[5] On *Contempt,* Godard complained of interference, and Joe complained about his uncommunicative director. On *Zulu,* Joe was similarly interventional, but relations were cordial.

Joe's concerns during the shooting of *Zulu* were the running time of the completed film, scheduling, budget, and the use (or lack thereof) of a second unit. In letters and telexes, he expressed himself forcefully but not impolitely. In a letter to Endfield and Baker, he demanded that the issues and concerns he had raised be dealt with as a matter of urgency, before offering his "kindest personal regards to you and your families."[6] Unlike Godard, producer and star Baker had a knack of writing diplomatic letters that would placate Joe: "I can only tell you Joe that Cy and myself are not out to prove anything to the world through *Zulu* but have the same interests in it as you do, that is to make a good picture of the right length that people will pay to go and see and therefore provide profit to us all."[7]

Joe did not visit the *Contempt* set, but he did visit the South African set of *Zulu.* His letters to Endfield and Baker do reveal a certain amount of frustration, and a visit was deemed necessary. That visit lasted less than seventy-two hours: he arrived, shouted at everyone who needed to be shouted at, posed happily for some publicity photographs, and then went on his merry way. R. H. Harrison, chairman of Paramount British Pictures, reported to Jack Karp of Paramount: "Up to the time that Mr Levine visited South Africa . . . I had been getting somewhat concerned at the slow tempo of the scenes that had been shot and the general pace at which the production seemed to be moving. . . . However, the effect of Mr. Levine's visit seems to have been reflected in subsequent scenes, both in the tempo of the shooting and the number of scenes taken."[8] Colin Lesslie, whom *Zulu*'s completion guarantors had brought in to oversee budget and scheduling, was also impressed by Joe's firecracker intervention: "Joe's visit was a tonic to us all, only it was too brief. . . . I think his visit was most opportune and did a lot of good. It certainly speeded Cy up."[9]

Once filming was completed, Joe pronounced the qualities of the finished film with his own peculiar wit: "Every bit of it is authentic," he told Katherine Hamill. "There's not one Zulu in it who isn't a Zulu."[10] This may be true, but, Zulus aside, there is much more in the movie for the viewer's pleasure. There is plenty of violence, blood, and bravery, and the action scenes are marvelously staged. It is also a *Boy's Own* showcase of the Best of British. Along with the acting talent, *Zulu* shows its British heroes with the odds stacked against them; officers with stiff upper lips lose their class-bound delusions and get stuck in alongside plucky, salt-of-the-earth battlers with regional accents from lower down the social order. These themes would have appealed to Joe. He was a considerable Anglophile. He was also a fan of Stanley Baker and would make three more films with him, the African adventure *Dingaka* (1965), *Sands of the Kalahari* (1965), and the British heist thriller *Robbery* (1967).

Following the failure of *Jack the Ripper,* Joe continued to invest in British films. These films, such as *Spare the Rod* (1961)—a sort of British *Blackboard Jungle* (1955) starring Max Bygraves—made little dent in the U.S. box office but show Joe's commitment to seeking out interesting films. *Spare the Rod* had been the subject of some controversy in the United Kingdom for its depiction of sadistic teachers and rioting schoolchildren in the state school system. It was a minor entry in Britain's emerging school of social-realist dramas, and it was this school that would provide Joe with critical, financial, and Oscar success with *Darling* in 1965.

Darling was the archetypal British 1960s movie. Serious, maybe a little didactically high-minded, it is a zeitgeisty exposé of the hypocrisies of the metropolitan celebrity jet set. *Darling*'s success at the box office and at awards ceremonies is testament to how the movie caught the mood of the times. Its exploration of the rottenness that lies beneath glamorous facades was ideal intellectual fodder for the time and led to its being a little overpraised at the time; nowadays, it is often unfairly disparaged for its heavy-handedness and modishness. But its heavy-handed modishness was to be the key to its success. Embassy bought the rights to its worldwide distribution, except for in the United Kingdom, and aggressively promoted it and its star, the charismatic, talented, and very beautiful Julie Christie, in the United States. The critics were mostly onside—Crowther was a notable detractor ("a totally corrosive film"[11])—and *Darling* won Oscars for its screenplay, costume design, and heavily hyped star, for whom Joe had lobbied hard.

More cynical British glamour appeared on Joe's schedule with *The Idol* (1966). This tale of youthful arrogance and sexual betrayal among the student set stars Michael Parks and British pop idol John Leyton. Hollywood glamour was provided in the form of Jennifer Jones as a beautiful divorcée, a role that had been previously assigned to Joan Crawford, then Shelley Winters, and then Kim Stanley. It was directed by Canadian Daniel Petrie, who would work for Embassy on his next film, the rather more lightweight *The Spy with the Cold Nose* (1966).

Joe had sought to capitalize on the James Bond–inspired secret-agent fever of the mid-1960s by buying the rights to films such as *Licensed to Kill*, a daft British Bond rip-off that Embassy released in the United States under the title *The Second Best Secret Agent in the Whole Wide World* (1965). Its equally silly sequel, *Where the Bullets Fly* (1966), was also released by Embassy in America. *The Spy with a Cold Nose* saw Embassy taking a production role as opposed to merely distributing a finished product. It was yet another Bond spoof, which took its punning title from John le Carré's novel *The Spy Who Came in from the Cold.* As with *The Idol,* its U.K. production was overseen not by Joe, but by Leonard Lightstone—vice president of Embassy and Joe's trusted second in command.

The Spy with a Cold Nose was written by Ray Galton and Alan Simpson, the writing partnership behind the radio and television shows *Hancock's Half Hour* (1954–1961) for British comedian Tony Hancock. Though the duo had few dealings with Joe, they do remember him speaking of his admiration for British cinema and culture.[12] Joe's admiration for Galton and Simpson's work is further evidenced by his attempt to adapt their television comedy series *Steptoe and Son* (1962–1974) for an American audience. Working again with Clarence Greene and Russell Rouse, the team behind *A House Is Not a Home* and *The Oscar,* a pilot of *Steptoe and Son,* starring Aldo Ray and Lee Tracey, was made for NBC, but NBC did not commission the series. In the 1970s, however, NBC would adapt *Steptoe and Son* for American audiences in the form of the hugely popular *Sanford and Son*, created by Norman Lear and Bud Yorkin.

Looking farther afield, Joe kept up his investments in European productions. He commandeered Ann-Margret to star in two Italian coproductions, *The Tiger and the Pussycat* (1967) and *The Prophet* (a.k.a. *Mr. Kinky,* 1968). Joe also maintained his presence on the European arthouse scene. Arthouse investments had been profitable for Embassy, and cracking the art market was something major studios were keen to do in the 1950s and 1960s. In 1957, Columbia acquired the foreign-film distributor Kingsley International; United Artists acquired Lopert Pictures in 1958; and Paramount certainly had its eye on the arthouse market when it entered into its deal with Joe and Embassy.

The art market was a risky proposition but could pay dividends in terms of awards, prestige, and profits. According to film historian Tino Balio, "Lopert released an average of five pictures a year during the sixties. Almost without exception, they failed to attract an audience."[13] When it came to guiding art films to success, however, few could match Joe and Embassy's track record. Although few foreign stars had box-office staying power, the two exceptions were Marcello Mastroianni and Sophia Loren. In the mid-1960s, Embassy had contracts with both as well as with Loren's producer husband, Carlo Ponti, and her favorite director, Vittorio de Sica.

The talents of all four of these major Euro-players were brought together in the Embassy release *Yesterday, Today, and Tomorrow.* Following the considerable success upon its release in the United States and its Oscar success as best foreign film, *Variety* announced that its release in the United Kingdom would be handled by Paramount; the same agreement would apply with a subsequent release from the same ensemble, *Marriage—Italian Style* (1964). This deal represented the first time Joe had allowed Paramount to handle any of his foreign-made art films.[14] The *Variety* article notes that because of Joe's success in handling "top foreign product, his touch has been watched with interest by majors seeking entrance into the foreign distribution field," before commenting on a power play: "Of interest is the fact that Levine is set up to distribute in England and had almost guaranteed success with *Yesterday, Today, and Tomorrow* at least which is already a proven winner. The name of the game could be 'give a little, get a little' since Embassy has 10 pix as yet uncommitted which it plans to produce within the next couple of years. But it also demonstrates Paramount's deeper penetration into Embassy's operations and a growing willingness on Levine's part to keep feeding Par bits of bait."[15]

Despite Joe feeding Paramount "bits of bait," the Paramount deal was not as mutually beneficial as it might have been. In addition to gaining entry into the art market, Paramount sought to capitalize on Joe's ability to keep product flowing and his unparalleled skills in working on multiple projects at a time. But the studio failed to fully get behind Joe's more ambitious projects, and the Paramount years saw the announcement of a number of big projects but no follow-through.

Among these unmade projects was *Runaway Train,* which was to be produced by Joe and directed by Japanese master Akira Kurosawa, who would be making his first film in America. Although *Runaway Train* was not made in the 1960s, it was eventually produced in 1985, without Joe, and directed by Andrei Konchalovsky, with Kurosawa's script adapted by, among others, Eddie Bunker. *Imperial Woman*—a proposed biopic of China's empress dowager Cixi to be adapted from Pearl Buck's novel, produced by Run Run Shaw, and directed by Ted Danielewski and to star Sophia Loren in the title role—also never made it to the screen. *Boomers,* from a nonfiction work published by Gay Talese in 1964 about the construction of the Verrazano-Narrows Bridge in New York, was another aborted project; at the time of writing, this film is in preproduction. Two more films slated or rumored at this time saw Joe seeking to move into unfamiliar genres with a big-budget sci-fi, *Only Tomorrow,* and a Broadway musical, *Little Me.* Other significant unmade projects had a British flavor. *Gandhi,* Richard Attenborough's labor of love, which would win eight Oscars at the ceremony in 1983, but without Joe's involvement, did not get beyond the preproduction stage during Joe's Paramount tenure. Joe was also set to produce the British adventure writer Wilbur Smith's debut novel, *When the Lion Feeds* (1964), alongside Stanley Baker, with Sidney Poitier to star alongside Baker, but the proposal came to naught.

Perhaps the most interesting of Joe's unmade Paramount projects is *Will Adams.* Adams was an English sailor who traveled to Japan in 1600 and became the first white samurai. The project was the brainchild of producer Eugene Frenke and was set to be directed by John Huston and scripted by Dalton Trumbo. The three had collaborated previously on *Heaven Knows, Mr. Allison* (1957), with Trumbo's scripting work uncredited because he was blacklisted at the time. Joe was to be executive producer, and Peter O'Toole was to play the title role. O'Toole's involvement in *Will Adams* was secured by Jules Buck, who came on board during the preproduction stages and was to coproduce alongside Frenke. But the production collapsed in a mess of infighting, grudges, acrimony, and clashing egos. Trumbo was moved to complain to Joe about the grudge bearing between Peter O'Toole and producer Jules Buck on one side and Eugene Frenke on the other.[16] Once the project had collapsed, John Huston wrote a poisonous letter to Buck, his now former friend:

> Now I'll address myself to you about yourself. What's going on in your shallow spirit. You're pissing with fear, dear Jules, lest your newly won success be snatched out of your hands. You don't really believe in it yet anyway. The past, with its slaps and humiliations, its vast uncertainties, is still too recent. That's why you like to tell

> about letting Joe Levine, for instance, "really have it" . . . pouring it on until he felt like jumping out of a window to escape your wrath. As though importance could be measured by who you can shout at and get away with it. . . . You made it a condition of Peter's appearance in *WA* that you would run the show. But the show never got started even. Paramount laid out the dough and time passed and absolutely nothing happened . . . thanks to your own efforts you were in the position of responsibility when the storm broke.[17]

It would be interesting to know how much of an impression this debacle left on Joe. In a rough, earlier draft of this letter (there were several), Huston accuses Buck of suffering from "vertigo" from having climbed too high too quickly. According to Trumbo, Eugene Frenke had spent seven years trying to get *Will Adams* to be realized on-screen, only to see his labor of love scuppered by Buck's power plays. In this context, it should be noted that when Joe came to put his own labor of love, *A Bridge Too Far,* onto the screen in 1977, he did so without ceding any control to any other producer and without any studio backing whatever.

Although some of the blame for the failure of these projects can be attributed to Paramount, it is also fair to say that Joe was not quite at the stage in his career where he would drop everything and devote himself to a single large-scale production—he was spinning too many plates. Alongside his aborted ambitious productions, he was still busily taking care of the lower end of the market. His Christmas offering in 1964 was the low-budget kiddie film *Santa Claus Conquers the Martians,* a film that was quite well reviewed at the time but is now affectionately regarded as one of the worst films ever made.

With Paramount failing to back his more ambitious ventures, Joe threw himself and Embassy's money into an expanded production schedule. In August 1965, he told the *Hollywood Reporter* of his intention to expand operations at Embassy: "We're going to produce and distribute with a greater intensity. . . . [W]e're going to produce and distribute every conceivable type of picture . . . American and foreign . . . high budget and low budget . . . for the entire family and with special themes for adults."[18]

Embassy's new program saw Joe investing heavily in low-budget films, most of which were unsuccessful at the time, but many of which have attracted a cult following since. Bert I. Gordon, an alumnus of Arkoff's

American International Pictures, made two films for Joe in this period. *Village of the Giants* (1965) is a teen weirdie starring a young Beau Bridges and a ten-year-old Ron Howard; and *Picture Mommy Dead* (1966) is an enjoyable *Psycho* rip-off with quite a stellar cast that includes Don Ameche, Martha Hyer, Zsa Zsa Gabor, and Wendell Corey.

More low-budget films came from Videocraft International, including a portmanteau film of Hans Christian Anderson stories titled *The Daydreamer* (1966), a part live-action, part puppetry family film that features the vocal talents of stars such as Tallulah Bankhead, Victor Borge, and Boris Karloff. Karloff also lent his voice to another Videocraft effort, *Mad Monster Party* (1966), a stop-motion animation. Both were directed by Jules Bass and produced by Arthur Rankin Jr. Even more low-budget fare came from Circle Productions in 1966, with *Billy the Kid versus Dracula* and *Jesse James Meets Frankenstein's Daughter.* Both were directed by William Beaudine, a versatile director who worked across film and television and is now wrongly remembered among cultists for his supposed incompetence and unfairly dubbed "William 'One Shot' Beaudine."

Alongside the genre-bending Westerns of William Beaudine, Joe invested in low-budget Westerns from America, such as *The Bounty Killer* (1965) and *Requiem for a Gunfighter* (1965), as well as spaghetti Westerns from Europe. In America, Westerns, in particular low-budget Westerns, were far from the audience draw they had been in previous decades. This was not, however, the case in Italy, where the massive success of *A Fistful of Dollars* in 1964 had sent spaghetti Western production into overdrive, and the genre replaced peplum as a model for high turnover–low budget production. With films such as *The Tramplers* and *A Pistol for Ringo* in 1965, Joe was a little too far ahead of the curve. United Artists had bought the rights to *A Fistful of Dollars* but did not release it in the United States until 1967. Having whetted the public's appetite for spaghetti, UA then capitalized by releasing two sequels, *For a Few Dollars More* (1964) and *The Good, the Bad, and the Ugly* (1966) later the same year. Joe had released his own spaghetti products in 1965—much too early for a cash-in.

Embassy's low-budget dabblings at this time bore little fruit, and Joe would subsequently admit that he had judged the market wrongly. In a speech to the New York Sales Executive Club in November 1969, he commented, "It's hard to tell in my business. In 1966 I made seven family films. Nobody—but nobody—went to see them, including my own family. It was obvious that this wasn't what the public wanted."[19] Even in 1966 he had noted that his strategies regarding family and exploitation films were not working. He dismissed his low-budget actioners as "an experiment," said that he would be making no more films of this type, and predicted a general decline in low-budget production.[20]

With his family films, Joe misjudged not only the market but also the budget. According to Maury Laws, who wrote the scores for the Videocraft films, the relationship between Joe and the Rankin–Bass partnership was "positive enough during the making of the films. I don't think it was very positive after Levine saw the finished pictures. . . . I think he thought he was buying films he could market to the *Mary Poppins* audience, but he expected to make them with a budget that would make that impossible. He was disappointed with the pictures when he saw them and hardly promoted them at all."[21]

While the Videocraft efforts failed to attract the family audience, the Bert I. Gordon films, the Westerns, and the Circle productions were none too successful with the drive-in crowd. According to Sam Manners, production supervisor on both *Billy the Kid versus Dracula* and *Jesse James Meets Frankenstein's Daughter,* Joe "expected to clear more than $5 million on each film."[22] Joe's expectation that he would more than quintuple his investments on these films shows either naïveté in the extreme or optimism far beyond ebullience. But there was another source of income for Joe's low budgeters beyond the kiddie matinees and drive-ins: television, and that was another market that Joe managed to misjudge.

According to the *Hollywood Reporter*, Joe's low-budget features were made for "quick liquidation theatrically followed by TV, now suffering from a scarcity of features."[23] Whereas in the 1950s many in the film industry had seen television as an enemy, by the mid-1960s the former adversary had revealed itself to be a powerful ally. In 1965, the *Los Angeles Times* reported that in the week ending 5 September around 235 films had been shown on Los Angeles TV screens and noted that NBC was adding an extra night of prime-time movies, on Tuesdays, to complement its *Saturday Night at the Movies* strand.[24]

The following year, amid the scramble for more films on the small screen, television began to emerge as the junior partner in a relationship in which movies were gaining the upper hand, a situation exemplified by ABC's decision not to renew Milton "Mr. Television" Berle's contract because of a drop in ratings as TV viewers chose to watch films rather than made-for-TV fare.[25] By 1968, as NBC added a third night of movies to its schedule, feature films were being shown on television every night of the week,[26] and the studios, having seemingly conquered television, were fighting in the courts to prevent television companies from making films for theatrical release.[27]

Throughout his career, Joe had maintained a belief in the power of television and its capacity to help, rather than hinder, the development of the motion-picture industry. As early as 1958, he was stressing the importance of having a high turnaround of product based on television's rapacious consumption of movies.[28] However, by the mid-1960s, he was beginning to discover that TV was not quite the indiscriminate glutton he had hoped, displaying little appetite for Embassy's lower-end productions. Television was hungry for films, but not *those* films.

Nonetheless, Embassy invested heavily in television during the mid-1960s, with some modest successes alongside the hubristic failures. The year 1965 saw a fondly remembered television run of fourteen of Embassy's peplum films featuring a variety of Herculeses, Macistes, and Ursuses, repackaged with a stirring theme song and inaccurately titled *Sons of Hercules.* Also in 1965, Joe secured a deal with NBC that gave NBC the rights not only to fifty of Embassy's films but also to a number of unmade projects. There was also *DoDo—the Kid from Outer Space,* a cartoon series from British animators John Halas and Joy Batchelor. For Joe, then, television represented a future source of revenue for completed projects and a new ally and valuable contributor to the funding of the production process itself.[29] Later that year he bought twenty-nine Italian films for television and announced a coproduction deal for television product with Britain's Harmony Films,[30] a company run by Robert Maxwell, a Czechoslovakian-born British member of Parliament and media mogul who is now best remembered for stealing his employees' pensions.

The myriad deals that Joe and Embassy engaged in, along with the regular announcements and scuttlebutt, kept Joe's name in the trades and the popular press. But he was spreading himself thin, and many of his investments were gambles—a substantial portion of which did not pay off. In 1966, Joe cashed in his Paramount chips, sold his shares, and ended his association with the studio. Paramount had capitalized on Joe's ability to keep product flowing but treated him with disdain. George Weltner recognized Joe's importance, but Paramount's powerful former president Barney Balaban resented the studio's reliance on the types of films Joe was making (but presumably welcomed the arthouse prestige). Despite the fact that Joe had brought *The Carpetbaggers, Where Love Has Gone, Zulu,* and *Harlow* to the studio, nobody there had yet seen fit to provide him with office space, and he had to make do with whatever was available when he visited the studio.[31] Upon leaving Paramount, Joe was characteristically droll about his time with the studio: "The way it worked at Paramount is that I had what they call consultative control. And the way that worked is that somebody would call up and say 'what do you think about so-and-so for such-and-such part in the film?' I would say 'No.' They would say 'Okay,' and the next day they would go and hire so-and-so for the part. I got consulted on everything."[32]

Joe needed a hit. He may not have craved critical acceptance, but he certainly enjoyed financial success and the attention it brought. "*Carpetbaggers* is grossing $25 million first time around," he had told Paramount executives. "I like to be associated with a picture like that."[33] He also needed a hit to pay for the misjudgments and misfires of the previous couple of years—Embassy was amassing horrifying debts.

While Joe was busy catering to television, families, drive-ins, and many other audiences, the young and hip were looking to the movies played in theaters. Just as the youngsters of the previous decade had become familiar with the screen monsters of the 1930s in preparation for the screen monsters of Hammer horror, so the Baby Boomers of the 1960s had been schooled in cinema on college campuses, in repertory art houses, and in front of the television, developing a cineliteracy alongside a boomer narcissism that led to a collective desire to see themselves and their lives reflected on-screen. In 1967, Joe would satisfy this desire and give them *The Graduate.*

The showman prepares. Joe in his New York office in 1965.

Joe shakes hands with an exhibitor while hyping *Gaslight Follies* in 1945.

A couple in period costume ride in tandem to promote *Gaslight Follies* in Boston in 1945.

Press book cover for *Godzilla: King of the Monsters,* 1956, Joe's first big, nationwide saturation campaign. (Courtesy of the Academy of Motion Pictures Arts and Sciences)

Joe with Steve Reeves, the muscular star of *Hercules* and *Hercules Unchained,* in 1959.

Press book cover for *Hercules Unchained,* 1960. (Courtesy of the Academy of Motion Pictures Arts and Sciences)

Joe and his wife, Rosalie, pose with Sophia Loren's Oscar for Best Actress at the Academy Board of Governors' Ball in 1962. (Courtesy of the Academy of Motion Pictures Arts and Sciences)

Joe and Sophia Loren celebrate her Oscar win for *Two Women* in Rome, 1962.

Joe clowns around with his friend Sophia Loren in Rome.

Joe with Carroll Baker, star of *The Carpetbaggers*, *Sylvia*, and *Harlow*, at the Academy Board of Governors' Ball in 1964. (Courtesy of the Academy of Motion Pictures Arts and Sciences)

Federico Fellini, Joe, and Piero Gherardi with their Oscars for best foreign film and best costume design for *8½*. "A great love affair between two conmen" was how a mutual acquaintance described Joe's friendship with Fellini. (Courtesy of the Academy of Motion Pictures Arts and Sciences)

Rosalie, Joe, and Howard Koch of Paramount at the Academy Board of Governors' Ball with the Oscar for *Yesterday, Today, and Tomorrow.* (Courtesy of the Academy of Motion Pictures Arts and Sciences)

Joe with Rex Harrison backstage at the Thirty-Seventh Academy Awards ceremony in 1965, where Joe picked up the Best Foreign Film Oscar for *Yesterday, Today, and Tomorrow* on behalf of Carlo Ponti and Vittorio de Sica. (Courtesy of the Academy of Motion Pictures Arts and Sciences)

Joe with director Vittorio de Sica in 1965.

Joe lights Carroll Baker's cigarette while costumer Edith Head inspects her outfit on the set of *Harlow* in 1965.

Joe chats with Sammy Davis Jr., star of *A Man Called Adam,* in 1965.

A brief moment of laughter during the filming of *The Graduate* in 1967.

Joe, Dustin Hoffman (seated), and others on the set of *The Graduate* in 1967. (Courtesy of the Academy of Motion Pictures Arts and Sciences)

Sidney Glazier, Joe, and Mel Brooks on the set of *The Producers* in 1967. (Courtesy of the Academy of Motion Pictures Arts and Sciences)

Press book cover for the controversial revisionist Western *Soldier Blue,* 1970. (Courtesy of the Academy of Motion Pictures Arts and Sciences)

Peter Rosen and Joe in Joe's ornate New York office with the Gold Hugo Award for *Bright College Years,* 1970. (Courtesy of Peter Rosen)

Press book cover for *The Day of the Dolphin,* 1973, a film about talking dolphins that would be Joe's last film with Mike Nichols. (Courtesy of the Academy of Motion Pictures Arts and Sciences)

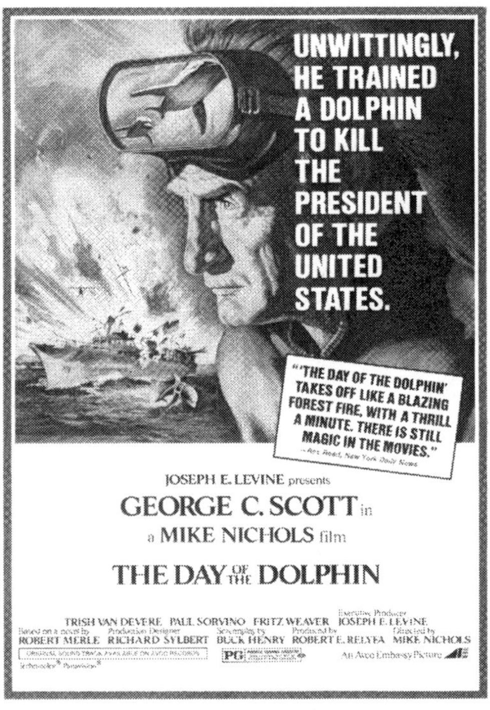

Press book cover for *The Night Porter*, 1974, featuring quotations cannibalized from Vincent Canby's scathing review of the film. (Courtesy of the Academy of Motion Pictures Arts and Sciences)

Director Richard Attenborough with Joe on the Netherlands set of *A Bridge Too Far* in 1976.

Dirk Bogarde as Lieutenant General Sir Frederick "Boy" Browning with Joe on the U.K. set of *A Bridge Too Far* in 1976.

Gene Hackman as Major General Stanislaw Sosabowski with Joe on the set of *A Bridge Too Far* in the Netherlands in 1976.

Robert Redford as Major Julian Cook on the Netherlands set of *A Bridge Too Far* with Joe in 1976.

Joe showing off his walking cane to Robert Redford. The handle is a molded replica of the bridge at Arnhem that gave the film its title.

Joe rallies the troops from a tank on the Netherlands set of *A Bridge Too Far* in 1976.

A seventy-five-year-old Joe with Bruce Dern on the set of *Tattoo* in 1980.

10

Graduating Class

> Those close to Levine have made it clear that, at this stage in his career, the boss is anxious to have his name associated with "class" product only.
>
> —Variety

While busily producing and promoting a wide range of films from all over the world and from all points on the cultural spectrum, Joe was making investments in the legitimate theater. These investments yielded one catastrophe, David Susskind's musical *Kelly* in 1965, which closed after only one night, but other avenues of investment were rather more profitable for Joe. In 1962, Sybil Burton of the Establishment Theatre Company, a U.K.-based company that included David Balding and Peter Cook, came to Joe through her friend Stanley Baker to obtain funding for *The Knack,* a play by Anne Jellicoe, to be produced off-Broadway. Joe agreed and built up ties with the Establishment, and Burton praised Joe in *Variety:* "he calls the group 'Reservoir of Talent' and I think that is Levine's greatest quality. He recognizes and uses talent."[1] One member of this reservoir was the director of *The Knack,* Mike Nichols, whom Joe would subsequently hire to direct *The Graduate.*

By the time Joe signed Nichols to direct *The Graduate,* Nichols was attracting a great deal of attention as a theater director. The recording of his first Broadway production with his improvisational comedy partner, Elaine May, *An Evening with Mike Nichols and Elaine May,* had won the Grammy for best comedy album in 1962, and his production of Neil Simon's *Barefoot in the Park* in 1963 had received rave reviews. By 1964, having scored another success with his production of Murray Schisgal's *Luv,* he was the toast of Broadway. Barney Lefferts of the *New York Times* had this to say about the hotshot young director: "Show folk, like other emotionally disoriented citizens who are forever straining to devise new ways of lassoing still another buck, are quick to notice when one of them becomes a front runner, a fellow possessed of that dark and inexplicable talent that translates . . . into box office receipts."[2]

Joe was quick to notice Nichols's talent and quick to capitalize, signing Nichols as *The Graduate*'s director in 1964. Following that film's success, Joe would, not unusually, take rather more credit than he deserved for "discovering" Nichols and would routinely portray Nichols as the initiator of *The Graduate,* but all the evidence suggests that it was Lawrence Turman, the film's producer, who was the driving force. It was Turman who bought the rights to Charles Webb's novel in 1963. For Turman, Joe's eagerness to be involved with Nichols was motivated by factors other than Nichols's talent as a director, suggesting that Joe was keen to advance his own artistic reputation: "*The Graduate* was his entree into a classier world of film than he was used to. . . . I think [Joe funded *The Graduate*] to be associated with Mike Nichols, who was already hot stuff in the NY world of chic."[3] This is perhaps an overly cynical view that overlooks Joe's track record of discovering and supporting new talent, but it is not entirely without merit. In August 1966, *Variety* reported: "It is noted that the now celebrated line JOSEPH E. LEVINE PRESENTS . . . has been absent from [Embassy's] low budget entries, and those close to Levine have made it clear that, at this stage in his career, the boss is anxious to have his name associated with 'class' product only."[4]

This was a remarkable change of tack for Joe, who had hitherto gloried in being associated simultaneously with both prestige pictures and exploitation pictures. His main source of pride had always been his multifariousness, and his eagerness to plaster his name on any and every film that came near him was legendary. Nonetheless, his name was notably absent from the publicity material for films such as *Picture Mommy Dead, Mad Monster Party,* and *Jesse James Meets Frankenstein's Daughter.* Furthermore, the 1966 *Variety* article gives hints of the "class" product Joe wished to be associated with, such as the abortive *Runaway Train* and *The Graduate.*

This desire to be associated with "class" was not merely an about-face for Joe; it indicated a massive policy overhaul at Embassy. With the commercial failure of the low-budget and family films, Embassy would concentrate its future energies in making "nothing but 'big' English language films."[5] There would be no more low-budgeters for the drive-ins and kiddie matinees. There would be no more coproductions with indies or majors. There would be no more overseas productions. There would be no more Italian art house. On this latter point, the shift marked the end of an era for Embassy. As if describing a mopping-up exercise at the era's end, Vittorio de Sica recalled the genesis of his last movie for Embassy, a portmanteau film made in collaboration with screenwriter Cesare Zavattini: "*Woman Times Seven* [1967] was a compilation of sketches that Zavattini had lying about. We were among the first to make films of sketches, and when Joseph Levine asked us to make another of them, Zavattini pulled some out of his drawer."[6] *Woman Times Seven* and *Shoot Loud, Louder . . . I Don't Understand* (1966) were the last Italian productions Embassy would be involved in for the time being.

This willingness and ability to enact such a major about-face, to completely abandon a policy in favor of a new, more expensive policy, shows Joe's nimbleness and readiness to take risks, alongside his reckless gambler's streak and the panic occasioned by recent failures. Joe's new policy of making fewer films and ensuring the ones made were "expensive and in English" was a strategy that, for *Variety,* represented the "biggest gamble of his career."[7] Joe's expensive English-language films would be *The Graduate* and *The Producers* in 1967 and *The Lion in Winter* in 1968.

The Graduate stars Dustin Hoffman, Anne Bancroft, and Katherine Ross, and it tells of a young man's sexual escapades in 1960s California, escapades motivated by post–college graduation ennui and alienation from the materialist world of his parents and their friends. Though its place in movie history is assured for its apparent uniqueness and revolutionary credentials, *The Graduate* was initially a low-budget affair on Embassy's crowded mid-1960s production schedule, a fact that adds yet another layer of romanticism to its unlikely bargain-basement beginnings. Turman, for example, rather exaggerates Embassy's penny-ante pedigree when he says it was "the end of the line" in terms of production companies. But Nichols, who had directed on the New York stage for Joe and would make two more films with him, has also said that Turman's approaching Joe was a matter of "scraping the bottom of the barrel . . . in every possible sense."[8] Joe, for his part, routinely disparaged the source novel as a way of emphasizing his discovery of Nichols's genius: "Well, with *The Graduate,* I met Mike Nichols . . . when he was doing *The Knack* in a theatre I owned off-Broadway. I watched him rehearse. He was a genius of Broadway then and still is. I said, 'Why don't you make a movie?' The next day he brought in the book *The Graduate* by Charles Webb, and I read it. He asked, 'How'd you like it?' I said it was the worst thing I'd ever read in my life. 'Then you won't make it?' I said, 'I'll make it if *you* want to make it.'"[9]

Nichols's genius notwithstanding, *The Graduate* was to be a fairly low-budget effort. By the time Turman and Nichols approached Joe for funding, *The Graduate* had, in Turman's account, been rejected by "every single studio."[10] According to Turman, Joe agreed to fund it because "I told him I could make it for a million bucks, which was my honest hope/intention at the time."[11] By the time the film was completed, however, its budget had risen to $3.2 million. But two things had occurred during the intervening years. First, Joe had abandoned his strategy of making low-budget films and seemed intent on increasing the production values for Embassy product. Second, Mike Nichols's stock as a director, both in theater and in film, had continued to rise. He had another major hit on Broadway in 1965, Neil Simon's *The Odd Couple*, and cinematic success with *Who's Afraid of Virginia Woolf?* (1966), which earned him a best director nomination at the Academy Awards.

That Joe allowed Nichols to direct *Who's Afraid of Virginia Woolf?* for Warner Bros. became the source of a typically self-aggrandizing one-liner: "I let him learn on Jack's money."[12] Though this is something of a Levineism, it demonstrates that by the time *The Graduate* began filming, Nichols had proved his mettle; and before it was even made, Joe was calling Nichols a genius in the press. Admittedly, hyperbole was part and parcel of Joe's approach, but what is interesting is how he presented his association with Nichols as a vindication of his new production strategies. Speaking in December 1966, he told Calvin Tomkins of the *New Yorker*, "We won't be doing as many things as we've done in the past, but they'll all be big budget pictures. Like this picture Mike Nichols is doing for us now—*The Graduate.* Mike is a genius, and we may really have ourselves something there. It all depends on how things break of course."[13]

The huge success of *The Graduate* indicates, in hindsight, that the movie was opportune for Joe and Embassy, but Joe was attuned to cultural and cinematic mores in spite of, or even because of, his recently failed policies at Embassy. In an interview with Charles Champlin, Joe pithily encapsulated the outbreak of discernment among movie audiences: "People don't go to the movies, they go to *a* movie."[14] The audience was fragmenting, and cinema attendance was declining. One demographic that was expanding, however, was the under thirties, and it was this increasingly discerning market at which *The Graduate* would be squarely aimed.

Against a backdrop of youthful sophistication, films such as *Blow Up, Tom Jones* (1963), *Alfie* (1966), *Morgan! Or a Suitable Case for Treatment* (1966), and Embassy's *Darling* became popular with young audiences. These films represented a new generation of European art films from Britain, whose success with audiences was aided in no small part by the fact that they were in English as well as by their smart and savvy treatment of "adult" themes.

Although all these films fit broadly into the arthouse category, they all achieved great success in the United States despite receiving mixed reviews. The under thirties have never been known to seek critical approval for their tastes, and, as an increasingly important demographic, young audiences became more powerful when exercising their own judgment. By 1967, a much romanticized yet still significant cultural shift appeared to be under way, a shift exemplified by *Bonnie and Clyde* and capitalized on by *The Graduate.*

Many regard *Bonnie and Clyde* as a watershed film in American cinema, and it is understood as marking the birth of a new Hollywood. It stars Faye Dunaway and Warren Beatty as the eponymous Depression-era robbers and killers. Violent, funny, exuberant, and stylized, Bonnie Parker and Clyde Barrow are reimagined as sympathetic symbols of counterculture alienation, yearning for freedom in a repressive society. Despite half-hearted marketing and lackluster distribution, *Bonnie and Clyde* was a huge success with young audiences. According to film historian Robert Sklar, "Audiences understood better than either the distributor or critics the emotional power of the film . . . a small victory for the independent judgement of audiences against the guiding advice of mass journalism, and it led to the unusual experience of mass periodicals, not wishing to lose their aura of omniscience, shaming themselves and coming out in favor of the film."[15] That *Bonnie and Clyde* could have overcome critical and industrial barriers and become successful constituted a triumph indicative of more progressive cultural tides in one of the most profoundly mythologized periods in American movie history.

Bonnie and Clyde was far from universally condemned, but it was condemned by the right people. Bosley Crowther, who, incidentally, had praised *Morgan!, Tom Jones,* and *Blow Up,* wrote three angry reviews of *Bonnie and Clyde* for the *New York Times.*[16] Crowther was hardly the most fashionable of film critics; his reviews of the film would make him even less so and may have done more to help than hinder the film's success.

Bonnie and Clyde was praised by the emerging fashionistas of film criticism, Andrew Sarris and Pauline Kael, who exalted it with gushing praise. According to Peter Biskind, one of the foremost chroniclers of this period, "Print critics had considerably more influence then than they do now. . . . [Film criticism] was a gentleman's sport dominated by Crowther's middle-brow taste. A bad review from him could kill a picture. . . . [Kael and Sarris were] two reviewers . . . waging war on 'Crowtherism,' as they called it."[17]

It is amazing how often a bumptiously oppositional barnstormer such as Joe found himself on the right side of intellectual movements. New Journalism, arthouse auteurism, and camp had paid dividends for Joe in one way or another. Now American film critics, like their cousins in New Journalism, were looking for whipping boys in the establishment to advance their own manifesto-driven interpretation of cinema, and they found their ideal candidate in Joe's old nemesis, Bosley Crowther.

If a culture war was being waged, most of the aggression came from one side. To be sure, Crowther's attacks on *Bonnie and Clyde* were repeated and somewhat hysterical, and another of the old guard, Dwight Macdonald, who had expressed admiration for *Bonnie and Clyde,* fired his own salvo by resigning in protest at Andrew Sarris's appointment as a film critic for *Film Quarterly.* (Macdonald claimed that Sarris was not a critic but "a systematic fool. His judgements have nothing to do with criticism, since he merely applies the party line to each movie."[18]) But, for the most part, the hip young-gun film critics such as Sarris and Kael advanced unhindered, their respective profiles magnified by repeated and highly public disagreements regarding the merits of auteur theory. ("We made each other," Sarris later said, "we established a dialectic."[19])

The critical sea change and the new generation's discerning tastes were not lost on Joe, who commented in June 1967, "We spent the last eighteen months making family films which no family saw. My son went to see *Blow Up.*"[20] Later that year, on 8 December, *Time* published "The Shock of Freedom in Films,"[21] an account of a new, franker, European-influenced Hollywood. The following week Embassy released *The Graduate.*

Given the market conditions, *The Graduate* was ideal fare for the emerging audience of youthful cognoscenti. It provided an accessible mix of freewheeling European filmmaking style and frankness, the jolly cynicism of the British New Wave, gestures toward the counterculture and the generation gap, as well as unmistakably American genre traditions. Like other counterculture films of the time, *The Graduate* is essentially a genre-formula film. Just as *Bonnie and Clyde* is a gangster movie, and *Easy Rider* (1969) is a biker-exploitation flick, so *The Graduate* is a screwball comedy, and one appealing factor of it is all too often overlooked—it is very funny. But the genre had been given a modern twist; it had been repackaged to incorporate the alienated-youth motifs of the previous decade's films, such as *Rebel without a Cause* (1955), and was aimed squarely at the expanding youth market.

Given that *The Graduate* was hardly a low-budget film, Joe granted an extraordinary amount of latitude to Turman and Nichols, displaying a great deal of faith in their respective talents. Perhaps even more remarkable than the free hand he granted to them in terms of filmmaking was the fact that he allowed them to participate in choosing promotional material: "It was Mike and myself . . . who arranged and selected the famous photo that became our logo, that of Dustin's figure underneath Anne Bancroft's leg. A Brit designer, Richard Williams, by the way, came up with that."[22] When it came to the actual selling of the film, however, Turman emphasizes that "Joe Levine was a high-powered kick-ass salesman, and he sure sold the hell out of *The Graduate.*"[23]

By the time *The Graduate* was released in December 1967, the success of *Bonnie and Clyde* had created a sympathetic press climate, with writers eager to embrace and be seen to embrace the idea of a new Hollywood. For Stanley Kaufman of *The New Republic,* "after months of prattle about the 'new' American film (mostly occasioned by the overrated *Bonnie and Clyde*) *The Graduate* gives some substance to the contention that American films are coming of age—of our age."[24] For Andrew Sarris, the success of *The Graduate* was organic: "The kids kept standing on line for a) Dustin Hoffman and b) Simon and Garfunkel. Then the adults stood on line to find out why the kids stood on line. Then the deep thinkers on the prestige publications stood on line to find out why the adults stood on line."[25] Crowther, the sworn enemy of the new breed of film critics, also praised the film, but *The Graduate* luckily found much needed opposition elsewhere. The venerable Hollis Alpert of the *Saturday Review* wrote, "What's all this about honesty and truth in *The Graduate*? The cards have been stacked against the middle class parent in favor of the rebellious 'now' generation. They darkly hint at the commercial motives of Levine, Nichols and company."[26]

The successes of *Bonnie and Clyde* and *The Graduate* contributed to the recognition of a new era in filmmaking, one that seemingly sprang from grassroots cinemagoers. According to Peter Biskind, "*Bonnie and Clyde* was a movement movie; like *The Graduate,* young audiences recognized it as 'theirs.'"[27] Yet *The Graduate*'s supposed organic evolution to megahit status was largely an illusion created by Joe. Whereas Joe had saturated the United States with *Hercules,* affording the opportunity for anyone with sufficiently aroused curiosity to see it, his strategy for *The Graduate* was to demand some effort from the audience.

In May 1967, the *Hollywood Reporter* hinted at how Joe planned to guide the film to success. "The film will open at Christmas with the usual Levine exploitation," ran the article. "He may play it hard ticket in smaller theatres. . . . 'Word of mouth,' says Levine, 'is still the best publicity.'"[28] Following *The Graduate*'s success, Joe recounted his technique to *Variety:* "I made sure it would kick off in the modern shopping center cinemas where the kids drive to; also that it would be in smaller houses, for longer sustained runs and the attendant ballyhoo that you 'can't get in.'"[29] Although such chicanery may not fully account for *The Graduate*'s phenomenal success, it does show that the appearance of Sarris's "lines" at the theaters was no accident.

Joe's approach to promotion had always been that of a carny barker, aggressively hyping his films while concurrently hyping himself and Embassy by presenting himself as the public face of all the projects with which he was involved. At this time, though, he was becoming choosier about what he would attach his name to, and, following the enormous success of *The Graduate,* he aggressively sought to associate himself with it and its young director and did so at the expense of Larry Turman, the film's producer, initiator, and driving force: "In my face-to-face negotiation with him for *The Graduate* I refused to allow him Executive Producer credit (commonplace today and for him at that time) and then once the film became a big hit he did everything he could to obliterate me, including at our celebratory party, attempting to seat me a mile away from himself with Mike Nichols and cast members. Mike had to intervene on my behalf."[30]

Joe's association with Nichols and *The Graduate* remained a frequently exploited source of self-promotion for the remainder of his career. Most significantly, he converted the kudos generated by his association with *The Graduate* and its director into an extremely valuable bargaining chip when he decided to sell his company.

11

Selling Up and Winning Trophies

Don't be stupid—be a smarty. Come and join the Nazi party!
—*Mel Brooks,* The Producers

In 1966, a wave of buyouts and corporatizations began rolling through Hollywood, beginning with Gulf and Western's takeover of the troubled Paramount Studios. With more corporate buyouts of Hollywood studios looking certain, Vincent Canby wrote in the *New York Times*, "Not since the Depression years has the motion picture industry—that strange and volatile business—experienced so many traumas, in number and in kind, as it did in 1966."[1] Following Paramount's takeover, Seven Arts Productions bought Warner Bros., and in 1967 Transamerica acquired United Artists. In 1969, Seven Arts sold Warner Bros. to Kinney National Services, and MGM sold out to real estate magnate Kirk Kerkorian. With corporations circling and sniffing around film companies, it was natural that Embassy should attract attention, especially given the dramatic makeover Joe had given his company over the previous months. In March 1967, Joe appeared to be pointedly noncommittal about the possibility of a merger, telling *Variety*, "We've had three offers from people who wanted to swallow us up completely, but we're too big to be swallowed."[2]

Joe had repeatedly talked of Mike Nichols's "genius" in interviews and clearly knew that *The Graduate* was going to be an important film. So he gambled and waited. In 1968, following the enormous success of *The Graduate* and against a background of industrial upheavals in Hollywood, Joe cashed in and sold Embassy to the Avco Corporation for $40 million. To put that into perspective, Seven Arts Productions had acquired the venerable Warner Bros. for $32 million in 1966.

The corporate takeovers of the Hollywood studios in the late 1960s were occasioned by three interrelated factors: first, the studios owned valuable real estate; second, they owned film libraries, which were increasing in value because of the demand from television; and, third, the film studios' stock was greatly undervalued. Peter Bart of the *New York Times* observed in 1966, "The libraries of old movies controlled by the studios have soared in value, yet the shares in movie companies have continued to sell at price-earning ratios below those of comparable companies in other industries. These depressed prices make them attractive for corporate takeovers."[3] Embassy owned no real estate or, indeed, equipment—something Joe had always been proud of: "I hope I never even own a camera."[4] Neither was Embassy's stock undervalued because Joe had never gone public. However, Embassy had a wide and varied library of films, and the value of such assets was rocketing.

Joe may have gone down a blind alley with his investments in low-budget family films and exploitationers, but Embassy had a vast television-friendly library. If television was hungry for product, the corporate world was hungrier. The studios' undervalued stock, combined with the burgeoning value of film libraries, sparked a feeding frenzy among corporations looking to get in on the action. This corporate feeding frenzy led, as it so often does, to an atmosphere of urgency whereby the objects of corporate desire became ever more enticing, which, in turn, led to a bubble from which Joe was able to profit hugely, and so he sold Embassy to Avco.

But it was not just Embassy's library of films that attracted Avco; it was Embassy's showman boss, and Joe accepted a position as president of Avco Embassy for an annual salary of $200,000 and a seven-year contract. He had just had a massive success with *The Graduate,* which put him in a strong position at the negotiating table. Whereas other companies were selling for less than their true value, Embassy's recent turnaround put the company in a commanding position, and helped to push up the asking price. A few months after the merger, James R. Kerr, Avco's president, wrote in *Variety,* "The question has been asked: would Avco have been interested in Embassy without *The Graduate*? The answer is an unqualified *yes.* Negotiations were already well advanced by the time *The Graduate* came out of the cutting room. The remarkable success of the film did, on the other hand, affect the eventual financial arrangement."[5]

It is extremely difficult to find any reliable financial information about Embassy from any point in its history. It was a private company and was essentially owner operated, so it was not required to make its financial records public. But it is certain that Embassy was in serious financial trouble at this time because of the failure of so many of Joe's scattergun investments in the 1960s. Gambling again, Joe gambled on the success of *The Graduate* to bail him out. By the time of the Avco takeover, *The Graduate*'s success had yet to make much of a dent in Embassy's sorry finances, but such a recent success made Embassy very attractive indeed in the takeover-hungry world of corporate Hollywood.

Tony Klinger, a young director-producer and son of British producer Michael Klinger, was close with Joe at this time and says Joe's financial situation was bordering on catastrophic when the Avco deal came through:

> Joe was literally having heart surgery when that deal came along to save his ass money wise. He thought the gig was up, he owed a fortune, with no prospect of payback. He was being wheeled to the operating theatre when the call with the deal came from Avco and he took the call before he was anaesthetized. He thought it was going to be to close his company down and he was, as ever, ready to fight, when he realized it was an offer way beyond his wildest dreams, to buy Embassy. He told us he couldn't fucking believe it![6]

Joe had gambled again, and it had paid off, as had his policy overhaul at Embassy, not only with *The Graduate.* As Avco's president further wrote in *Variety,* "We also had some knowledge of what Levine had up his sleeve in the way of projects and forthcoming releases."[7] During the negotiations with Avco, Joe had two future successes: *The Lion in Winter* and, rather farther up his sleeve, *The Producers.*

The Producers is the first feature by the now legendary comedian Mel Brooks, and it deservedly retains its status as a comedy classic. Brooks and Thomas Meehan readapted the film as a successful Broadway stage musical in 2001, which was subsequently adapted for the screen in 2005. In 1968, however, following a disastrous test screening, *The Producers* was not a priority on Joe's release schedule—shelved, if not buried.

What is often forgotten in discussions of *The Graduate* is that it is very funny, but it seems always to be remembered as revolutionary. By contrast, *The Producers* will always be remembered as being very funny, but it is also revolutionary—more so than *The Graduate* in many ways. The film's story concerns a scheme cooked up by a theater producer and his accountant to produce a Broadway flop and abscond with the investors' money when the play inevitably closes. *The Producers* stars Zero Mostel and Gene Wilder, both Jews, as the producer and his accountant. As detailed in chapter 6, the archetype of the Jewish huckster-impresario, stalwart of vaudeville and prewar Hollywood, had been largely absent from screens in the postwar era because of concerns about stereotyping—concerns that fueled the disquiet surrounding the depiction of Joe in the Maysles brothers' documentary *Showman,* not least from Joe himself. Nonetheless, *The Producers* revives the archetype with unshackled gusto, poking many other sacred cows along the way.

The Producers tells of how a nervous accountant, Leo Bloom (Wilder), spots an accounting loophole that suggests that producing a disastrous failure on Broadway could be a very profitable venture so long as the perpetrators are not caught in their fraud. Leo's boss, a greedy and deliciously corrupt showman named Max Bialystock (Mostel), is determined to exploit the possibility of a get-rich-quick scheme, and the two begin searching for the worst script they can find. They eventually settle for a musical entitled *Springtime for Hitler: A Gay Romp with Adolf and Eva at Berchtesgaden,* written by a lunatic Nazi. The play, deadly serious in its praise of Adolf Hitler, is subsequently misinterpreted as a pasquinade by the too sophisticated audience and becomes a huge success; thus, the scheme unravels.

By the time Brooks brought *The Producers* to Joe, he had already built up a successful comedy career. The 1961 comedy album *2000 Years with Carl Reiner and Mel Brooks* had been successful and won awards; he had won an Oscar, with Ernest Pintoff, for best animated short for *The Critic*—a satire of highbrow film criticism—at the Academy Awards for 1964; and his Broadway musical *All American* had won two Tony Awards. He had also helped to create the James Bond spoof television show *Get Smart* (1965–1970) with Buck Henry, who would later script *The Graduate.* But Brooks was unable to generate interest in *The Producers* from Hollywood studios, despite the best efforts by Brooks and Sidney Glazier, his producer, who had given Brooks his "vow" to get the movie made.[8] With the memory of slaughter of the Second World War still vivid, and bearing its original title, *Springtime for Hitler,* the project was deemed too tasteless by everyone but Joe.

Brooks and Joe were already connected by future success and past failure by the time they met to discuss *Springtime for Hitler.* Brooks's wife, Anne Bancroft, had been cast in the role of Mrs. Robinson in *The Graduate,* and Brooks himself had done rewrites on David Susskind's Broadway megaflop *Kelly,* which had lost Joe a quarter of a million dollars. At their meeting, says Brooks, "I did a 20 minute presentation of storyline, characters and highlights of the movie in his office."[9] Having faced rejection from so many studio executives, Brooks and Glazier were surprised to see their brazenly impertinent project get Joe's approval. There were, however, conditions. Joe wanted the movie's budget to be less than $1 million, and, more controversially, he demanded a title change. According to Brooks, "Mr. Levine explained that having been an exhibitor all his life, he knew 'Hitler' would not work on the marquee—especially in New York, Chicago and LA. It was Joe who suggested another title. At first I disagreed vehemently—almost violently—but slowly and surely I could see his point of view and in the end I simply had to concede to his savvy and wisdom."[10]

Barely twenty years after the Second World War, it was perhaps unwise to have the name "Hitler" on cinema billboards and advertisements all over America. Joe did later say that he regretted his veto, but it is worth noting that six decades after the war neither of the twenty-first-century reworkings of *The Producers* reverted to the much-argued-over original title.

Joe interfered very little in the production of *The Producers.* He had some doubts about Brooks taking on the director's role and insisted that he "audition" by directing a television commercial. Once a commercial for Frito-Lay snacks had been completed, Joe felt that Brooks had proved his competence, and the director's chair was his.[11] During filming, Joe took exception to Gene Wilder as Leo Bloom. "I don't know what the hell that Wilder guy is doing," Joe said to Brooks during a screening of rushes. "I got twenty-five thousand dollars for you to find another actor."[12] Brooks stood his ground, and Wilder, who was getting only $10,000 for *The Producers,* stayed in the picture.

Once *The Producers* was completed, a test screening was held in a small suburban theater in Philadelphia, an occasion that Brooks recalled as "the worst night of my life."[13] Few people attended, fewer laughed, Joe left without a word, and the film was found a shelf to sit on. A couple of months later, in January 1968, the film's fortunes changed thanks to an intervention by British comedy actor Peter Sellers. Sellers had attended what was to be a private screening of Fellini's *I Vitelloni* (1953) hosted by the actor Paul Mazursky. Fortunately for Brooks, Mazursky had forgotten to order a print of the film, but the projectionist happened to have a copy of *The Producers,* which he offered to screen for the frustrated guests. Sellers loved the film and, perhaps emboldened by the marijuana brownies on offer, telephoned Joe in the middle of the night to tell him so.[14] The next day, in a promotional coup even Joe could not have dreamed of, Sellers took out ads in the trade papers wherein he heaped praise on *The Producers* and Brooks.

> Last night I saw the ultimate film . . . *The Producers,* or as it was originally titled *Springtime for Hitler.* Brilliantly written and directed by Mel Brooks, it is the essence of all great comedy combined in a single motion picture. Without any doubt, Mel Brooks displays true genius in weaving together tragedy–comedy, pity, fear, hysteria, schizophrenia, inspired madness and a largess of lunacy with sheer magic. The casting was perfect.
>
> Those of us who have seen this film and understand it have experienced a phenomenon which occurs once in a life span.
>
> —Peter Sellers

By March, *The Producers* was in the theaters. The night before its New York opening, Joe took out his own ads in the *New York Times,* which reprinted Sellers's fulsome praise along with a hastily concocted promotional image in the form of a line drawing of a near-naked lady sporting a Hitler moustache.

The Producers is now often misremembered as a critical catastrophe, with critics outraged by its tastelessness. The reviews were mixed but far from damning. Many critics complained about the film's crudeness, both in humor and in technical prowess, but many more warmed to at least parts of the movie. Roger Ebert rated it very highly; Pauline Kael and Andrew Sarris were less enthused. Perhaps the most illustrative critical response came from Renata Adler of the *New York Times,* who wrote that it "leaves one alternately picking up one's coat to leave and sitting back to laugh."[15] *The Producers* was never going to find the critical consonance of *The Graduate.* Despite being much funnier, it is uneven and messy. But it is as anarchically inspired as the Marx Brothers' Paramount films of the 1930s, privileging caricature and zany humor over characterization and plot coherence.

Like *The Graduate* and *Bonnie and Clyde*, *The Producers* harked back to the Golden Age of Hollywood. But where *The Graduate* and *Bonnie and Clyde* were slick and knowing, *The Producers* contrived to cram as many gags as possible into its running time, leaving it too overstuffed for some tastes. In the era of flawed and moody antiheroes, from *Bonnie and Clyde*'s sexy rebel killers to *The Graduate*'s self-obsessed Benjamin Braddock, the protagonists of *The Producers* are uniformly rotten, cowardly, avaricious, and corrupt. Neither blockbuster nor bomb on its release, but daft, quotable, and filled with grotesque characters, *The Producers* found its audience among college boys—probably the same kids who had dragged their dads to see the mighty saga *Hercules* ten years earlier.

The appealing narrative of a badly handled, if not disregarded, film that found an afterlife as a cult classic tends to dominate writing about *The Producers*. In his autobiography, Wilder is understandably critical of Joe, given that Joe tried to get him fired from the production. Mel Brooks's assessment of Joe, however, is much more sympathetic: "In the promotion, he was pretty darn generous to a first time filmmaker. . . . He could be tough and obdurate in dealing with people, but I found him to be a pretty good guy. He was never arrogant or egotistical like a lot of other studio executives."[16]

When considering *The Producers* and the reductive assessments of the failings of Hollywood's "money men" that often form the discourse, it is important to remember that, like *The Graduate*, the project had been rejected many times by movie executives. Joe backed an ostentatiously inflammatory project from a first-time director based on little more than a twenty-minute performance from Brooks and a commercial for potato chips. Brooks says that *The Producers* "might never have been made" without Joe's backing.[17] Certainly, the film would have benefited from a more heavy-guns promotional campaign to put the movie over. Unfortunately, this did not happen. *The Producers* finally made it onto American screens while Joe was deeply involved in negotiations with Avco, the promotion of *The Graduate*, the production of *The Lion in Winter*, and heart surgery, so it rather slipped through the net. But Joe was instrumental in *The Producers*' inception and so must receive a good deal of credit for its afterlife.

Following *The Graduate* and *The Producers*, two comedies that were at once modern and nostalgic, Joe produced an old-fashioned prestige picture, *The Lion in Winter*. It was directed by Anthony Harvey, produced by

Joe alongside Martin Poll, and based on a play by James Goldman. Set in the Christmas Court of King Henry II, *The Lion in Winter* investigates the plotting and politicking of medieval Europe in a tale of disputed successions, matrimonial chicanery, and plans for war. It stars Peter O'Toole as Henry II, Katharine Hepburn as Eleanor of Aquitaine, and two interesting new faces, both belonging to Welshmen, in their big-screen debuts: Anthony Hopkins as Richard the Lionheart and Timothy Dalton, a future James Bond, as Philip II of France. After rehearsals in London, *The Lion in Winter* was filmed in Ireland. Rumors of trouble on set as well as of friction and flaring tempers between Hepburn and O'Toole circulated, but O'Toole later dismissed them with characteristic flair: "Trouble with *Kate?* I *worship* the bloody woman! I've never enjoyed working with anyone so much in my whole life, not even Burton. There were no problems, not a one. As a matter of fact, Kate came to see me in Ireland a few weeks ago—completely unannounced, as always. '*Hello,*' she said, looking in the window. My children thought it was a tinkerwoman."[18]

Although Joe never sought critical favor, he was partial to a spot of middlebrow prestige and had a great fondness for awards. *The Lion in Winter* brought him these things: most reviews were fairly positive; it was financially successful; and awards were won at the Golden Globes and the Oscars. Perhaps for these reasons, Joe often claimed *The Lion in Winter* as his favorite among his own films.

Joe won his first and last major filmmaking award for *The Lion in Winter.* At the Golden Globe Awards ceremony in February 1969, he, along with Marin Poll, was awarded the Golden Globe for best picture in the drama category. Other Globe recipients for *The Lion in Winter* were John Barry for his score and Peter O'Toole, who won the award for best actor in a drama for his portrayal of King Henry II, repeating his success of four years earlier when he had won the same award for playing the same character in *Becket.* Anthony Harvey was also nominated as best director but failed to win. At the Oscars, *The Lion in Winter* was nominated for best picture, Harvey for best director, and O'Toole for best actor, but none won. Katharine Hepburn, however, won the Best Actress Oscar for her performance as Eleanor of Aquitaine. The award, her third in total, made her only the second actress in history to win a Best Actress Oscar two years in succession, having won the previous year for her performance in *Guess Who's Coming to Dinner* (1967). It was also the only time in the award's history where the Best Actress Oscar has been shared—Barbra Streisand jointly won the Oscar for her performance in *Funny Girl.* In addition, James Goldman won for best adapted screenplay, and John Barry, repeating his Golden Globe success, won for best score. Meanwhile, Mel Brooks won the Best Original Screenplay Oscar for *The Producers,* and Gene Wilder, Joe's candidate for firing, was nominated as best supporting actor.

The Lion in Winter was Joe's first major release under the new Avco Embassy banner. The Oscar ceremony came less than twelve months after the deal with Avco had been struck and finalized in May 1968, and Avco's enormous investment was looking sound. Joe would have been well advised to push *The Producers* a little more, but its Oscar success, along with the financial, critical, and award success of *The Lion in Winter* in 1968 and *The Graduate* the previous year more than compensated for this lapse in judgment.

Having found himself on the right side of so many cultural movements, from monster movies to New Journalism, camp, and the Hollywood Renaissance, Joe now found himself of the right side of the corporate feeding frenzy that was engulfing Hollywood, a frenzy that had saved him from bankruptcy and made him a fortune. Embassy was not, like Paramount, a troubled studio; it was an essentially owner-operated concern with a promising future now that its debts had been taken care of. In September 1968, Joe became the head of a major, joining the other eight big Hollywood studios represented by the MPAA when Avco Embassy became the association's first new member in twenty-one years. Joe was now a corporate executive.

Avco was a highly diversified corporation involved in everything from insurance and banking to the manufacture of farm equipment and weaponry, so its association with Embassy added a vibrancy to the corporation's public image. That said, the glamour in the partnership reflected both ways. Avco's government contracts included some for NASA, thereby associating the corporation with the most glamorous and exciting endeavor of the twentieth century, the Apollo moon shot, which happened in 1969. The twin glamour of Tinseltown and space exploration was displayed in Avco Embassy's circular logo, the top half of which depicted the moon and the bottom half a film reel, accompanied by the slogan "Avco EMBASSY. A company on its way to the moon."

The movie business had been steadily improving throughout the 1960s. Box-office receipts were going up, thanks largely to the doubling of ticket prices since the war rather than to increased patronage. Corporations were looking to diversify, and investing in the film business was attractive not only because of the impressive figures and forecasts of box-office revenues and television sales but also because corporations wished to communicate better with the public. The corporate world had expanded significantly in the postwar period and appeared to replace the vibrant dynamism of American individualist entrepreneurial capitalism with vast, gray, faceless bureaucracies that were expanding into any and all sectors without bothering to distinguish themselves from one another. There is little doubt that at that time, as now, many of the gray faces of the corporatocracy were attracted to the glitzy world of showbiz.

More than any other figure in American cinema, Joe represented the can-do spirit of American moneymaking that informed the mythology of the American Dream. Corporations, in contrast, represented the might-as-well-do approach to amassing virtual capital. As the corporate world entered the movie world, it is interesting to compare Avco president James R. Kerr's unglamorous, rationalist assessment of the benefits of buying Embassy with Joe's streetwise film-flam. For Kerr, "Levine's company provides Avco with an enhanced public image. It strengthens notably our toehold in the leisure time field; it provides a firm base for further development in that field."[19] Joe, meanwhile, bragged about achieving major status with the MPAA and the "endless revolving credit" he had access to through Avco. He also predicted that 1968 would be a "record year," while Kerr predicted that Avco Embassy would generate fifty cents per share for the company.[20]

Joe's arrival at Avco made an odd sort of sense. His huckster charm gave Avco a sheen of rakish appeal, and Avco's billions gave Joe the stability to indulge his multifarious appetites. As Joyce Haber reported in the *Los Angeles Times,* "Now Joe Levine's manicured right hand knows exactly what his scruffy left hand is doing. For example, he has signed Mike Nichols to direct another movie, for which he'll pay him a record $1 million. But he also has some left-handers about to break, including something called *The Terrornaughts.* (Subtitle: *The Virgin Sacrifices to the Gods of the Ghastly Galaxies*)."[21] Produced by Joe's erstwhile partner, Max Rosenberg, at Britain's Amicus studios, *The Terrornaughts* had, in fact, already been released by Embassy a year before the deal was struck with Avco. But, alongside the Nichols announcement, the title provided the kind of juxtaposition that journalists associated with Joe by this time.

Indeed, one wonders if Joe bought *The Terrornaughts* for precisely that reason.

Following the success of his strategy of making fewer but more expensive films, evidence that Joe was about to return to his usual policy of a crowded production and distribution schedule that catered to all tastes and budgets came in *Variety,* which on 13 November 1968 carried an eighty-eight-page advertising broadside from Avco Embassy. It featured tributes from various influential individuals—James R. Kerr, MPAA president Jack Valenti, New York mayor John V. Lindsay, and Senator Jacob K. Javits—as well as a plethora of advertisements that gave Avco a chance to promote its development of a heat shield for the moon shot and Avco Embassy a chance to promote its upcoming cinematic endeavors. Pride of place for the film projects was MN2, or "Mike Nichols Two," an as yet untitled project that would be Mike Nichols's second film for Embassy, though his fourth in total. "Mike Nichols," ran the blurb, "Academy Award winning director of *The Graduate* will make his next film for Avco Embassy. ENOUGH SAID!"[22]

Nichols was not the only familiar face in Avco Embassy's starting lineup. Sidney Lumet, who had directed *A Long Day's Journey into Night* for Joe in 1963, was attached to two projects, Harold Robbins to three, Jules Dassin to one, and John Michael Hayes to one. Also included was a notable prestige project, an adaptation of Ken Kesey's novel *One Flew over the Cuckoo's Nest,* published in 1962, to star Kirk Douglas (the film was later made by United Artists and starred Jack Nicholson), and moderate potboilers such as *The Man Who Had Power over Women.*

The Lion in Winter had just been released; Joe had a vision for the future and Avco's billions to help him achieve it; box-office receipts were rising; and television was demanding more and more movies to fill up schedules. What could possibly go wrong?

12

The Corporate Gadabout

> This is no business for big business—it's an art form. You can't have endless meetings. Someone's got to have instinct. I never had a meeting in my life before I got here. Not because I was opinionated . . . but because I had confidence in my judgments.
>
> —*Joseph E. Levine*

In 1970, MGM sold the ruby-red slippers worn by Judy Garland's Dorothy in *The Wizard of Oz,* and the sale became a symbol of the recession Hollywood was in the midst of. The ruby slippers were the centerpiece of an auction of more than 350,000 props and costumes acquired from MGM by auctioneer David Weisz. Weisz paid $1.5 million to MGM and claimed to make more than $12 million on the sales. MGM's owner Kirk Kirkorian had appointed James T. Aubrey, also known as "the smiling cobra," as president in 1969, and Aubrey began a massive asset-stripping operation. He shut down many green-lighted productions and interfered in many more; he sold off the studio's real estate, its international theaters, and MGM Records. In 1971, he relocated the studio's New York offices to Culver City, California, and in 1973 shut down MGM's distribution operations. Still, the studio struggled to make it through the 1970s.

MGM is an extreme case but emblematic of the problems facing Hollywood. Joe used the accelerated disintegration of a once-great studio as the basis of one of his regular evaluations of the state of the movies: "The heads of MGM blamed their own inadequacies on the film business. Years ago, there was a mystique about the business. This business does less to promote itself than any I know. AVCO has divisions that sell horseshit—and they're more glamorous than the picture business."[1]

It was more than a lack of self-promotion that was troubling the industry by the late 1960s. Corporations had been attracted to Hollywood by, among other things, the revenues promised by the television market, but the television bubble had just burst. By 1969, movies were being shown on television seven nights a week, and audience figures were falling. In the late 1960s, television had seemed dependent on Hollywood product, but the voraciousness of television stations' appetite for new products to fill its schedules had led to a bloated inventory when the number of made-for-TV movies had increased dramatically. By the turn of the decade, the major broadcasters had purchased enough movies to last until 1972.[2] As Hollywood became reliant on money from television, complacency inevitably followed.

Hollywood's reliance on money from television was at least partly occasioned by the confusion caused by cinema audiences. Cinema was no longer a mass medium because the audience was no longer a mass, but rather an agglomeration of disparate niches with diverse and divergent tastes, sensibilities, and desires. Put simply, formulas were not working because audiences were not behaving how they should. The formulas that brought success in the 1960s also brought failure. Epic successes such as *Ben Hur* led to epic failures such as *Cleopatra* (1963); musical successes such as *The Sound of Music* (1965) led to musical failures such as *Paint Your Wagon* (1969); family successes such as *Mary Poppins* (1964) led to family failures such as *Dr. Doolittle* (1967). With many films of this time failing not because they were not popular but because box office takings could not match the bloated budgets, the discovery of the youth market, with its appetite for lower-budget films, must have seemed like a godsend, but it was another minefield. Capricious youths responded enthusiastically to counterculture fare such as *Bonnie and Clyde, The Graduate,* and *Easy Rider,* but not to the youth-oriented films *Head* (1968), *Zabriskie Point* (1970), and *The Last Movie* (1971). With such divergent tastes to appeal to, the Hollywood studios were not catering to audiences; they were chasing markets. As film historian Thomas Schatz observes, "Hollywood's cultivation of the youth market and penchant for innovation in the late 1960s and early 1970s scarcely indicated a favorable market climate. On the contrary, they reflected the studios' uncertainty and growing desperation."[3]

Avco Embassy, however, looked to have an ace in the hole with Joe. As Hollywood was worrying how to deal with an audience that had apparently transformed into a cluster of niches, Avco Embassy's president was a man who had amassed his fortune catering to niches. Joe was renowned for his versatility and ability to juggle projects and cater to multiple markets. He saw the importance of the youth audience, but that audience was just one patch in his proposed work, as he told *Variety* in October 1969: "I do not intend to stop production for general audiences but I am going ahead to make films for young people and encourage young talent as a program in itself."[4] Some months later Joe reiterated his commitment to cinema's youthful patrons but warned, "Neither *The Love Bug* or *Airport* is anti-establishment, so producers just can't afford to set their goals on youngsters."[5]

There is a perceptiveness behind these comments that recognizes changing tastes and audience unreliability. Joe had said of *Hercules* in 1966, "Of course, that kind of promotion, that kind of picture—you couldn't sell it now. People have become very skillful at smelling out what's good and what's lousy."[6] Younger audiences had become either too sophisticated to appreciate hokum or too unsophisticated to appreciate irony or maybe just that little bit more serious. The carnivalesque showmanship that defined Joe in the previous decade would no longer work in the era of Vietnam, and neither would the drive-in double bills, monster movies, and weirdies.

Drive-in theaters were on the decline, and the gimmickry and concessions that had defined them in the 1950s and provided diversions from the dodgy film were on the way out. Young cinemagoers wanted more serious productions with a political edge. Joe spoke of "nonconformist" and "anti-establishment" cinema, and while he may have been Hollywood's maverick outsider, he hardly cut an antiestablishment figure in the eyes of the Woodstock generation—unlike, say, Roger Corman. Joe had done more than most to put "antiestablishment" cinema into the mainstream with *The Graduate* and was greatly responsible for the acceptance of sexual frankness in American commercial cinema with his arthouse imports and films such as *The Carpetbaggers.* But as the 1960s turned into the 1970s, Joe, an old-fashioned flim-flam man, seemed like a man out of his time. For Joe, the Avco years were singularly undramatic, and although this is certainly a reflection of Hollywood's recession, it is also true to say that during this time Joe was uncharacteristically not firing on all cylinders.

Michael Klinger can be seen as England's answer to Joe. He described himself as "the best producer in England," no less than twice in a single short letter to Joe, and Joe would have certainly appreciated such a Levinian level of immodesty.[7] The son of Jewish immigrants, Klinger hailed from

London's Soho, where his father worked in the rag trade. He held many jobs, including a stint as an ice cream seller on the Isle of Wight, before gravitating toward the entertainment industry. He managed strip clubs in Soho (the Nell Gwynne and Gargoyle clubs) before becoming a movie exhibitor. Spotting a loophole in the law which allowed censored films to be shown in private members' clubs, Klinger and his partner, Tony Tenser, opened the Compton Cinema Club in Soho, which showed a wide variety of allowed and disallowed movies. At the Compton in the early 1960s, skin flicks alternated with peplum, monster movies, European arthouse films, and curious anomalies that demonstrated the capriciousness of Britain's censor such as *The Wild One,* the 1953 biker movie starring Marlon Brando, which, for no good reason, was banned by nannyish censors in Britain until 1968. In its heyday, the Compton built up an impressive celebrity clientele, including John Trevelyan, the secretary of the British Board of Film Censors, who would attend to watch the films that he himself had banned.

Klinger and Tenser graduated from exhibition to production and set up a production company, Compton Films. They produced a couple of nudie-cutie movies, *As Nature Intended* (1961) and *My Bare Lady* (1962), before moving into other exploitationers. Compton caught the *Mondo* craze by producing pseudoanthropological documentaries about the seamier side of 1960s London, *London in the Raw* (1965) and its sequel, *Primitive London* (1965). It also found a profitable niche in topical social issue exploitation films such as *That Kind of Girl* (1963), a drama about venereal disease, and *The Yellow Teddybears* (1963), a film about the loss of virginity among high school girls. With a couple of horror films besides, Klinger and Tenser gained a reputation as low-budget purveyors of the disreputable, with a company whose audience was, as one censor report had it, "only interested in strong meat."[8]

But Klinger was an exploitation man with an eye on arthouse prestige, and he persuaded Tenser to fund two Roman Polanski films, *Repulsion* (1965) and *Cul-de-sac* (1966). The financial failure of the latter prompted the dissolution of the partnership, and shortly thereafter Klinger began to build his reputation as one of England's most dynamic film producers. His production of *Baby Love* (1968) caught Joe's eye. The Hollywood recession had hit the British film industry hard as Hollywood studios quickly withdrew their investments. But Joe had a fondness for Britain and British films as well as a keen eye for talent, and *Baby Love* showcased a number of emerging British talents. It was the debut feature for both director Alistair Reid and star Linda Hayden, and it was put together by Klinger as he moved from exploitation to mainstream success. At a time when the British film industry was in distress, Klinger secured $1 million from Avco Embassy for the worldwide distribution rights to *Baby Love.* It was a tidy sum, but Klinger told the press that he had turned down even bigger offers, so keen was he to profit from Joe's showmanship.

Given the similarities in their backgrounds and the many career parallels, it would be surprising if Joe and Klinger had not worked together. Both were gifted showmen, raconteurs, and wits. Klinger's son, Tony, has many fond memories of fun and fights between Joe and his father. "Joe, my father, and I all crossed swords in many ways and on many occasions," he says. One of Tony Klinger's recollections involves a defecating horse and a quick wit: "One of my favorite moments was when we were all at the Dorchester lunch to launch Anthony Harvey's *The Lion in Winter,* and he had a horse with a knight come into the main dining room, and as it knelt, the knight offered the wife of Levine a silk tribute. As the horse stood back up it did a mighty number two. There was a shocked silence, and then Joe said, 'That's what they call showmanshit!'"[9]

Baby Love was no exploitation flick, but it had its fair share of exploitable elements. It tells the story of Luci, a troubled teenager raised in poverty in the North of England who, following her mother's suicide, moves into the family home of Richard, one of her mother's old friends, in England's affluent South. It is a tale of middle-class hypocrisy and destructive sexuality. Once in her new home, Luci proceeds to seduce Richard's wife and son, though her attempts to seduce Richard are rebuffed. The film centers on a brilliant performance by Linda Hayden, a fifteen-year-old English actress who had been chosen from among more than three hundred girls to play the part.

Soon after the distribution deal was sealed, problems began. A document from Klinger's papers provides a list of discussion points related to the *Baby Love* contract—details that were of concern to Klinger but about which Joe was intractable: Avco Embassy's right to delay payment instalments; a request for a three-year delay in and an improved share from U.S. and Canadian television sales; and the right of approval in various matters pertaining to exhibition and rentals. Klinger also believed that Joe had reneged on a promise of a pre-Christmas 1968 release date, which was postponed to March 1969. For most of these points, the document states that Avco Embassy was "adamant in refusing these rights to us. . . . Embassy would not relinquish these points even at the risk of killing the deal."[10] Klinger seemed to have struck a good deal with Joe, but he had sought a worldwide distribution deal to free himself to concentrate on other projects. This deal gave Joe the upper hand in all distribution matters, and there was little Klinger could do beyond vent his anger. Tony Klinger remembers his furious father telling Joe to "shove the contract up your ass—and don't forget the staples!"[11]

The U.S. promotional campaign was focused on Hayden. New York's Times Square hosted a huge sixty-by-eighty-foot poster featuring a grotesquely made-up Luci, along with the words "*Baby Love* is coming." As in the United Kingdom, much was made of Hayden's age; one press release from Avco Embassy reads:

YOUTH ON PARADE

> Screen sex kittens get younger and younger. If things keep going the way they are, Hollywood will soon literally be robbing the cradle.
>
> Latest of a long list of young girls to star in a sexy film is Linda Hayden. She is 15-years-old and English. She was selected from among three hundred applicants to play the part of Luci, the Lolita-like love-starved teenager in Joseph E. Levine's presentation of *Baby Love,* an Avco-Embassy film. Apparently there are more 15-year-old sexpots around than one would suspect.
>
> Of course, Linda Hayden looks older. Sixteen, at least.

Ever since Hayden's introduction to the U.K. press, very few press stories about her did not mention the fact that at fifteen she was too young to see her own film. Avco Embassy incorporated this fact into a trailer, which featured Hayden purring seductively to camera, "I'm old enough to make it, but not old enough to see it."

Following *Baby Love*'s London premier, Klinger and Hayden flew to New York to build on Avco Embassy's prepublicity with rounds of interviews and personal appearances. Joe knew how to play the media and had always had an immensely cozy relationship with the press. Interviews with Hayden were arranged with the New York media, as were television appearances. Hayden, Klinger, and Reid stayed in large suites in a plush hotel near Central Park. When the party moved to Los Angeles, however, they stayed in a much smaller hotel on Sunset Strip: "I was doing interviews in my bedroom," recalls Hayden. Klinger found the situation intolerable and moved the party, at his own expense, to a hotel in Beverly Hills.[12] A million-dollar investment notwithstanding, Joe had lost interest.

Both Tony Klinger and Linda Hayden feel that *Baby Love* was badly promoted in America, with publicity materials causing confusion. For Hayden, the image on the billboard in Times Square made *Baby Love* look like a horror film.[13] Klinger had to take up some of the promotional slack left by a muted Joe and intervened to change the emphasis of the advertising in the United Kingdom, which foregrounded Luci's threat to the sanctity of the family home to appeal to female audiences rather than relying on the young star's sexual attractiveness.

Klinger and Joe fell out over *Baby Love,* but they would work together again and remained alternately friends and foes for many years. Klinger would become England's most successful independent producer of the postwar era, producing blockbusters such as *Gold* (1974) and *Shout at the Devil* (1976) as well as a series of low-brow smut-coms in the *Confessions* series (1974–1977), but he will be best remembered for *Get Carter* (1971), a gritty thriller rightly considered to be one of Britain's best.

Baby Love marked the beginnings of Klinger's success as a reputable producer, but it also marked a turning point for Joe. According to Tony Klinger,

> During this entire period Joe was totally distracted, first by his money troubles, and then by the big deal, and then by the demands of the new boys in charge [at Avco]. . . . I think MK [Michael Klinger] would have sued Joe if he wasn't Joe and he actually personally liked him. The feud was serious more because Joe wasn't seemingly focused on his film business . . . and his one terrific gift for showmanship was no longer happening. The business was just not so important or vital to him and on *Baby Love* we knew we had a picture with big commercial potential since it had done so well in the UK.[14]

Capricious as Joe was, *Baby Love* was not the first film that he had lost interest in, but, following the frenetic activity and huge successes of the

1960s, along with the current Hollywood recession, his apparent indifference to a well-received film that Avco Embassy had heavily invested in points to a dampened enthusiasm for showmanship and cinema in a man defined by his energy. One would expect America's most flamboyant showman, now backed by Avco's billions, to become even louder and more boisterous, but Joe did not enjoy his time at Avco Embassy. According to Tony Klinger, "He was far too much the maverick to be happy reporting to the corporate guys."[15] Following his tenure there, Joe would complain about corporate strictures, bemoan his loss of independence, and recount the anxieties he felt when investing shareholders' money as opposed to money he had raised himself. Even during his Avco years, he complained about the bureaucratic procedures he was unused to: "This is no business for big business—it's an art form. You can't have endless meetings. Someone's got to have instinct. I never had a meeting in my life before I got here. Not because I was opinionated . . . but because I had confidence in my judgments."[16]

Joe had a seven-year contract with Avco; he served six years and later said that he had tried to extricate himself from the deal after only six months:

> Part of the deal was a seven year contract. At the end of six months I went to Jim Kerr, the head of the conglomerate, and I said "Jim, we both made a terrible mistake." I said, "I gave you three smash hits when I joined you but I doubt whether you'll ever get a hit from me again." I said, "I can't take the advice your accountants give me because I can't analyze anything. Here you had a company making manure spreaders, aero structures, and whatever the hell they're called, whirlybirds . . . Helicopters." But Kerr wouldn't let me go. He said "I'll release you in a couple of years." But then things got very bad in the motion picture industry and he couldn't let me go because, I guess, there was always this fear that if he *did,* the following year I'd come up with a big smash and he'd look bad to his stockholders and board of directors.[17]

The Avco years were productive cinematically but strangely quiet, although Joe did not disappear from the public's view. He and his wife made regular appearances in the society pages as prominent members of the jet-setting elite. If Joe had lost some of his enthusiasm for movies and was making fewer pronouncements about the state of the industry and what should be done about it, there were plenty of other diversions as the boy who grew up barefoot in Boston set about enjoying the vast wealth he had accumulated.

Like many wealthy men, Joe was a keen collector of art and sundry other items, and this led to his frequent appearance in the popular press, which reported on his attendance at auctions and charity events. He was usually accompanied by Rosalie, who gained a reputation for attending functions dripping with gems and jewels. Joe, meanwhile, was always pictured with his now trademark walking cane, which he would carry for the rest of his life because of an ongoing knee problem. Joe would never be accepted by the cultural elite, nor would his public image allow it, but he certainly enjoyed his membership of the social elite that his wealth gained him entry to. He bought expensive goodies, and his purchases made the press, maintaining his profile. In 1969, he spent more than $20,000 on three vintage cars at an auction in New York[18] and bought the sketch that he himself was auctioning at a charity event in aid of the Police Athletic League and Catholic Youth Fund, which he attended with Rosalie, "dressed in diamonds and sapphires."[19] Rosalie became so notable for her bejeweled appearance at social events that she became a target for professional thieves. During a stay at one of Joe's homes, Sophia Loren was robbed of $650,000 worth of jewelry; an anonymous phone call followed, with the caller telling Rosalie, "You're next," at which point, she claimed in the press, she sold all her gems.[20]

The early 1970s saw the Levines attend a succession of glittering events, theater openings, gallery openings, auctions, charity balls, a piano recital by Joan Kennedy, a Thanksgiving excursion to an exclusive private resort unimaginatively named Xanadu ("I think it's vulgar to gamble in an emerald necklace and a cotton dress," quoth one lady guest[21]), and lunch with David Frost, the British broadcaster who would later find fame for his penetrating television interviews with Richard Nixon, when Frost flew sixty of his close friends to Bermuda for cocktails and carousing.[22] As a showman socialite, Joe was becoming famous for being famous, attracting press attention for doing little more than leaving the house.

Besides cinema and high society, Joe made more investments. In the legitimate theater, he invested $100,000 in the Repertory Theatre at Yale,[23] and his financial support of New York's Circle in the Square Theatre was recognized when it was renamed in his honor as the Circle in the Square–

Joseph E. Levine Theatre (occasioning some murmured objections from regular patrons). Joe also continued to expand his art collection with much publicized purchases, including his acquisition of the Olsen House, the farmhouse in Cushing, Maine, that is depicted in Andrew Wyeth's most famous painting, *Christina's World* (1948). Joe refurbished the house and opened it as a museum for Wyeth's paintings in 1972. But the project was short-lived as locals complained about tourists bespoiling their community with litter and general disturbances. "You know," Joe commented, "I've made 400 movies in my life, but I can't seem to make one little museum."[24] In politics, he made contributions to both the Republican Party and the Democratic Party, corresponded with Spiro Agnew, and was approached by Richard Nixon for suggestions of suitable "leaders" for appointment in his upcoming administration. He lent one of his New York properties for use as campaign headquarters to Jane Pickens Langley, a former popular singer and conservative Republican who was challenging Ed Koch in New York's Eighteenth Congressional District. She lost, and Koch would later become mayor of New York.

Back at Avco Embassy, Peter O'Toole was in litigation after Joe had refused to pay him monies due for his work on *The Lion in Winter*, accusing him of drunkenness and "disgraceful conduct" during filming. O'Toole won the case and was awarded $750,000 and 10 percent of the film's receipts.[25] Following an unpleasant court dispute, Joe picked up the distribution rights to O'Toole's next film *The Ruling Class* (1972). "I think it's delightful that Joe is distributing our film," said O'Toole. "It's hilarious! Marvelous! Everyone should settle their disputes this way."[26] The film, a broad satire on hereditary privilege among Britain's ruling elite, was produced by Jules Buck, Joe's coproducer in the failed *Will Adams* adaptation. It received some good reviews and some bad ones and failed to find an audience. Failure to find an audience was a problem that was general in Hollywood.

13

New Haven, 'Nam, Nichols, and Nazis

Burn down the theater! Hang Joe Levine!

—*Audience in Paramus, N.J.*

The best way to understand Joe's Avco years is not so much as a downturn, but as a plateau. Avco Embassy's production slate during Joe's tenure included two films from Mike Nichols, *Carnal Knowledge* (1971) and *Day of the Dolphin* (1973); a film from de Sica, *Sunflower* (1970), which starred Sophia Loren and Marcello Mastroianni, was produced by Arthur Cohn and Carlo Ponti, and was filmed in the Soviet Union; and a couple of Harold Robbins adaptations, *Stiletto* (1969) and *The Adventurers* (1970). Alongside these continuities was a varied roster ranging from *Mondo*-exploitation (*Sweden: Heaven and Hell,* 1968) to star comedy vehicles such as *Don't Drink the Water* (1969, starring Jackie Gleason) and *The Stoolie* (1972, starring Jackie Mason in his first feature); a biker flick starring Joe Namath and Ann-Margret entitled *CC and Company* (1970); and an entry into the popular blaxploitation cycle, *Book of Numbers* (1973), directed by Raymond St. Jacques. On the distribution front, there were spaghetti Westerns such as *A Bullet for the General* (1966) and *They Call Me Trinity* (1970), plus its sequel, *Trinity Is STILL My Name* (1971); European art-house films such as *The Swimming Pool* (1969), from Jacques Deray, and *Woman in Chains* (1968), Henri-Georges Clouzot's final film. There were also a few horrors, and some more oddities from Britain—including *Monique* (1970), a sort of bawdier *Baby Love* produced by Michael Klinger's erstwhile partner, Tony Tenser. Avco Embassy also distributed and promoted Klinger's production *Something to Hide* (1972) in the United Kingdom—again not to Klinger's satisfaction.[1]

Despite the warning to the industry about putting too much faith in "antiestablishment" films, it is interesting that two of Joe's notable films from this period can be described as such. *Bright College Years* (1970) is a documentary about the May Day Strike at Yale University in 1970, and *Soldier Blue* (1970) is a violent Western about the massacre of a Cheyenne tribe by the U.S. Cavalry in 1864. The former is little known, the latter notorious, and the political context adds to their power because both films were made during the period of widespread anti–Vietnam War protests, unrest on college campuses, and America's invasion of Cambodia.

In 1968, Joe began the Joseph E. Levine Fellowship Program at Yale University, and fellowships were awarded to talented young playwrights and filmmakers for entry into the university's "Writing for the Camera" course. One fellowship recipient was Peter Rosen, a young documentary maker who became close friends with Joe. Once Rosen finished his course at Yale, he showed Joe his graduation film, *I'm a Man*. "Then I told him about the events that were about to unfold on the Yale campus leading up to Mayday," says Rosen, "and he agreed it would be a good documentary. He gave me about $100,000 to make it, and I hired student crews."[2] The "events that were about to unfold" were student strikes to protest the arrest of Bobby Seale, the chairman of the Black Panthers, who was accused of ordering the murder of an alleged FBI informant within the Panthers, Alex Rackley. Seale, already serving a four-year sentence for contempt of court, was ultimately acquitted.

Rosen's film, entitled *Bright College Years* in ironic reference to the title of Yale's sentimentally duteous school song, details the embryonic phase of what would become more widespread student strikes and campus protests in 1970. According to Bart Whiteman, a senior at Yale in 1970, "New Haven prepared for this event like it was an approaching hurricane. Almost all shops downtown were closed and boarded up. The National Guard was mobilized and placed in position in large numbers throughout the area. Military jeeps and troop carriers rolled through downtown in an open display of force. There were rumors of tanks being parked and ready at the perimeter of the city. I never saw any."[3]

The situation was tense. Calls for strikes and protests were accompanied by calls for violent action from less-temperate voices, and a large cohort of protesters was expected from out of town. Also, Yale's faculty appeared to be complicit. Yale suspended "academic expectations" for the semester and confirmed that students involved in the strikes would not be punished. This stance outraged the conservative minds within and without Yale, and more outrage followed when it was revealed that Kingman Brewster, Yale's president, had said in a faculty meeting, "I am appalled and ashamed that things should have come to such a pass in this country that I am skeptical of the ability of black revolutionaries to achieve a fair trial anywhere in the United States."[4] In response, many people, including U.S. vice president Spiro Agnew, called for Brewster's resignation.

The simmering tensions in New Haven are clearly depicted in Rosen's movie, alongside passion, idealism, and naïveté from some of the most privileged students in the land: "Upper-middle class white students are going to support the Panthers," says one striker; "they are not alone." But Seale's arrest appears as a catalyst for other concerns—chiefly the ongoing war in Vietnam. On 30 April, the day before the strike began, President Nixon had announced the invasion of Cambodia, causing consternation among those participating in America's antiwar movement. *Bright College Years* memorably shows one student's boundless optimism at the efficacy of campus strike action as he issues a demand that "the US government end repression of dissidents and withdraw from South East Asia." The day after the strike and the filming of *Bright College Years* finished, four unarmed antiwar protesters were shot and killed by the National Guard at Kent State University in Ohio.

Bright College Years should be better known than it is. The expansion of the Vietnam War into Cambodia, the exposure of the My Lai massacre cover-up, the Kent State shootings, which prompted both countrywide campus protests and pushback from the pro-government "silent majority," all combine to make the film a fascinating glimpse into a moment in American history. Joe toured college campuses with the film and Rosen, and the movie won a Gold Hugo Award.

Rosen speaks very warmly of Joe, and he was thrilled to have Joe's backing at that time in particular because "it is not the kind of film you would associate him with." Joe had had some experience with documentaries such as *Discovery; The Sky Above, the Mud Below;* and *John F. Kennedy: Years of Lightning, Day of Drums,* but one can see Rosen's point. "I don't think he cared especially for documentaries, just films that had a good story," says Rosen. He describes Joe as broadly "apolitical" but suspects he may have had left-of-center sympathies.[5] But they never discussed the major issues of the day, such as the student strikes, the civil rights movement, and Vietnam.

Joe was not around to see the actual events of the Yale strike unfold because he was in London attending the Showmanship 70 International Convention to promote his wares. He and Avco had a number of new films to sell, and the most prominent on the Avco stand was *Soldier Blue,* another film inextricably bound up in the ongoing war in Vietnam. A Western, *Soldier Blue* tells the story of a brutal retaliatory attack by the U.S. Cavalry on a Cheyenne village. The climactic massacre is based on the Sand Creek massacre in 1864 and is widely seen as an allegory for American intervention in Southeast Asia. Author P. B. Hurst wisely observes, "Of course, there are certain passages that can be heard as a condemnation of the then American presence in Southeast Asia. . . . But the truth is something can be read into anything. If *Soldier Blue* had been released in 2003, it would have been possible to see it as a parallel for the invasion of Iraq."[6] Hurst, who has extensively researched just about every aspect of *Soldier Blue,* finds the evidence for it being an intentional Vietnam allegory sketchy at best. Nonetheless, allegory rooted in viewer interpretation is no less valid than allegory rooted in author intentionality, and many reviewers of the time found condemnations of America's current actions in *Soldier Blue*'s condemnations of America's past crimes.

Soldier Blue was directed by Ralph Nelson, who had a varied résumé as a director, including Westerns, thrillers, and comedies, alongside more socially progressive films such as *Lilies of the Fields* (1963) and the rather harder-hitting *. . . tick . . . tick . . . tick* (1970). It stars Peter Strauss, Candice Bergen, and Donald Pleasance and was promoted, with some justification, as the "Most Savage Film." But there was some concern from Nelson himself that *Soldier Blue* was *too* savage.

After a screening of a workprint for Joe, Nelson decided that the violence of the final sequence was too much and announced that he wished to make some cuts. The on-screen savagery, it should be noted, not only was very bloody but also included rapes, mutilations, and infanticide. Joe told Nelson that he was being "chicken."[7] Alterations were made nonetheless, in part to bring down the film's running time before a handful of press screenings and sneak previews took place in Britain and America. One of these sneak previews, in Paramus, New Jersey, reportedly turned into a "near riot," with the appalled audience chanting, "Burn down the theater! Hang Joe Levine!"[8] Joe was fortunately not in attendance.

The violence in *Soldier Blue* is shocking, necessarily so because of the film's furious condemnation of the atrocities committed against Native

Americans and because of the film's stark revisionism. Cavalrymen had been heroes on the screen since the dawn of American cinema, and *Soldier Blue* is uncompromising in its repudiation of the deeply entrenched cowboys-and-Indians myth. But the cinematic violence was also to be a key selling point for the film. Joe and other Avco executives, noting the success of films like *The Wild Bunch* (1969), wanted to capitalize on the mainstream American audience's increasing appetite for violent spectacle. *Soldier Blue* was not a box-office success in the United States, but it was a huge success in Britain, becoming the third-biggest grosser of 1971, behind *The Aristocats* and the TV spinoff *On the Buses.*

Behind the scenes, Joe was deeply involved in the making of *Soldier Blue* and its promotion within the industry. But the public promotional campaign for the film lacked his personal touch. Given its controversial subject matter, exploitable elements, and the opprobrium heaped upon it by many critics, *Soldier Blue* was ideal fodder for Joe's oppositional, barnstorming showmanship. But he was curiously absent. Much of the promotion came from Nelson as he traveled the world selling the movie. In an article in *Variety,* Nelson paid warm tribute to Joe and positioned him as showman-mentor: "Joe Levine is a showman. He is also a salesman. His *Hercules* campaign is a legend. . . . [H]e also makes salesmen out of the people who make pictures for him."[9] Joe sent Nelson off on a world tour to promote *Soldier Blue,* and it seemed that as Joe approached his seventies and increasingly indulged his appetites in the arts and on the social scene, his drum banging for the movies was to become ever more muted as he taught his protégés the secrets of ballyhoo and then took a back seat.

If there was one key relationship for Joe during the Avco years, it was with Mike Nichols, though it was not to be quite as fruitful as the success of *The Graduate* had indicated. Nichols's second film for Joe was *Carnal Knowledge.* Film scholar J. W. Whitehead accusingly and wrongly asserts that "the prurience of subject and the prospect of Candice Bergen and Ann-Margret in bedroom scenes were reason enough for crusty Levine's eye-winking patronage,"[10] but the collaboration with Nichols had been set in motion long before the subject matter was chosen or any actors cast.

Following *The Graduate,* Nichols had directed *Catch-22* (1970) for Paramount, and during production Avco Embassy acquired Nichols's production company Friwaftt (an acronym for "fools rush in where angels fear to tread") and signed Nichols to direct two films. The first was *Carnal*

Knowledge, written by Jules Feiffer, which started life as a play but which Nichols thought would work better as a film. "Nichols will be the boss," announced Joe, "the director *and* the producer—for the first time. And he richly deserves it. We don't even care who's in the film. We don't need stars in a Nichols film."[11] Joe occasionally bragged that *Carnal Knowledge* was the only time he had granted total artistic control to a director, a questionable claim, but Joe still retained a producer credit.

Starring Jack Nicholson, Art Garfunkel, Candice Bergen, and Ann-Margret, *Carnal Knowledge* tells of the romantic and sexual exploits of two college friends over a twenty-five-year period. One of the friends, Sandy (played by Garfunkel), is gullible, and the other, Jonathan (played by Nicholson), is cynical. The film is marked by brilliant acting, mannered direction, and a dull script. By way of promotion, Joe released a short elliptical synopsis: "*Carnal Knowledge* takes two young men from their college days in the mid-40s and follows them into the 1970s, exploring through the years the way they dream about, talk about, think about, behave with, and love or hate women." He then forbade any more leaks about the content of the movie in order to create a buzz around the mysterious forthcoming project from Nichols. After the film was released, Gary Arnold of the *Washington Post* felt finagled: "That Joseph E. Levine certainly is a caution. For the past several months he's been stringing the film press along on his latest production, *Carnal Knowledge,* implying that the content was so original and candid that it had to be classified information."[12]

Arnold was scathing about *Carnal Knowledge* and the critics who admired it—whom he accused of falling for "Levine's little joke."[13] But many others, including Vincent Canby and Bosley Crowther, admired the film, especially the acting. It caused some controversy, too, with some exhibitors objecting to the frankness of the title, some feminists objecting to misogyny, and some critics objecting to pretentiousness. *Carnal Knowledge* is an unabashed American arthouse film and succeeded where it was supposed to—big metropolitan cities and campus towns. It certainly did not receive the box-office takings and plaudits of *The Graduate,* but it gave Nichols a useful critical and commercial lift following the critical and commercial failure of *Catch-22.* Having impressed serious movie critics and intellectual audiences with a forensic character study of the sexual mores of the American male, and with their partnership bearing fruit, Joe and Nichols somehow decided that their next film would be about talking dolphins that attempt to assassinate the president of the United States.

The Day of the Dolphin is an enjoyably ridiculous film that brought an end to Nichols's filmmaking partnership with Joe. Loosely based on a novel by Robert Merle, it tells of a marine biologist, played by George C. Scott, who is training dolphins to communicate with humans in spoken English. His trainees arouse the interest of a shady organization and are subsequently dolphin-napped and used in an assassination attempt on the president, but of course the marine biologist foils the plan. It failed at the box office and was lampooned mercilessly by critics. According to Joe,

> We had two scripts we were considering. One picture was about a rabbi, and the other was *The Day of the Dolphin.* We took a long time before we decided whether we should make, with no disrespect, the Jew picture or the fish picture. Unfortunately, we chose the fish picture. I thought it was great when we were making it, and even when I saw it finished, but it just didn't work. Even when you have a picture like that, you're able to get advances and sell the television rights, so we came out on the whole. All we left behind was Mike's dignity.[14]

The Day of the Dolphin was originally to be made at United Artists and directed by Roman Polanski, but the film fell into trouble during the scripting stage. Joe then stepped in and bought the rights from UA for Nichols because, according to the *New York Times,* he "knew of Nichols' devotion" to the project.[15] Many years later, however, Nichols said that *The Day of the Dolphin* "really came about because I needed to find something to get out of my contract with Joe Levine."[16] Joe was also dismissive of the film and said of the director in a rare, if oblique, public criticism of Nichols, "People went to see the film expecting to see Nichols's grim 'schticula,' but instead saw an adventure film. Mike Nichols' name on the film hurt it."[17] Joe also blamed the star, George C. Scott, for many of the problems of the production, calling him a "jerk" in *Variety*[18] and later launching "into a tirade against Scott's character and personal habits which scorched the tablecloth at the Beverly Hills Hotel" during an interview with a provincial reporter.[19] Joe was furious at Scott for, among other things, disappearing on a three-day drunken bender while the cast and crew waited for him. He blamed Scott for the cost overruns on *The Day of the Dolphin* and for his failure to properly promote the movie—despite his $750,000 paycheck. In response, Scott called Joe "an old cunt."[20]

The Day of the Dolphin was the last major film Joe produced at Avco Embassy. Six months after its Christmas 1973 release, a year before his contract was due to expire, he stepped down as president of Avco Embassy. After nearly forty years, at the age of sixty-eight, Joe retired from the film business in May 1974.

Shortly after his retirement, Joe came out of retirement. He set up a new independent company, Joseph E. Levine Presents, and started selling films again under that banner. Relishing his newfound freedom from corporate strictures, Joe said, "I didn't like being an executive. . . . I like to make pictures, I like to wheel and deal."[21] He returned to wheeling and dealing with some gusto once he had left the corporate world behind, reconnecting with his peculiar talent for film promotion. He bought three movies from Europe: "I bought 'em all in about six days," he said, "and felt better than I had in years."[22] Joe was free to promote as an independent—Avco, meanwhile, took care of the distribution for Joe.

The three movies Joe brought back from Europe look like his career in microcosm. *This Time I'll Make You Rich* (1961) was written and directed by Gianfranco Parolini, a graduate of the peplum craze that Joe did so much to popularize. Joe described it as "an exploitationer, which won't win an Academy Award."[23] *And Now My Love* (1974) was a respectable art-house film by a reputable French director, Claude Lelouche, and received enthusiastic reviews in both the *New York Times* and the *Los Angeles Times* upon its release.[24] But it was the campy and kooky *The Night Porter* (1974), directed by Liliana Cavani, that would put Joe back in his element as he took to the press to promote the film with an enthusiasm not seen since before his partnership with Avco.

Using this controversial tale of a kinky relationship that develops between a concentration camp survivor (Charlotte Rampling) and a former Nazi camp guard (Dirk Bogarde) in postwar Vienna, Joe repositioned himself as the master flim-flam man of the movies. Complaining of "a sore lack of showmanship in the current film industry," he promised that the film he dubbed "*Last Tango in Vienna*" would be opened with "the greatest campaign seen in recent years."[25] When the film opened to good box office and bad reviews, Joe commented, "The bad reviews all seem to mention the same words—sado-masochistic—I never knew what they meant before. Now I know. It's money!"[26]

Despite the bad reviews, *The Night Porter* is an interesting film and remains much beloved by cultists; its iconography was incorporated into many subsequent films of the Italian Nazisploitation cycle and Madonna's *Justify My Love* video (1990). Joe promoted the movie with more energy than he had put into any of his Avco Embassy output, and the bad reviews allowed him to return to his hobby of critic baiting. "It's a people's picture," said Joe of *The Night Porter*, "just like *Hercules* was, and critics should remember that."[27] The critics, in Joe's estimation, had savaged *The Night Porter* unfairly. "Nora Sayre reviewed it in *The New York Times* and she really tore it apart," he complained. "Then, just in case it was still alive and twitching there on the floor, Vincent Canby did a Sunday piece and shot it through the head."[28] But Joe schemed to turn the bad reviews to his advantage and advertised his film with quotations cannibalized from Vincent Canby's damning review, as Canby explains:

> The quote in question took the headline of my piece ("*The Night Porter* is romantic pornography") added a bit of a sentence from the first paragraph (" . . . a hectic love affair") and then a long sentence from the seventh paragraph ("Among the film's various definitions of decadence is a strong preference to do on a floor what most people would do on a chair, table or bed"), winding up with a phrase from the ninth paragraph ("what a kinky turn-on!"). . . . What Levine knew—and the critics did not—was that *The Night Porter* was the kind of silly movie that could excite the public's imagination by being accurately described. . . . Junk presented as junk still sells.[29]

Evidently pleased with himself for using a bad review to promote his film, Joe boasted to Charles Champlin about the repurposed quotations: "we didn't even have to lift them out of context."[30] Canby took the chicanery in good humor and applauded his tormentor: "My admiration for Joe Levine as a picker of movies may not be great, but I do admire the boldness of his full frontal assault on the critics. Like a character in a Tom and Jerry cartoon he has neatly folded back the barrels of the critics' guns so that the buckshot hits them in *their* faces, not his."[31]

Canby's good humor is revealing. Despite Joe's repeated broadsides against critics, intellectuals, and eggheads, by this time much of the press was fond of him, as if his carefully constructed public image had left him tamed. For all his boisterous bluster, he was a known quantity. He had been quiet and probably missed during the Avco years. Now American cinema's most rambunctious big mouth was back and rejuvenated, selling hard and hurling insults. Once again he was taking the industry to task for its lack of showmanship, and once again he was about to change direction: this time to embark on the biggest project of his career—*A Bridge Too Far.*

14

Joe's Baby

> It would be rather nice to shove some of the screwers' noses in the shit by grossing a couple of hundred million.
>
> —*Sean Connery*

In some ways, by the mid-1970s Hollywood had caught up with Joe. He had pioneered the summer blockbuster, saturation openings, and blunderbuss multimedia marketing with *Hercules,* and Hollywood was now using the same techniques, most notably with *Jaws* (1975). Steven Spielberg's film about a killer shark is often wrongly cited to be the first ever summer blockbuster, but the techniques used to sell it show Joe's influence. Like *Godzilla, Hercules,* and many of the saturation openers of the 1950s, *Jaws* is a creature feature, and, like those films, the star is the creature. It was the shark that formed the basis of the promotion, not the acting talents of Roy Scheider, Robert Shaw, and Richard Dreyfuss. It was released in a saturation pattern with around four hundred prints (far short of the 635 prints of *Hercules*) and was ballyhooed with stunts, promotions, tie-ins, and television advertising.

But *Jaws* is a different kind of film from its predecessors. It is a taut, compelling, and frightening film directed by a genius with the backing of a major studio—Universal. This respectability also, oddly, speaks to Joe's legacy, though. Saturation openings and blunderbuss publicity seem natural today, when films can be opened all over the world at the same time, but these techniques were not so natural in 1975. They were seen as vulgar overtures that compromised the prestige of the product. The hard sell and the engagement with lower media (television, children's comics) were the stuff of exploitation. It was Joe, more than anyone else, who made saturation openings disreputable for two decades.

When David O. Selznick released *Duel in the Sun* in a saturation pattern in 1947, he was widely believed to be sneakily using the technique to circumvent bad reviews for what many felt he knew to be a lackluster film. In 1962, when Fox suggested offsetting its losses on *Cleopatra* by releasing Darryl Zanuck's *The Longest Day* in a saturation pattern, Zanuck, Fox's former head, was so appalled that his film should be treated in such a manner that he flew back from Europe and retook control of the studio. Saturation openings and blunderbuss publicity were synonymous with chicanery and low-brow entertainment, and Joe did more than anyone else to cement the synonyms. By the mid-1970s, however, Hollywood had come through a recession and was beginning to find general audiences again—and blockbusters such as *The Godfather* (1972) and *Jaws* were key. Hollywood discovered what Joe always knew: with the right product, it is good to sell—and sell hard.

Jaws was produced by David Brown and Richard Zanuck, Darryl Zanuck's son, and just as Zanuck Junior was preparing to follow in Joe's footsteps, Joe was preparing to follow in Zanuck Senior's footsteps and produce a star-packed war epic that, like *The Longest Day*, is based on a best-selling book by historian Cornelius Ryan. *A Bridge Too Far*, published in 1974, is the story of Operation Market Garden, a failed attempt by the Allies to affect a final big push to end the Second World War in 1944 by capturing a series of bridges in Holland and moving through to Berlin. The plan initially met with some success, when bridges in Eindhoven and Nijmegen were successfully secured; the operation's full objectives, however, were not realized. Because of strong resistance from the Germans and the plan's overambition, relief forces were unable to make it to Arnhem, where the British First Airborne Division, led by Lieutenant Colonel John Frost (played by Anthony Hopkins in the film), were attempting to hold the Arnhem road bridge. Overwhelming resistance meant that the bridge could not be taken, thus proving it to be the "bridge too far" of the title.

Joe was friends with Ryan and promised the dying writer that he would ensure that his book would be realized on-screen, just as the writer had promised himself that he would not die before he had finished his book. "He was a tough Irish son of a bitch," said Joe of his friend. "He willed himself to finish that book. He knew he was dying of cancer, but he was determined to finish the writing. . . . I remember visiting him at the hospital. . . . I can see him now shaking his fist in the air, raging at God, I suppose, and vowing that he wasn't about to die until he'd finished his work. And he didn't."[1] Joe enlisted Richard Attenborough as director with the promise that Attenborough's long-cherished biopic of Gandhi would be the next film they made.[2] Joe did not keep that promise.

Prior to *A Bridge Too Far,* Joe's typical modus operandi was to work on a variety of projects in a variety of roles, sometimes for a variety of companies, simultaneously. When *A Bridge Too Far* was announced in 1975, it was one of a number of projects he was working on. The Hollywood rumor mill predicted an announcement from Joe that Frank McCarthy would be the producer,[3] but the announcement never came, and Joe, along with his son, Richard, assumed the producer's mantle. Joe had close-hand personal experience of how the fickleness of producers could see a project placed on indefinite hiatus. He had been through the debacle of *Will Adams* with Jules Buck and Eugene Frenke, and it was, in part, his own delaying tactics and lack of commitment that had kept Richard Attenborough's long-nurtured project, *Gandhi,* off the screen. When Joe came to make his own labor of love, however, he ensured that from an early stage he was in an unassailable leadership role.

In 1966, Joe had suggested to Calvin Tomkins that he might "drop everything one of these days and make the big one."[4] Upon leaving Paramount, he complained about the lack of control he had had at the studio.[5] In theory, his association with a major studio should have allowed him greater scope to pursue more ambitious and more expensive projects; such, however, was not the case. Similarly, when Joe sold Embassy to the Avco Corporation in 1968, becoming the president of Avco Embassy, he looked to be able to take advantage of the corporation's assets in order to invest in bigger productions. Once again, the ambitious ventures failed to materialize. It seems fitting, then, that when Joe came to make "the big one," he would do so without any backing or interference from a studio or other major financial source.

A Bridge Too Far would have been a mammoth undertaking for anyone, but as Joe entered his seventies, his experience as a producer was in some ways quite limited. He was one of American cinema's great packagers. He knew how to cast a film, both with acting and production talent; he knew which exploitable elements would appeal to which audience; he had a dramatic flair for story contributions; and he was more than willing to perform explosive interventions if necessary. But he generally left the day-to-day minutiae of production arrangements to others. Attention to detail is perhaps the minimum requirement for a film producer, and Joe was not very interested in details. His approach allowed others to attend to detail, while he gave himself the freedom and distance to oversee multiple projects and intervene only when necessary. This way of working changed on *A Bridge Too Far,* when he and his son, Richard, assumed all the functions and responsibilities of a focused, one-project, workaday producer.

Joe was not about to make things easy for himself, either. William Goldman, who scripted *A Bridge Too Far,* recalls the sense of urgency from the very beginning: "The first time I met [Joe] he was totally convinced of one thing: *A Bridge Too Far* was going to open on June 15th 1977."[6] Goldman is at a loss to explain why Joe was so fixated on this particular date. The film had not yet been cast, the script had not yet been written, and funding had not yet been secured, but he had decided upon a release date. The date may have something to do with Joe's deathbed promise to Ryan, but it is neither Ryan's anniversary (23 November) nor his birthday (5 June). Nor does the date correspond with any date for Operation Market Garden. *A Bridge Too Far,* however, is a largely British film about a largely British operation, and Joe could have had his showman's eye on a royal celebration.

Queen Elizabeth II's Silver Jubilee, marking her twenty-five years as monarch, would be celebrated in 1977. She had ascended the throne on 6 February 1952 upon the death of her father, King George VI. The anniversary of her coronation, however, would be quite close to the release date Joe had chosen, 2 June 1953, so it is probable that he wished to release his film in the summer of 1977 to capitalize on the Jubilee celebrations. But that still does not quite explain his specificity. Nonetheless, the film had its world premiere in Washington, D.C., on Joe's date, 15 June 1977. There was royalty in attendance in the form of Princess Anne, and later in the year the queen herself attended the London premier. Unfortunately, Joe was unable to fully capitalize on a royal coup from the previous year when he had met the queen at a function with Richard Attenborough. The queen had asked Joe about the handle of his walking cane—which was a molded replica of the bridge at Arnhem. "At this point," recalled Attenborough, "the photographer who had been trailing the Queen was nowhere to be seen. 'Where's that goddam lousy photographer?' said Joe between clenched teeth. 'Of all the goddam stinking lousy pictures he's ever taken, there was a great one. Me, the bridge, and the Queen of England in the same picture. . . . I'll kill the bastard!'"[7]

With a release date decided upon, Joe hired William Goldman to write the script and Richard Attenborough to direct. Goldman was a successful screenwriter who had already won an Oscar for *Butch Cassidy and the Sundance Kid* (1969) and would win a second for *All the President's Men* (1976) during the production of *A Bridge Too Far.* Attenborough, by contrast, was a much admired actor but had directed only two films, neither of which had been commercially successful nor approached anywhere near the scale of *A Bridge Too Far.* But Joe and Attenborough had been planning *Gandhi* for more than ten years by this time; they knew each other well, and Joe counted Attenborough's directorial debut, *Oh! What a Lovely War* (1969), among his favorites. Nonetheless, choosing Attenborough to direct the film appeared an odd decision, and Goldman recalls one Hollywood executive who described Attenborough's hiring as an act of "total committable lunacy." Goldman goes on to say, "Since he [Levine] has always done things his own way, his own money, his own publicity sense—he is very resented in the movie business, something I didn't realise until I started work on *Bridge,* and people came out of the woodwork to wonder why I was working on 'that piece of shit'—Hollywoodese for 'property.' Everyone told me that the entire exercise was going to be futile, because Levine was retired, old, past it, washed up, done."[8]

Joe reveled in being the great outsider of American cinema, but some of what Goldman says can be seen as fair comment. Joe had not had a really big hit since *The Graduate;* the Avco years had been very quiet for him on the film front as society soirees and charity balls seemed to take precedence; and never before had he embarked on a project of such magnitude. "We have concluded that we do not wish to invest in such a motion picture"[9] was the response of his former company, Avco, when Joe approached it for funding, nor could he find funding from anywhere else. The solution, then, was to saturate the movie with star names to generate interest among distributors. Joe planned to fund the movie entirely from preselling distribution rights. These tactics, of course, would push the budget up, and Joe would have to pay these costs out of his own pocket.

The gross-point deal meant that Hollywood's biggest star names would be guaranteed a percentage of box-office takings in addition to their fee. Joe could not offer this deal because with so many stars in the film—fourteen in all—giving each of them a percentage would wipe out all the profits. So Joe had to offer huge sums as salary, and he had to pay these sums using his own money because many agents had doubts about the viability of the project and demanded advance payment. "I'd never screamed louder in my life!" he told Goldman. "I'd never given in to a guarantee demand before, I swore I never would—but I didn't have much room to manoeuvre; if I did I didn't see it."[10]

By the end of 1975, British star power had been secured. Attenborough wrote to Joe, "As far as the British are concerned, it appears that we may count on commitments from Sean Connery, Michael Caine, Dirk Bogarde, Anthony Hopkins and Lawrence Olivier."[11] American involvement was then needed, and in order to facilitate it Joe and Attenborough journeyed to Hollywood to conduct what William Goldman dubbed "The Raid"[12]—procuring star power with large sums of money. James Caan, Elliott Gould, Ryan O'Neil, and Gene Hackman were courted before signing on to make the movie. The other stars enlisted later were Liv Ullman, Maximilian Schell, Hardy Krüger, and Edward Fox.

Of the major Hollywood stars of the time, Joe focused his attention on Robert Redford and Steve McQueen for the part of Major Julian Cook, and after negotiations with both, during which McQueen's demands rose to exceed $3 million, a deal with Redford was struck in January 1976 that would see him paid $2 million for four weeks' work.[13] Not only was this fee an astonishing (though not unheard of) amount for the time, but also an astonishing amount to pay an actor who was not in a starring role. In terms of screen time, the star of the film is Connery in his role as Major General Robert Urquhart.

With the script written, star power secured, and preproduction work completed, Joe's troupe decamped to the Netherlands in March 1975. Once shooting began, Rosalie Levine paid a visit to the set and recorded the event in her diary: "Set is staggering. When I saw the first actor in German uniform I felt like I was stabbed in the stomach. Before shooting started directors chairs were set out—one Joseph E. Levine, next Richard P. Levine and big thrill—Mrs Joseph E. Levine."[14] Once they were in the Netherlands, more fiscal inflations occurred because, with the film's enormous budget now common knowledge, shops and suppliers in the various locations in the Netherlands pushed up their prices accordingly.

Once shooting commenced, the film's big budget provoked criticism from the press. The *Economist,* for example, warned that "Hollywood may be taking the inflationary road to ruin once again," as it had done in the 1960s, and concluded, "Few very expensive films make money."[15] But the atmosphere on set was buoyant. Joe had sold some distribution rights before shooting began, but he held back key territories in a characteristic gamble. By holding back distribution rights, he was able to ignite a bidding war among companies keen to distribute the star-filled, widely publicized spectacle.

Joe embarked on the unconventional tactic of selling on set. He had editing suites and screening rooms set up in the Netherlands so that distributors interested in the rights could view portions of the uncompleted film. On paper, *A Bridge Too Far*'s commercial potential is not immediately apparent. Operation Market Garden was neither a resounding victory nor a catastrophic defeat. It was a failure. But exhibiting spectacular star-studded sequences on set, and presenting the project in a more realized form provided prospective investors with a fuller idea of its potential. On seeing the early footage, Arthur Krim of United Artists told Attenborough that the film "looks like one of the biggest winners of all time."[16] The following month, UA paid $17 million for the North American distribution rights.[17] Joe's success in selling the unfinished film had a direct, positive impact as the universally enthusiastic response from distributors helped to maintain high morale among the cast and crew.[18]

Joe was on set throughout the 133-day shoot, save for a six-week period when he had to return to the United States to recover from complications with his ongoing knee problem. Communications with Attenborough at the time reveal not only Joe's confidence in the comparative novice director but also his frustration at being laid up: "Thank God for you. I feel safe with our film safe in your hands. Notwithstanding I would give one of my legs to be with you."[19] Despite his obvious faith in Attenborough, Joe was determined to get back to the Netherlands, and Rosalie's diary reveals plans for the provision of doctors, nurses, oxygen, an emergency ambulance at the airport, and a stretcher for her husband on the plane, along with evidence of Joe's tenacity and irrepressible nature: "Both doctors advise against transporting him. [The Dutch airline] KLM doctor refuses to be part of worsening condition."[20] Leg injury or not, Joe returned to the set.

Although Joe and Attenborough's friendship ended acrimoniously, Attenborough maintained his admiration for Joe as a producer and wrote about Joe's generosity toward him and of how Joe kept a "meticulous eye on production affairs" but never interfered with the artistic decisions made by his director.[21] During filming, Joe was fulsome in his praise for Attenborough: "All the credit belongs to you," he wrote on seeing the early rushes. "This of course does not preclude me from screaming at you, but I will scream a little softer."[22] Attenborough's characteristically flowery response was similarly gushing: "Have just read your telex and am completely bowled over by your wonderful but monstrously over generous reaction to the sequences you saw."[23] Goldman, too, was enthused as the film began to take shape, writing to Attenborough, "It is better than I ever dreamed it would be."[24]

Once *A Bridge Too Far* was complete, more praise for Attenborough flowed from Joe, praise that emphasizes not only a deep sense of partnership occasioned by working so closely together on such an ambitious project but also Joe's complete devotion to and belief in the film. More than any other film, *A Bridge Too Far* was his labor of love. "You have created an atmosphere of absolute harmony and optimum productivity among fourteen highly individual stars, hundreds of crew members and extras in the thousands," Joe told Attenborough. "All the hopes and dreams I have held for the past 30 months have been realized, not just for spectacle, not just for entertainment, but for a film that expresses and inspires humanity. . . . For this I will be forever proud forever grateful and forever your friend."[25]

In private correspondence and on set reports, the sense of camaraderie among the huge team that collaborated on *A Bridge Too Far* is palpable and stands in contrast to the many press reports that sniped about the project's budget, overambition, and inevitable failure. But the press reports served only to stiffen the cast and crew's resolve. Once shooting was over, Sean Connery wrote to Joe: "It would be rather nice to shove some of the screwers' noses in the shit by grossing a couple of hundred million."[26] Despite the reckless rush into production, shooting on *A Bridge Too Far* was completed just one day over schedule and, according to a press release from distributor United Artists, under budget.

As befitting the film's scale, Joe took to the press with a blunderbuss publicity drive. The lack of any major source of outside funding was a point of pride for him throughout the campaign, allowing him to play up his role as hustler supreme, working outside the system: "In Hollywood they've been saying that I ought to be carted off in a strait jacket," he told Victor Davis upon the film's completion. "But I want them to know that I already have every dollar back."[27] There was little about the film that could not be publicized, and Joe set about publicizing it all. The press book is filled with brags about how much meat (240 pounds) and potatoes (260 pounds) were prepared on an average day during the shoot and contains information regarding tea consumption on this most British of productions (3,880 pounds during preproduction and shooting.)

"You're never going to see 900 men jump out of the sky ever again," Joe told Earl Wilson, simultaneously emphasizing the film's antiwar message and the vastness of the production. "You're never going to see 800 tanks ever again, unless you go to war, and you ain't if you see this picture."[28] More antiwar sentiment appeared in Joe's idiosyncratic prediction of the movie's audience: "Teenagers will love *A Bridge Too Far*. . . . Teenagers hate Vietnam and the people who started the war there," he told Guy Flatley, adding, "They'll love it in Japan too," but for less-pacifist reasons: "the Japanese love to see white men kill each other."[29] Still another reporter was treated to a rather more aggressive quip: "We thought of declaring war on Russia . . . we had the men and equipment to do it."[30]

Lavish spending, the engineering of a bidding war between distributors, an abundance of stars, and a blunderbuss publicity drive led by America's most notorious showman combined to characterize *A Bridge Too Far* prior to its release. Given that the film dealt with war and human tragedy, depicting events that were within living memory, such excess may well have served to damage the film's reputation even before it had been seen, with the carnivalesque flim-flam appearing unseemly when laid alongside the film's weighty subject matter.

That the media drive was, arguably, inappropriately ostentatious for the subject matter, and that the press voiced fears of historical inaccuracy meant that *A Bridge Too Far* inevitably attracted criticism. Viscount Montgomery, son of Operation Market Garden's architect, Field Marshal Montgomery, complained that his father was not even portrayed in the film.[31] This absence gave rise to further criticism from novelist Daphne du Maurier—the widow of Lieutenant General Sir Frederick "Boy" Browning, who was portrayed by Dirk Bogarde. It was Browning's famous line that gave the book and film its title: He warned Montgomery that his plan may involve going a "bridge too far."[32] But with no Monty to give his warning to, Bogarde delivers the line to General Urquhart *after* the failed operation, icily enunciating, "You know I always thought we tried to go a bridge too far." This led to du Maurier's accusation that the filmmakers were looking for a "fall guy," complaints from Urquhart, and some criticism from Bogarde himself—who had served alongside both Montgomery and Browning during the war.[33]

Another key scene in the film that attracted considerable criticism was the capture of the Nijmegen Bridge by Major Julian Cook (Robert Redford) when in fact the bridge had been captured by the British Grenadier Guards without Cook's involvement. Colonel John Waddy, one of the film's technical advisers, protested on set at the historical inaccuracy of the scene, but Richard Levine told him, "The facts, John, would be more difficult and more expensive. . . . Doing it this way means an awful lot at the box office."[34] In a lengthy article about the making of the film, Waddy is full of praise for Attenborough, but his attitude to Joe is considerably cooler.[35]

Many in the British press used the fact that Joe was American as evidence of a cavalier attitude to historical fact. Viscount Montgomery's suggestion that the film he had not yet seen "seems clearly another film of how the Americans won the war"[36] is emblematic of British wariness of Hollywood's version of military history, and many British critics accused the film of aiming toward the U.S. market. Douglas Orgill wrote that he left the cinema "feeling nationally resentful" and complained of the stereotyping of the British officers,[37] as did Patrick Gibbs, who posed the question, "The producers are American. Could a desire to angle the film towards American audiences have been an issue?"[38]

On the other side of the Atlantic, U.S. critics had similar complaints about the stereotyping of *their* countrymen. "Whatever is lively and memorable in the film . . . is provided by the English members of the cast. Their Yank allies . . . have dim, brief lives on the screen," observed Richard Schickel.[39] Andrew Sarris had similar concerns: "The British players, with their ancestral stiff upper lip, come off much better than the American stars, who have a slack jawed, gee-whiz approach to the action."[40]

Though some reviews positively glowed, most did not. *A Bridge Too Far* was neither a success nor a catastrophe, critically or commercially. Had the film been better received by the critics, then Joe's campaign may have been better complemented. In the absence of critical adulation, his heavy-guns marketing appeared incongruous. Even Joe seemed to accept that he had gone overboard, as Earl Wilson noted of the promotional campaign for Joe's next film, *Magic* (1978): "[Joe] doesn't talk about picture budgets anymore. He quit after there was a rash of publicity about *A Bridge Too Far* costing $26 million. 'People think I'm talking about a bank instead of a movie.'"[41] Joe would not, however, accept that the film was a box-office failure, as Joe Baltake suggested to him: "'What do you mean *A Bridge Too Far* was a flop? That (expletive deleted) film made $21 million!' He stops and stares, then he pokes the reporter with his walking stick. 'Write that down!'"[42]

Joe had done more than most to forge the template of the summer blockbuster. He did so with *Hercules,* a cheap movie for kids with a great title and no stars. As he unleashed his heavy-guns promotion of the expensive, star-laden, prestige picture *A Bridge Too Far,* critics and audience alike were in the thrall of *Star Wars* (1977)—a movie for kids with a great title and no stars. Its groundbreaking special effects notwithstanding, *Star Wars* would not have looked out of place on a drive-in screen twenty years earlier. Having found himself on the right side of so many movements in American culture, Joe now found himself on the wrong side of one he helped to create. The action movie that fits into the holiday mood was now more likely to be taken seriously by critics, perhaps as a corrective to the stuffy attitudes of their forebears.

"*Bridge* is Joe's baby," wrote William Goldman, "There is simply no way it would have ever seen the light of any day without him."[43] It was a huge, collaborative production, but it was Joe's labor of love, and labors of love are often marked by flaws and folly. For all its strengths and weaknesses, *A Bridge Too Far* is very much a Joseph E. Levine film. It began with a quick decision based on sentimentality and a deathbed promise; it was guided into being by vast ambition and a gambler's sense of indestructibility and hubris—the initial stages of the production could have easily ruined Joe. Momentum was maintained by Joe's knack of keeping product flowing; just as he had done with multiple pictures simultaneously in the past, so he did with a single massive picture. Momentum was also maintained by a bloody-minded belief that powerful people expected or wanted him to fail.

A Bridge Too Far was ballyhooed when it was announced and ballyhooed throughout the casting process when stars were signed and their salaries disclosed. It was ballyhooed on the very set it was being made on as distributors journeyed to the Netherlands, afraid of missing out on something big. Then it was ballyhooed on its release with an incessant campaign that prompted one *New York Times* reader to wonder if exposure to Joe's promotional tactics constituted "cruel and unusual punishment."[44]

Joe was justifiably proud of *A Bridge Too Far,* writing, "I've never left a bigger piece of myself in a film than I did with this one."[45] It is a showman's war movie. It is overblown, overlong, and overstuffed; it is filled with exploitable elements and is even a little camp in its seriousness. *A Bridge Too Far* could be *A Budget Too Big, A Star Too Many,* or *An Hour Too Long,* but it is infused with the sincerity of people who believed in the importance of what they were doing, and much of that belief can be attributed to Joe's leadership. The film is the result of a fixation and a belief that it needed to be made. For all its flaws, it remains one of the best war films ever produced.

15

Leaving the Exploitation Business

> This is film. This isn't real. This film is hokum. Nobody kidnaps somebody and tattoos them!
>
> —*Joseph E. Levine*

A Bridge Too Far may not have been the success Joe expected it to be, but the production was a masterpiece of efficiency. Having spent so many years in so many roles, Joe was now, at seventy-two years old, a working producer—one who had guided an enormous and complex project to completion with minimal setbacks. His position as producer and supervisor of such an ambitious project meant that he could now take potshots at others in the industry who he felt were not up to his exacting standards.

With *A Bridge Too Far* in the can, Joe offered his observations on Francis Ford Coppola's troubled production of *Apocalypse Now* (1979): "Look at the spot Coppola's got himself in with this *Apocalypse* thing. He should be thinking of nothing but making movies, for God's sake. A terrific talent but instead of directing, he spread himself thin trying to be a deal-maker. What's he doing trying to copy my act?"[1] Later, following press reports that the budget on Michael Cimino's *Heaven's Gate* (1980) had spiraled out of control and that United Artists might pull the film from cinemas, Joe took aim at the studio: "Trusting $50 million to that kid, they gotta be crazy!"[2] It is worth noticing that in neither case did Joe blame the directors, but rather pointed to a lack of proper production support.

Following *A Bridge Too Far,* Joe, Attenborough, and Goldman reconvened to make *Magic* based on Goldman's novel of the same title. It is a much smaller-scale production than *A Bridge Too Far,* costing around $7 million. It resurrects the old horror trope of the ventriloquist's evil dummy possessing its supposed master, as seen in films such as *The Great Gabbo* (1929) and *Dead of Night* (1945). Joe had bought the rights to *Magic* shortly before shooting of *A Bridge Too Far* began in the Netherlands and had Norman Jewison in mind to direct and Jack Nicholson to star. Both Jewison and Nicholson passed on the project, so Attenborough took the director's chair, and Anthony Hopkins took the starring role, alongside Ann-Margret. It was Hopkins's third film with Joe and Ann-Margret's fifth.

Having made *A Bridge Too Far* as an independent, Joe found a studio home for *Magic* through a coproduction and distribution deal with Fox. Reconvening with the director and screenwriter of *A Bridge Too Far* and changing his production schedule to make one film at a time made it appear as if Joe were settling into a more stable life as he entered his mid-seventies. At a seminar for the Center for Advanced Film Studies in Los Angeles, he told students about his change of approach: "I used to make as many as twelve pictures at a time. I wanted to learn something about the business. On *Magic* and *Bridge,* I lived with the picture. I was on the set early in the morning with Dickie [Attenborough]. . . . It was a marvelous experience."[3] *A Bridge Too Far* was an epic movie accompanied by epic promotion. *Magic* was a more intimate film and was accompanied by more intimate promotion. Prior to its release, the indefatigable seventy-three-year-old Joe set off on a whirlwind promotional trip around America in which he visited twenty-seven cities in less than a month. "Here are the tickets for you and Mrs. Levine for your back-breaking tour," wrote Mike Hutner of Fox in a letter to Joe. "Just take it easy."[4]

Many of the interviews Joe gave to reporters around the country during this tour show him at his most rambunctious and entertaining. He hustled around America being bossy to young provincial reporters, complaining that "people don't hustle anymore," and telling old and new stories about the movies he had made and the people he had worked with. When one reporter inspected the sensitively worded promotional material for *Magic,* Joe chastised him: "Don't print any of that. . . . It's a lot of garbage. It doesn't even begin to describe the movie. What you should write is that Attenborough is one hell of a director, that Ann-Margret is at her finest, and that Hopkins will get at least an Oscar nomination out of it."[5] Hopkins was not nominated for an Oscar, but *Magic* performed well at the box office and was largely well received critically.

Following *A Bridge Too Far* and *Magic,* Joe was once again accused of trying to, in the words of film scholar James Monaco, "redeem his reputation."[6] In his review of *Magic,* the critic John Desplas also took aim, as many had before him, at Joe's supposedly bourgeois aspirations and confuses Joe with director and producer William Castle: "I suppose it's the tireless lusting after respectability. He wants to make pictures that appeal to the unwashed masses, but he wants it to look highbrow. The showman's desire for respectability fared much better during the sixties when he would satisfy such urges by importing Fellini's *8½.* . . . Joe Levine should go back to giving out insurance policies to those attending the latest horror movie. At least if he didn't believe in *Magic* in the old days, he still believed in keeping the show lively."[7]

As if Joe were indeed lusting after respectability, per Desplas's reductive analysis, next up was *Gandhi,* to star Anthony Hopkins as the Mahatma and to be directed by Attenborough. *Gandhi* had been first announced in 1964, and by the time it was released Attenborough had nurtured the project for twenty years. During those years, Joe had often talked about the project in interviews and in private, but he would ultimately pull out during preproduction. Quite why he did so is difficult to ascertain. Attenborough has said that Joe's decision was motivated by the Indian government's decision to grant full diplomatic status to the Palestine Liberation Organization in March 1980.[8] As a Jew, Joe found the decision unjustifiable. However, more than a year earlier Joe had expressed doubts about *Gandhi* to his friend Peter Rosen—director of *Bright College Years.* Rosen had been corresponding with Joe about the possibility of producing a "making of" documentary about *Gandhi,* and Joe wrote to him: "I must tell you now that at this time I am not sure whether *Gandhi* will or will not be made. If it is made, I very much doubt whether I will make it."[9] Joe was, however, deeply involved in casting arrangements with Attenborough for much of 1979.

It seems fair to say that, whatever the reasons, Joe's heart was just not in the project, as it clearly had been for *A Bridge Too Far.* When Joe backed out, Attenborough continued—now both director and producer—but with Ben Kingsley in the title role. In order to do so, however, Attenborough first had to buy the rights to his own labor of love from Joe, who demanded $1 million from Attenborough, bringing their close friendship to a bitter end. As noted in the introduction to this book, Joe was certainly not the nicest man in show business. By contrast, many accounts and reports suggest that Attenborough could have laid claim to being precisely that, which makes Joe's *Gandhi* dealings all the more shameful. It was a particularly brutal business deal that bordered on blackmail.

Gandhi was met with both box-office success and universal critical acclaim, eventually winning eight Oscars. There is little doubt that Joe would have appreciated the prestige and plaudits had he remained involved with the project, but for Joe to have produced *Gandhi* as his final film would have given his career in the movies a too logical trajectory—exploitation hawker to Oscar glory. His versatility and peculiar talents preclude his career being understood as a satisfying character arc, and it makes an odd sort of sense that his final film was *Tattoo* (1981), a mad exploitationer that won no awards, failing even to win the Worst Actor Award for Bruce Dern at the Razzies in 1982. *Tattoo* scuppers all insinuations that Joe at the end of his life wanted to redeem his reputation among critics and scholars or was lusting after respectability. "People in this business think I'm nuts," he once said. "That's OK, because this is not a logical business. If I was logical, I wouldn't be in this business."[10]

Tattoo was directed by Bob Brooks, an American director best known for his advertising work in Britain, where he was the driving force behind the fondly remembered Cadbury's Smash aliens; and it was written by Brooks and Joyce Buñuel—daughter-in-law of director Luis Buñuel. It tells the unlikely tale of a deranged tattoo artist (Bruce Dern) who becomes obsessed with a model (Maude Adams) and kidnaps her in order to cover her in tattoos. The production ran fairly smoothly, though some power struggles emerged during the editing stage.

While *Tattoo* was in postproduction, Joe decided to change Brooks's edits, apparently without informing him beforehand. Brooks became angry about the interference and wrote a furious letter to Joe in which he, among other things, attacks Richard Levine's abilities as a coproducer and accuses Joe of privileging the opinions of "assholes in Los Angeles" over those of a "real audience." Brooks also, revealingly, compares Joe to his own father:

> About ten years ago my father died. He was strong willed and obstinate in his beliefs and what he thought was best for me. I have always felt that there was a great similarity between him and you. It was only when I really removed myself from him completely that I began to see the real Sam Brooks, a gentle man forced

> by poverty to quit school at an early age to support a family and fiercely desirous of success for himself and his family. . . . Unlike you he never really made it.
>
> Just once in my relationship with you did I feel that I actually glimpsed the real Joe Levine. I liked what I saw and it reminded me of my father as I came to understand him. I will try to keep that image of you with me.[11]

Brooks later wrote to apologize to Joe and to thank him for supporting him in the making of *Tattoo*.[12] But this assessment of Joe's character, by someone who worked closely with him and whose father came from similar circumstances, rings true.

Joe could be distant in his dealings with colleagues, sometimes brusque, sometimes humorous, and sometimes hidden behind a showman's mask. On occasion, however, he could display a paternal warmth toward younger filmmakers, as he did with Brooks. That Joe remained haunted by his poverty-stricken upbringing and that this lingering feeling resulted in the cultivation of public and private personas as protective shields should not be dismissed as Pagliacci cliché. Joe had spent much of his life in a world that was vastly different to the world he grew up in. He enjoyed his success and notoriety, and he loved being rich, but even in later life a sense of disorientation remained, resulting in a warmth tempered by wariness or, perhaps, in a wariness punctuated by warmth. Let us not assume that loneliness was a dominant characteristic, but others interviewed for this book have attested that Joe was vulnerable to such feelings.

As *Tattoo* was geared up for release, there was more trouble, but this trouble was more to Joe's liking. He found himself at the center of a controversy because of the promotional poster, which showed a woman's tattooed body and legs, bound at the ankles, raising a storm of objections from feminist groups. "This kind of sexually violent advertising is founded on the notion that women aren't even human beings," protested Dorchin Leidholdt of Women Against Pornography. "You see a body that's simply an object to be tormented and degraded." Joe's response, without any apparent irony, was, "I'm in the exploitation business."[13]

With feminist opposition creating stories for the popular press and protestors vandalizing and defacing the hundreds of *Tattoo* posters gracing the walls of New York's subway system, Joe reveled in the controversy and free publicity: "I used to hustle every picture. I'd do anything but piss on the sidewalk to get a little publicity. . . . Here we are spending all this money for full page ads and now we've got them for nothing. If your paper runs a picture of the poster with the story, that's something I didn't have to pay for. The poster's already been shown on every television station in New York—for free. . . . What will they hit next—The Metropolitan Museum of Modern Art and destroy a Picasso?"[14]

Throughout Joe's career, many influential people and organizations had criticized both him and his films, and he enjoyed it. Industry watchers, arthouse directors, highbrow intellectuals, auteurist critics, the MPAA, the Catholic Legion of Decency, and now the women's liberation movement—all unwittingly helped Joe in his publicity drives. As a result of the protests, the New York Transport Authority removed the posters from the city subway system—but not before Joe squeezed some free publicity from the furor. He threatened to sue the Transport Authority, but nothing came of it. He did, however, storm out of a television interview when he was accused of making an antifeminist film: "I felt like I was a poor Jew at Gestapo headquarters."[15]

Gandhi is a solid, respectable, and renowned film. It would seem a logical step for Joe to make it, but it makes more sense that he walked away from it and chose to make *Tattoo* instead. *Tattoo* received some good reviews and some bad ones, and it did not make much of a dent at the box office. But it is fitting that Joe's final film should see him provoking controversy, and fitting, too, that his final film was thematically ambitious, outré, and macabre.

Responding to the *Tattoo* poster protestors, Joe pointed out, with faultless common sense and some faux exasperation, "This is film. This isn't real. This film is hokum. Nobody kidnaps somebody and tattoos them!"[16] This matter-of-fact distinction between reality and hokum is important. Joe was a showman; exaggeration and hyperbole were his stock in trade. Blurring the lines between reality and hokum was his specialty. Yet one can draw a distinction between Joe's carnivalesque, populist showmanship and the sometimes arbitrary value systems of those who criticized him. Of course, some of the criticism directed at him may have been valid, but he had a peculiar talent for using condemnation to his own advantage. "I used to resent criticism," he once told Pat O'Haire of the *Sunday News,* "but never outwardly. I learned years ago not to resent openly. Very early I adopted the slogan that he who lives by the sword . . . y'know . . . and I live by publicity."[17]

Following *Tattoo,* Joe remained a prominent figure in the press until his death. Many projects were mooted in his final years: *The Lonely Passion of Judith Hearne,* to star Liv Ullman; *Verna: USO Girl,* to star Bob Hope (because, according to Joe, "it's about time he won an Oscar"[18]); *Phyllis and Me,* a semiautobiographical script by Katharine Hepburn; *Boomers,* from Gay Talese's book; and *All the Tea in China,* a rollicking period adventure on the high seas to star Roger Moore and Michael Caine. There was even talk of a *Hercules* remake. None came to pass.

Through the 1980s, Joe became more and more frail. A few weeks before his death, he was interviewed by Donna Rosenthal for the *New York Times.* Rosenthal wrote that "the man who's spent a lifetime out-hyping the biggest hucksters in the industry is less ferocious and more cantankerous." The interview sees Joe, as usual, bragging about his past, trumpeting his upcoming projects, and bemoaning the state of the current industry. But he also reveals his frustrations: "If only I could have 10 more healthy years, I'd gladly give up my entire bank account—because I know I could fill it up again quickly. . . . It's easy as hell to make a picture now. With so much more money around, and with cable TV and video, producers have many more opportunities and escape routes that they don't have to be as smart as they were years ago. As Mike Todd said, 'It's a hard way to make an easy living.' Now it's an easy way to make an easy living."[19]

As ever, Joe is an entertaining interviewee. His wit and ability to deliver a one-liner were hallmarks of his showmanship, and in his final interview he poignantly sums up both his peculiar talent and inevitable demise in a single sentence: "I can cope with changing patterns in films and audience tastes . . . but I can't cope with getting older—it's hell."[20] Less than a month later he was dead.

Joe was a little man with a bad leg and a big belly. Health problems had visited him during the previous two decades, but they never seemed to slow him down in any significant sense. He had walked with a cane for nearly twenty years, something that compromised his distinctively kinetic waddle, and his rotund plumpness had given way to a leaner figure from diets and increasing frailty. Joe had been a ball of energy, but as he entered his eighties, although his mind remained agile, his body did not.

Joe was a dazzling showman and an aggressive hustler who grew up in a world where complacency meant hunger. Even as one of the most successful men in the film business, his ambitions often exceeded his grasp—in part because those ambitions were so many, so varied, and so changeable. The film he talked most about making toward the end of his life was *All the Tea in China,* to be filmed in Hong Kong and on the Pacific Ocean in an audaciously hubristic denial of his own advancing decrepitude; equally, however, his next film could have just as easily been a bizarre deflection into the backwoods territory of cinema, another mad exploitationer or some crazy gamble. But the next film was not to be. Joe's motors had wound down.

Joseph E. Levine died on 31 July 1987 at age eighty-one in Greenwich Hospital, Connecticut, following a short, unspecified illness. Writing in the *New York Times,* Nan Robertson correctly called Joe "a towering figure in movie making" and wrote how he "relished the accoutrements of his power and fame: the obsequious retinues of hangers-on, the 96-foot yacht, the sumptuous hotel suites, the Greenwich estate, the enviable collection of paintings, the power lunches in the Four Seasons—Mr. Levine's 'favorite fast food restaurant.'"[21] In the *Los Angeles Times,* Jack Jones recalled "the one-time shoe-shine boy who became a multi-millionaire with saturation screenings and intense publicity campaigns" and provided a quotation from Joe that could serve as a fitting epitaph: "I've made some good ones. But I've made my share of lousy ones too."[22]

As if to confirm his peculiar talent for self-promotion, some of Joe's achievements are a little overestimated in various obituaries. But his peculiar talent for film promotion is well drawn by all, as is his extraordinary versatility. Joe had finally left the exploitation business, and like P. T. Barnum and Mike Todd before him, his death left a showman-shaped hole in American culture.

Epilogue

A Peculiar Talent

Whatever happened to showmanship?

—*John Waters*

Showmanship was an essential feature of cinema from its inception. Early films were shown in fairground sideshow tents. Carnival barkers stood outside, making their pitch, encouraging passers-by to "step right up to see the marvel of the modern age." Later, exploitation roadshowmen continued this tradition, plastering towns with promotional posters promising all manner of shocking but unmissable attractions for an evening's delectation. The show went on, the crowd went home, and the exploiteers packed up and moved to the next town. American cinema was birthed by independent entrepreneurs. They built Hollywood and the studio system, but the studio system made it more difficult for independent entrepreneurs to operate outside it.

In his recent book about the film exhibitor and radio broadcaster Samuel "Roxy" Rothafel, Ross Melnick uncovers the life and work of another great American showman who, like Joe, was internationally famous, profoundly influential, and, following his death in 1935, forgotten in unsentimental haste. Rothafel recognized that film was an integral, or even incidental, part of an overall entertainment experience. He attracted patrons to his movie palaces with carefully planned, lavishly orchestrated shows that enhanced the film program in a manner that was more genteel but not dissimilar to Joe's later blunderbuss campaigns. It is perhaps unsurprising, then, that Rothafel was a very early experimenter in saturation openings (in 1919) and unsurprising, too, that Rothafel's influence and achievements waned with the advent of block-booking and the increasing rigidity of the studio system.[1]

It is no coincidence that Joe—along with Sam Arkoff, Roger Corman, and William Castle—came to prominence following the *Paramount* case in 1948. As the studio system crumbled, and Hollywood feared the threat from television, the window of opportunity reopened for the entrepreneurial showman, independent and unbound, ready to capitalize on Hollywood's anxieties and take advantage of the new opportunities afforded by television, youth culture, and drive-ins. This window of opportunity remained wide open until the corporatization of Hollywood in the late 1960s, when it began to slowly close before shutting almost entirely when Hollywood emerged from its recession. The corporatization of Hollywood also coincided with the rise of auteurism in American cinema. The director became the star, the film object became fetishized, and the objectifier, the showman, was increasingly regarded as a relic from less-sophisticated times.

In his essay "Whatever Happened to Showmanship?" (1983), the director and exploitation aficionado John Waters asks whether showmanship is a thing of the past.[2] When Joe first entered the national consciousness with *Hercules,* he appeared like a man from the past, the "big selling days" of Hollywood's Golden Age in the 1930s. In the 1950s and 1960s, he sought to make a name for himself by waking up an industry he felt was sleeping on the job. Even then he recognized that showmanship may have had its day, but he nonetheless declared his belief that the hard sell is the only way to sell and told the press, "Exploitation appears to have gone out of style . . . but you can't hide behind a lot of fancy Madison Avenue words."[3]

Protesting against the professionalization and bureaucratization of ballyhoo, Joe was a blast from a positive past. Toward the end of his career, however, he noticed that something fundamental had changed in the business he loved. Though he spoke positively about the emergence of cable television and video (which he called "opportunities and escape routes" but would now be called "ancillary revenue streams"), he also lamented, "They have this concept called marketing. I don't know what it means and I certainly don't think they know how to bring an audience to a film."[4] Joe was an exploitation man, not a marketing man, and he arrived on the scene when it was possible for a showman to be distinctive. He believed in exciting an audience by banging the promotional drum. Modern blockbuster marketeers are banging the same drum to the same beat—and it is Joe's beat.

Corporate Hollywood caught up with Joe with *Jaws.* Joe should rightly be positioned as the man who pioneered the techniques that were used to sell *Jaws*, but it is worth reiterating that it is even more befitting to Joe's legacy to remember that it was his hucksterish approach and persona that tarnished the technique and made saturation methods appear downmarket for more than fifteen years. Yet another fourteen years passed before Hollywood would truly match the merchant carnival of Joe's *Hercules* campaign when *Batman* was released in 1989. *Jaws* was backed by hype and merchandising, but the movie was still the thing. *Batman,* however, appeared to be just one component of a wider campaign and cultural event—Batmania. The swirl of hype surrounding it may have, as Thomas Schatz observes, "created a new paradigm for Hollywood blockbusters,"[5] but it also harked back to the all-encompassing spectacle of earlier times.

Every modern blockbuster release can trace its lineage back to *Hercules.* In 2014, two Hollywood-made *Hercules* films and one *Godzilla* were released in cinemas. Joe's influence lies not only in the methods used to sell movies but also in the very titles of the movies themselves. Campaigns may be sterile and safe and lack the personal vulgar touch, but Joe's ghost is there. With Joe, it was not just about the movies; it was about everything else. And Joe gave the movies *a lot* of everything else.

In his essay, Waters wonders, "Who is to follow in the footsteps of the great low-rent Samuel Z. Arkoffs and Joseph E. Levines who used to hype films?"[6] Many people who worked with and were influenced by Joe took the exploitation route. In addition to those mentioned thus far, sexploitation queen Doris Wishman, a cousin of Max Rosenberg, who worked with Joe in the 1950s, was so impressed by his success in promoting the nudie-cutie film *Garden of Eden* (1954) that she made her career in sexploitation cinema and remains one of the best-loved filmmakers in that genre. Jonathan Demme, who went from small-time film critic to Embassy press agent thanks to his positive review of *Zulu,* started out as a director, making *Caged Heat* (1975) and *Crazy Mama* (1975) for Roger Corman before going on to Oscar success with *Silence of the Lambs* (1991) and *Philadelphia* (1993). And Michael Lynne, who worked in the legal department of Avco Embassy for Joe, set up New Line Cinema with his college friend Robert Shaye. Lynne and Shaye distributed old exploitation and arthouse films to college campuses in the 1960s and 1970s and were responsible for making *Reefer Madness* (1938) the cult classic it is today. New Line produced many of John Waters's films but is most famous for its success with Peter Jackson's *Lord of the Rings* trilogy (2001–2003).

As an exploitation man, Joe worked extensively in the arthouse, and it is here that we find his most obvious successor—Harvey Weinstein. As head of Miramax, Weinstein, like Joe, cultivated his reputation as American cinema's great independent, even after Miramax was acquired by the Disney Corporation. Alisa Perren's recent book about Miramax reveals many other parallels. Weinstein baited censors over ratings and used censorial condemnations to publicize himself and his wares; he also flagrantly and controversially campaigned for Oscar nominations and awards for his films and sought to bring arthouse cinema to a wide audience. "Although we make artistic films," he said, Levine-like, following Miramax's release of *sex, lies, and videotape* (1989), "we don't use the starving artist mentality in our releases. Other distributors slap out a movie, put an ad in the newspaper—usually not a very good one—and hope that the audience will find it. And most often they don't. It's the distributors' responsibility to find the audience."[7] Notably, Anthony Hopkins, having based his film-producer character in *Slipstream* (2007) on Joe, named him "Harvey" and asked Weinstein to play the part.[8]

Like many successful men who grew up in poverty, Joe was always impeccably attired, his tailored suits a sartorial rejection of former circumstance and a visible manifestation of an upward social journey. In his spick-and-span New York office, you would find Joe seated behind an enormous desk and around him ornate fittings, shelves displaying awards, and walls featuring photographs of him with the stars of showbiz, politics, and elsewhere.

Joe's office, where he met the world, was a monument to both his achievements and his personal fastidiousness. One reason he did not smoke cigars, speculates Peter Rosen, was that they were "too messy for him. . . . The office was always spanking clean and neat. Bottle of Perrier on silver tray, crystal glass, etc."[9] For today's producers, notes filmmaker and scholar John Caldwell, the emphasis is more likely to be on a downward social trajectory, as the gurus of American primetime television, bearded and barefoot Ivy League alumni, renounce their own privileged pasts in faded band T-shirts and messy offices.[10] The contrast could not be more stark, but here, also, we can find Joe's spirit, inverted and everted.

For Caldwell, "producers and directors actively organize their professional spaces as presentational tableaus for public consumption,"[11] and this was as true for Joe's office pomp as it is for today's office jumble. Joe may have been neat, but it is the "creativity inducing mess" found in the modern producer's office that speaks most to Joe's legacy. In this clutter, in the haphazard strewing of CDs, DVDs, books, comics, and artworks, Caldwell sees "culturally coded tableaus . . . an impressively odd intellectual pedigree formed by combinations of high culture, low culture, prestige and kitsch."[12] This is Joe's scattergun inventory. Joe's output is the modern producer's input. Where Pierre Bourdieu once observed a sacrilegious reuniting of tastes,[13] recent years have seen formerly dissonant clatterings become consonant and cultural omnivorousness become the hallmark of both Bourdieu's possessor of legitimate culture and Caldwell's impressive intellectual pedigree. That such studied eclecticism has become an intellectual cliché should not detract from how distinctive and controversial Joe's variegated output was in America of the 1960s.

The postmodern normalization of diversity points to another answer to Waters's question about the dearth of modern showmanship: the vanishing of the public intellectual. Joe needed criticism. He needed the intolerance of an intellectual elite to define him as a maverick outsider. In the middle of the twentieth century, members of the cultural elite were self-identifying, passionate, and sincere, and they made ideal sparring partners for Joe. In modern times, the pop-culture maverick has little opposition. There is little for cultural gatekeepers to get upset about, aside from the occasional moral panic. Nowadays superhero films are reviewed with the same thought and care as arthouse fare, and the gaudy aesthetics and lowbrow histrionics of *The Carpetbaggers* are replicated in critic-friendly, quality television shows such as *Mad Men* (2007–2015). But showmanship needs opposition—without that, it is just marketing.

Joe's influence on movies and movie-going culture should not be underestimated, and it should be more recognized. Joe was a showman. Perhaps showmanship is a forgotten talent, but it was a talent that made him hugely important and influential. Trying to understand American cinema in the postwar era without understanding Joseph E. Levine is like understanding Hollywood's Golden Age without understanding Irving Thalberg. Joe made fast decisions, great decisions, and bad decisions. He made commercial art, and he made art commercial. He was influenced, and he influenced. Nonetheless, he was a one-off, a peculiar talent. To paraphrase the *New York Times* bio of him, *Joseph E. Levine was . . . well . . . Joseph E. Levine.*

Acknowledgments

I must first thank Julian Stringer for his efforts and support when I first started working on the material that went into this book. I also thank Andrew Spicer for helping me to develop my research skills and for teaching me how to write a book. Thanks to Mark Jancovich for advising me in the initial stages of this project and to Yannis Tzioumakis for the advice he offered toward the end.

I am also grateful to everyone I interviewed or corresponded with for this book: Mel Brooks, Alan Brown, Ray Galton, Linda Hayden, Tony Klinger, the late Albert Maysles, Peter Rosen, Elizabeth Rosenberg, Alan Simpson, Gay Talese, and Larry Turman. Their insights have been invaluable.

My thanks also go to the staff of the various libraries and archives I have visited: the Hallward Library at the University of Nottingham; the British Film Institute Library in London; the Howard Gottlieb Research Center in Boston, especially Alex Rankin; the West End Museum in Boston; and the Margaret Herrick Library in Beverly Hills, especially Kristine Krueger and my dear friend Jenny Romero.

Thanks also to colleagues past and present at the University of Nottingham in Ningbo, China, especially Margaret McDonald, for her advice and feedback on draft chapters, as well as Doug Bell, Robert Beveridge, and Richard Silburn for their help and support. And thanks to the staff of the University Press of Kentucky—especially Anne Dean Dotson and Patrick O'Dowd—for their help and patience.

Thanks to Christine Troughton and her family for giving me a place to stay on London research trips and to Lauren G. and family for giving me a place to stay on Los Angeles research trips. Thanks to my dad for his proofreading and, of course, to my wonderful wife, Kiki Tianqi, for her love, support, patience, and encouragement.

Select Filmography

It is very difficult indeed to compile a comprehensive list of every film that Joseph E. Levine was involved with, but I have made this filmography as inclusive as possible.

The list is organized chronologically according to the date of the film's U.S. release. For the sake of simplicity, distribution details refer to the United States unless noted otherwise, though Joe dealt extensively in other territories. Titles provided refer to the title given to a film for its release in the United States, with original or alternative titles provided in parentheses.

Un Carnet de bal (a.k.a. *Christine*) (Julien Duvivier, 1937). This was the first film Joe presented at the newly acquired Little (Lincoln) Theatre in New Haven, Connecticut, in 1938.

How to Undress in Front of Your Husband (Dwain Esper, 1937). An exploitation short shown on the same bill as *Un Carnet de bal* at the Lincoln Theatre.

The Body Beautiful (c. 1938). Sex-hygiene exploitation film distributed by Joe in New England.

Ravaged Earth (c. 1940s). Exploitation film about Japanese atrocities committed in China during the Second World War. Exhibited by Joe in Boston in the late 1940s.

Gaslight Follies (a.k.a. *The Good Ol' Days* or *The Good Old Days*, 1945). A comedy compilation film of recycled (mostly silent) material coproduced by Joe and Max Rosenberg, who used the pseudonym "Max Finn" for this production. Produced and distributed by Motion Picture Ventures.

Discovery (1947). A documentary of footage of Admiral Richard E. Byrd's Antarctic expeditions produced and distributed by Joe through a deal with Filmways.

Duel in the Sun (King Vidor, 1946). Distributed by Joe in New England for its re-release in 1954. Joe's first big saturation opening.

Gangbusters (1955). Four episodes of the popular television show spliced together for theatrical release. Distributed and promoted nationally by Joe and Terry Turner through Embassy.

Wiretapper (Dick Ross, 1955). Crime thriller. Distributed and promoted nationally by Joe and Terry Turner through Embassy.

Godzilla: King of the Monsters (Ishiro Honda, Terry Morse, 1956). A reedited and reworked version of *Gojira* (Ishiro Honda, 1954). Distributed and promoted by Joe, Terry Turner, and Edward Barison through Transworld.

Walk into Hell (a.k.a. *Walk into Paradise* or *L'Odyssee du Capitaine Steve*) (Lee Robinson and Marcello Pagliero, 1956). French-Australian coproduction. Jungle thriller starring Chips Rafferty. Distributed and promoted nationally by Joe and Terry Turner through Embassy.

The Mysterians (a.k.a. *Chikyū Bōeigun*) (Ishiro Honda, 1957). Embassy acquired the rights and promoted this film nationwide alongside Terry Turner. MGM handled distribution.

Attila (a.k.a. *Attila, il flagello di Dio* or *Attila fléau de Dieu*) (Pietro Francisci, 1954). Produced by Carlo Ponti and Dino De Laurentiis. Starring Sophia Loren and Anthony Quinn. Distributed and promoted by Embassy in 1958.

Hercules (a.k.a. *La Fatiche di Ercole*) (Pietro Francisci, 1958). Italian peplum film starring Steve Reeves that made Joe famous. Embassy acquired the rights and handled promotion; Warner Bros. handled the film's distribution in 1959.

Jack the Ripper (Robert S. Berman, Monty Berman, 1959). British horror acquired by Embassy. Distributed by Paramount.

Hercules Unchained (a.k.a. *Ercole e la regina di Lidia*) (Pietro Francisci, 1959). *Hercules* sequel starring Steve Reeves. Acquired by Embassy, distributed by Warner Bros.

Where the Hot Wind Blows (a.k.a. *La Legge* or *The Law*) (Jules Dassin, 1959). French-Italian drama starring Gina Lollobrigida, Yves Montand, and Marcello Mastroianni. Acquired by Embassy, distributed by MGM.

Morgan the Pirate (a.k.a. *Morgan il pirata*). (Primo Zeglio, Andre de Toth, 1960). Italian-French-U.S. coproduction starring Steve Reeves. Coproduced by Embassy. Distributed by MGM.

Two Women (a.k.a. *La Ciociara*) (Vittorio de Sica, 1960). Produced by Carlo Ponti and starring Sophia Loren. Distributed by Embassy.

The Thief of Baghdad (a.k.a. *Il Ladro di Bagdad*) (Arthur Lubin, Bruno Vailati, 1961). Italian-U.S. coproduction starring Steve Reeves. Coproduced by Embassy and distributed by MGM.

The Wonders of Aladdin (a.k.a. *Le Meraviglie di Aladino*) (Mario Bava, Henry

Levin, 1961). Italian-U.S. coproduction starring Donald O'Connor and Vittorio de Sica. Coproduced by Embassy and distributed by MGM.

Spare the Rod (Leslie Norman, 1961). British social issue drama about corporal punishment in schools. Starring Max Bygraves. Distributed by Embassy.

Divorce, Italian Style (a.k.a. *Divorzio all'italiana*) (Pietro Germi, 1961). Starring Marcello Mastroianni. Distributed by Embassy.

The Sky Above, the Mud Below (a.k.a. *La Ciel et la boue* or *The Sky Above, the Mud Beneath*) (Pierre-Domonique Gaisseau, 1961). Oscar-winning documentary distributed by Embassy.

The Last Days of Sodom and Gomorrah (Robert Aldrich, 1962). Italian-U.S. coproduction starring Stewart Granger, Anouk Aimee, and Stanley Baker. Coproduced by Embassy and distributed by 20th Century Fox.

Love at Twenty (a.k.a. *L'Amour a vingt ans*) (François Truffaut, Andrzej Wajda, Renzo Rossellini, Shintaro Ishihara, Marcel Ophuls, 1962). One of many portmanteau art films acquired by Embassy in the 1960s. Distributed by 20th Century Fox.

Seven Capital Sins (a.k.a. *The Seven Deadly Sins* or *Le Sept peches capitaux*) (Philippe de Broca, Claude Chabrol, Jacques Demy, Sylvain Dhomme, Max Douy, Jean-Luc Godard, Edouardo Molinaro, Roger Vadim, 1962). One of many portmanteau art films acquired by Joe in the 1960s. Distributed by Embassy.

Long Day's Journey into Night (Sidney Lumet, 1962). Based on the play by Eugene O'Neill. Starring Katharine Hepburn, Ralph Richardson, Jason Robards, and Dean Stockwell. Distributed by Embassy. Joe received an executive-producer credit in return for funding the production.

Boys' Night Out (Michael Gordon, 1962). Sex comedy starring Kim Novak, James Garner, and Tony Randall. Produced by MGM. Joe was involved in promotion and received an executive-producer credit.

The Devil's Wanton (a.k.a. *Fängelse* or *Prison*) (Ingmar Bergman, 1949). A "vintage Bergman" distributed by Embassy in 1962.

Night Is My Future (a.k.a. *Musik i mörker* or *Music in Darkness*) (Ingmar Bergman, 1947). A "vintage Bergman" distributed by Embassy in 1963.

Madame (a.k.a. *Madame Sans-Gene*) (Christian-Jacque, 1961). Starring Sophia Loren. Distributed by Embassy in 1963.

Boccaccio 70 (Vittorio de Sica, Luchino Visconti, Federico Fellini, Mario Monicelli, 1963). The most successful of the many multidirector portmanteau art films acquired by Joe in the 1960s. Coproduced by Embassy and Carlo Ponti. Starring Sophia Loren, Romy Schneider, Anita Ekberg, and Marisa

Solanis. Mario Monicelli's segment, which stars Marisa Solanis, was excised from the U.S. release in 1963 because of concerns about running time.

The Bear (a.k.a. *L'Ours*) (Edmond Sechan, 1960). A film about a talking bear. Distributed by Embassy in 1963.

Women of the World (a.k.a. *La Donna nel mondo*) (Gualtiero Jacopetti, 1963). *Mondo* film made up of footage left over from *Mondo Cane* (Gualtiero Jacopetti, 1962). Distributed by Embassy.

8½ (a.k.a. *Otto e mezzo* or *Eight and a Half*) (Federico Fellini, 1963). Oscar-winning Italian art film starring Marcello Mastroianni. Promoted and distributed in the United States by Embassy through a deal with Columbia.

Contempt (a.k.a. *Le Mépris* or *Il Disprezzo*) (Jean-Luc Godard, 1963). French-Italian-U.S. coproduction starring Brigitte Bardot, Michel Piccoli, Fritz Lang, and Jack Palance as a philistine American producer widely believed to be based on Joe. Coproduced by Embassy, Carlo Ponti, and Georges de Beauregard. Distributed by Embassy. Perhaps Joe's most notorious production.

The Empty Canvas (a.k.a. *La Noia*) (Damiano Damiani, 1963). U.S.-Italian coproduction starring Bette Davis, Horst Buchholz, and Catherine Spaak. Coproduced by Embassy and Carlo Ponti. Distributed by Embassy.

Yesterday, Today, and Tomorrow (a.k.a. *Leri, oggi, domain*) (Vittorio de Sica, 1963). Oscar-winning Italian comedy. Coproduced by Embassy and Carlo Ponti. Starring Sophia Loren and Marcello Mastroianni. Distributed by Embassy.

Zulu (Cy Endfield, 1964). Produced by Stanley Baker. Starring Stanley Baker and Michael Caine. Embassy–Paramount coproduction.

The Carpetbaggers (Edward Dmytryk, 1964). Starring George Peppard, Alan Ladd, and Carroll Baker. Embassy–Paramount coproduction. Joe's first Harold Robbins adaptation and his first major producer credit.

Santa Claus Conquers the Martians (Nicholas Webster, 1964). Starring Pia Zadora. Fondly regarded as one of the worst films ever made. Coproduced and distributed by Embassy.

Marriage, Italian Style (a.k.a. *Matrimonio all'italiana*) (Vittorio de Sica, 1964). Starring Sophia Loren and Marcello Mastroianni. Coproduced by Embassy and Carlo Ponti. Distributed by Embassy.

Casanova 70 (Mario Monicelli, 1965). Starring Marcello Mastroianni. Coproduced by Embassy and Carlo Ponti. Distributed by Embassy.

A House Is Not a Home (Russell Rouse, 1964). Based on Polly Adler's autobiography. Starring Shelley Winters. Produced and distributed by Embassy.

Only One New York (Pierre-Domonique Gaisseau, 1964). Documentary from the director of *The Sky Above, the Mud Below.* Distributed by Embassy.

Where Love Has Gone (Edward Dmytryk, 1964). Harold Robbins adaptation starring Susan Hayward and Bette Davis. Embassy–Paramount coproduction.

Dingaka (Jamie Uys, 1965). South African drama starring Stanley Baker. Coproduced and distributed by Embassy.

Sands of the Kalahari (Cy Endfield, 1965). British adventure starring Stanley Baker. Coproduced by Embassy, Baker, and Endfield. Distributed by Paramount.

Seaside Swingers (a.k.a. *Every Day's a Holiday*) (James Hill, 1965). British comedy musical featuring John Leyton and Freddie and the Dreamers. Distributed by Embassy.

A Pistol for Ringo (a.k.a. *Una Pistola per Ringo*) (Duccio Tessari, 1965). Spaghetti Western distributed by Embassy.

The Bounty Killer (Spencer Gordon Bennet, 1965). Low-budget Western distributed by Embassy. Shown on a double bill with *A Pistol for Ringo.*

Requiem for a Gunfighter (Spencer Gordon Bennet, 1965). Low-budget Western distributed by Embassy.

The Tramplers (a.k.a. *Gli uomini dal passo pesante*) (Albert Band, 1965). Spaghetti Western starring Gordon Scott and Joseph Cotten. Distributed by Embassy.

Darling (John Schlesinger, 1965). British drama starring Julie Christie. Distributed by Embassy.

Village of the Giants (Bert I. Gordon, 1965). Low-budget family sci-fi. Coproduced by Embassy and Bert I. Gordon. Distributed by Embassy.

Sylvia (Gordon Douglas, 1965). A Paramount production starring Carroll Baker. Joe had some input on the production side and in his role as Baker's self-appointed Svengali.

The 10th Victim (Elio Petri, 1965). Italian-French-U.S. coproduction starring Marcello Mastroianni. Coproduced by Embassy and Carlo Ponti. Distributed by Embassy.

The Second Best Secret Agent in the Whole Wide World (a.k.a. *Licensed to Kill*) (Lindsay Shonteff, 1965). British Bond spoof. Distributed by Embassy.

Harlow (Gordon Douglas, 1965). Biopic of Jean Harlow starring Carroll Baker. Embassy–Paramount coproduction.

Git! (Ellis Kadison, 1965). Children's film about a boy and his dog. Coproduced and distributed by Embassy.

The Cat (a.k.a. *Cat!*) (Ellis Kadison, 1966). Children's film about a boy and his cat. Coproduced and distributed by Embassy.

The Idol (Daniel Petrie, 1966). British drama starring Jennifer Jones and John Leyton. Produced and distributed by Embassy.

Nevada Smith (Henry Hathaway, 1966). Harold Robbins adaptation. Prequel to *The Carpetbaggers.* Starring Steve McQueen as Nevada Smith, who had been played by Alan Ladd in *The Carpetbaggers.* Embassy–Paramount coproduction.

The Oscar (Russell Rouse, 1966). Cameo-filled drama about the Academy Awards. Coproduced and distributed by Embassy.

John F. Kennedy: Years of Lightning, Day of Drums (Bruce Herschensohn, 1966). Distributed by Embassy for free because of Joe's admiration for President Kennedy. The director, Herschensohn, is now better known as a conservative Republican political commentator.

Jesse James Meets Frankenstein's Daughter (William Beaudine, 1966). Starring John Lupton as Jesse James and Narda Onyx as Baron Victor von Frankenstein's granddaughter, rendering the film's title incorrect. Embassy–Circle coproduction. Distributed by Embassy.

Billy the Kid versus Dracula (William Beaudine, 1966). Starring Chuck Courtney as Billy the Kid and John Carradine as Count Dracula. Embassy–Circle coproduction. Funded and distributed by Embassy.

An Eye for an Eye (Michael D. Moore, 1966). Western coproduced by Embassy and Circle. Funded and distributed by Embassy.

A Man Called Adam (Leo Penn, 1966). The story of a jazz trumpeter's turbulent life. The project was brought to Joe by the star, Sammy Davis Jr. Also starring Louis Armstrong and Ossie Davis. Joe was executive producer. Distributed by Embassy. Joe was later rumored to be collaborating with Ossie Davis on a biopic of the controversial black comedian Stepin' Fetchit (a.k.a. Lincoln Perry), but Davis quashed the rumors amid criticism from Perry.

Where the Bullets Fly (John Gilling, 1966). Bond spoof sequel to *The Second Best Secret Agent in the Whole Wide World.* Distributed by Embassy.

The Spy with a Cold Nose (Daniel Petrie, 1966). British Bond spoof scripted by Ray Galton and Alan Simpson, starring a wide range of British comedy and character-acting talent. Embassy–Associated London coproduction. Distributed by Embassy.

Romeo and Juliet (Paul Czinner, 1966). Film of the Royal Ballet Performance of Prokofiev's adaptation of William Shakespeare's play in 1965. Starring Rudolph Nureyev and Margot Fonteyn. Distributed by Embassy.

Shoot Loud, Louder . . . I Don't Understand (a.k.a. *Spara forte, piu forte, non capisco*) (Eduoardo de Filippo, 1966). Light-hearted crime caper starring Marcello Mastroianni and Raquel Welch. Italian-U.S. coproduction. Coproduced and distributed by Embassy.

Picture Mommy Dead (Bert I. Gordon, 1966). Horror starring Don Ameche, Martha Hyer, Susan Gordon, and Zsa Zsa Gabor. Embassy–Bert I. Gordon coproduction. Distributed by Embassy.

Hellbenders (a.k.a. *I crudely*) (Sergio Corbucci, 1966). Spaghetti Western starring Joseph Cotten. Produced by Albert Band, director and producer of *The Tramplers* (1965). Distributed by Embassy.

The Daydreamer (Jules Bass, 1966). Family fantasy starring Tallulah Bankhead and Victor Borge. Embassy–Videocraft coproduction. Distributed by Embassy.

Mad Monster Party (Jules Bass, 1966). Animated children's film scripted by Harvey Kurtzman of *Mad* magazine and featuring the voices of Boris Karloff and Phyllis Diller. Embassy–Videocraft coproduction. Distributed by Embassy.

The Terrornaughts (a.k.a. *The Terrornaughts! The Virgin Sacrifice to the Gods of the Ghastly Galaxies*) (Montgomery Tully, 1967). British sci-fi horror produced by Joe's erstwhile partner Max Rosenberg at Amicus Studios. Distributed by Embassy.

They Came from beyond Space (Freddie Francis, 1967). British sci-fi horror produced by Joe's erstwhile partner Max Rosenberg at Amicus Studios. Distributed by Embassy.

The Tiger and the Pussycat (a.k.a. *Il Tigre*) (Dino Risi, 1967). Starring Ann-Margret. Coproduced and distributed by Embassy.

The Caper of the Golden Bulls (a.k.a. *Carnival of Thieves*) (Russell Rouse, 1967). Produced and distributed by Embassy.

Woman Times Seven (a.k.a. *Sette volte donna*) (Vittorio de Sica, 1967). Comedy-drama anthology starring Shirley MacLaine, Michael Caine, and Peter Sellers, among others. Italian-U.S. coproduction. Produced and distributed by Embassy.

Robbery (Peter Yates, 1967). British crime thriller starring Stanley Baker. Coproduced and distributed by Embassy.

The Graduate (Mike Nichols, 1967). Counterculture comedy-drama starring Dustin Hoffman and Anne Bancroft. Coproduced and distributed by Embassy.

The Producers (Mel Brooks, 1967). Comedy starring Zero Mostel and Gene

Wilder. Coproduced by Embassy and Sidney Glazier. Distributed by Avco Embassy.

The Lion in Winter (Anthony Harvey, 1968). Period drama starring Katharine Hepburn, Peter O'Toole, and Anthony Hopkins. Coproduced and distributed by Avco Embassy. Joe's favorite among his own films.

Baby Love (Alastair Reid, 1968). British drama starring Linda Hayden. Distributed by Avco Embassy.

Woman in Chains (a.k.a. *La Prisonniere*) (Henri-Georges Clouzot, 1968). Clouzot's final film. Distributed by Avco Embassy.

Sweden Heaven and Hell (a.k.a. *Svezia, inferno e paradiso*) (Luigi Scattini, 1968). Italian *Mondo* film about Sweden. Funded in part and distributed in America by Avco Embassy.

A Bullet for the General (a.k.a. *Quien sabe?*) (Domiano Domiani, 1966). Spaghetti Western starring Gian Maria Volonte, Klaus Kinski, and Martine Beswick. Distributed by Avco Embassy in 1968.

Stilletto (Bernard L. Kowalski, 1969). Harold Robbins adaptation starring Alex Cord and Britt Ekland. Coproduced and distributed by Avco Embassy.

12+1 (a.k.a. *The Thirteen Chairs*) (Nicholas Gessner, 1969). Based on *The Twelve Chairs,* a satirical novel by Ilya Ilf and Evgeny Petrov. Starring Sharon Tate (in her final film), Vittorio Gassman, Orson Welles, and Vittorio de Sica. Distributed by Avco Embassy. Curiously, in 1970 Mel Brooks released a film based on the same novel, giving it the title *The Twelve Chairs.* Following the success of *The Producers,* Brooks offered Joe *The Twelve Chairs* as a possible next project, but Joe turned him down.

Don't Drink the Water (Howard Morris, 1969). Based on a play by Woody Allen. Distributed by Avco Embassy.

A Nice Girl Like Me (Desmond Davis, 1969). British sex comedy. Distributed by Avco Embassy.

The Swimming Pool (a.k.a. *La Piscine*) (Jacques Deray, 1969). Italian-French drama. Distributed by Avco-Embassy.

Generation (George Schaeffer, 1969). Comedy starring David Janssen. Produced and distributed by Avco Embassy.

The Adventurers (Lewis Gilbert, 1970). Harold Robbins adaptation. Avco Embassy–Paramount coproduction. Paramount's production credit relates to its stake in the rights to the Robbins novels Joe had brought to the studio.

Soldier Blue (Ralph Nelson, 1970). Controversial revisionist Western starring Candice Bergen, Peter Strauss, and Donald Pleasance. Avco Embassy–Katzka/Loeb coproduction.

CC and Company (a.k.a. *Chrome Hearts*) (Seymore Robbie, 1970). Biker movie starring Ann-Margret and Joe Namath. Avco Embassy coproduction.

Rider on the Rain (Rene Clement, 1970). Thriller produced by Serge Silberman, starring Charles Bronson. Distributed by Avco Embassy.

Sunflower (a.k.a. *I Girasoli*) (Vittorio de Sica, 1970). Starring Sophia Loren and Marcello Mastroianni. Filmed in the Soviet Union. Coproduced by Avco Embassy and Carlo Ponti. Distributed by Avco Embassy.

Monique (John Bown, 1970). Low-budget British sex drama. Distributed by Avco Embassy.

Macho Callahan (Bernard L. Kowalski, 1970). Civil War Western starring David Janssen, Jean Seberg, and Lee J. Cobb. Distributed by Avco Embassy.

The Man Who Had Power over Women (John Krish, 1970). British sex comedy starring Rod Taylor. Distributed by Avco Embassy.

Bright College Years (Peter Rosen, 1970). Documentary about the May Day strike at Yale University in 1970. Coproduced and distributed by Embassy.

Road to Salina (*La route de Salina*) (Georges Lautner, 1970). French thriller. Distributed by Avco Embassy.

Promise at Dawn (a.k.a. *La Promesse de l'aube*) (Jules Dassin, 1970). Distributed by Avco Embassy.

They Call Me Trinity (a.k.a. *Lo Chiamavano Trinità*) (E. B. Clucher [Enzo Barboni], 1970). Comedy spaghetti Western starring Terence Hill and Bud Spencer. Distributed by Avco Embassy.

Carnal Knowledge (Mike Nichols, 1971). Drama starring Jack Nicholson, Art Garfunkel, Ann-Margret, and Candice Bergen. Avco Embassy production.

The Nightcomers (Michael Winner, 1971). British horror film starring Marlon Brando and Stephanie Beacham. Distributed by Avco Embassy.

The Steagle (Paul Sylbert, 1971). Comedy starring Richard Benjamin. Produced and distributed by Avco Embassy.

Trinity Is STILL My Name (a.k.a. . . . *Continuavano a chiamarlo Trinità*) (E. B. Clucher [Enzo Barboni], 1971). Sequel to *They Call Me Trinity.* Starring Terence Hill and Bud Spencer. Distributed by Avco Embassy.

The Ski Bum (Bruce D. Clarke, 1971). Based on the novel by Romain Gary. Produced and distributed by Avco Embassy.

The Ruling Class (Peter Medak, 1972). Comedy based on Peter Barnes's play. Starring Peter O'Toole. Distributed by Avco Embassy.

What? (a.k.a. *Che?* or *Quoi?* or *Was?* or *Diary of Forbidden Dreams*) (Roman Polanski, 1972). Comedy produced by Carlo Ponti and starring Marcello Mastroianni. Distributed by Avco Embassy.

The Stoolie (John G. Avildson, 1972). Comedy starring Jackie Mason. Avco Embassy production.

Book of Numbers (Raymond St. Jacques, 1973). Period thriller of the blaxploitation cycle, starring Raymond St. Jacques, Philip Michael Thomas, and Freda Payne. Coproduced and distributed by Avco Embassy.

A Touch of Class (Melvin Frank, 1973). British sex comedy starring George Segal and Glenda Jackson. Distributed by Avco Embassy.

Hurry Up, or I'll Be 30 (a.k.a. *I Am Waiting No More*) (Joseph Jacoby, 1973). Comedy-drama starring John Lefkowitz. Coproduced and distributed by Avco Embassy.

Day of the Dolphin (Mike Nichols, 1973). Thriller about talking dolphins. Starring George C. Scott. Produced by Avco Embassy. Joe's last film with Mike Nichols.

This Time I'll Make You Rich (a.k.a. *Questa volta ti faccio ricco!*) (Gianfranco Parolini [Frank Kramer], 1974). Italian-German low-budget thriller coproduced by Hong Kong's Shaw Brothers' Studio. Acquired by Joseph E. Levine Presents. Distributed by Avco Embassy.

And Now My Love (a.k.a. *Toute une vie* or *A Whole Lifetime*) (Claude Lelouche, 1974). Romantic saga. Acquired by Joseph E. Levine Presents. Distributed by Avco Embassy.

The Night Porter (a.k.a. *Il Portiere di notte*) (Liliana Cavani, 1974). Controversial Nazi-themed erotic drama starring Dirk Bogarde and Charlotte Rampling. Acquired by Joseph E. Levine Presents. Distributed by Avco Embassy.

A Bridge Too Far (Richard Attenborough, 1977). Star-studded war epic. A Joseph E. Levine Presents production. Produced by Joe and his son, Richard P. Levine. Distributed in the United States by United Artists.

Magic (Richard Attenborough, 1978). Horror starring Anthony Hopkins, Ann-Margret, and Burgess Meredith. Produced by Joe alongside his son, Richard P. Levine. Joseph E. Levine Presents–20th Century Fox coproduction. Distributed by 20th Century Fox.

Tattoo (Bob Brooks, 1981). Thriller starring Bruce Dern and Maud Adams. Produced by Joe and his son, Richard P. Levine. Joseph E. Levine Presents–20th Century Fox coproduction. Distributed by 20th Century Fox. Joe's final film.

Notes

Introduction

1. Neil Harris, *Humbug: The Art of P. T. Barnum* (Chicago: University of Chicago Press, 1973), 3.

2. Quoted in Chuck Kramer, "You Seen My Art Pitchas?" *Phoenix Star,* May 1970.

3. Quoted in "Joe Unchained," *Time,* 24 February 1961.

4. Eric Schaeffer, *Bold! Daring! Shocking! True! A History of Exploitation Films, 1919–1959* (Durham, N.C.: Duke University Press, 1999).

5. Quoted in Katherine Hamill, "The Supercolossal—Well, Pretty Good—World of Joe Levine," *Fortune,* March 1964.

6. Quoted in "The Last of the Movie Barons," *Newsweek,* 2 May 1966.

7. Paramount Inter-Office to Edmund R. Rosencrantz, 1 July 1964, Paramount Collection, Association of Motion Picture Arts and Sciences, Margaret Herrick Library, Beverly Hills, Calif.

8. Victor Davies, "How the Bridge at Arnhem Came to Be Paved with Gold," *Daily Express* (London), 7 February 1977.

9. Quoted in Guy Flatley, "Cary—from Mae to September," *New York Times,* 22 July 1973. *A Touch of Class* was coproduced by Joseph E. Levine Presents and Brut Productions—the latter company was a subsidiary of Faberge, of whom Grant was a director. When Flatley interviewed Joe in 1977, he reported that Joe was "still smarting from an old wound," quoting him as saying, "Cary was a *friend* . . . I don't know what prompted him to say that" (Guy Flatley, "At The Movies," *New York Times,* 10 June 1977, 61).

10. Arthur L. Mayer, letter to the editor, *Los Angeles Times,* 24 November 1974.

11. Lawrence Turman to the author, personal correspondence, 8 March 2006.

12. Richard Davis, "Review of *The Oscar,*" *Films and Filming,* July 1966.

13. Nan Robertson, "Joseph E. Levine, a Towering Figure in Movie Making, Is Dead," *New York Times,* 1 August 1987.

14. Quoted in Art Murphy, "Joe Levine Unchained, or, How *Hercules* Made Hollywood Tremble," *Swank,* n.d. [c. 1965], newspaper clipping in the Joseph E. Levine Collection, Howard Gotlieb Archival Research Center, Boston University.

15. Robert Sklar, *Movie-Made America: A Cultural History of American Movies* (New York: Vintage Books, 1994), 271.

16. Quoted in Bernard F. Dick, *The Merchant Prince of Poverty Row: Harry Cohn of Columbia Pictures* (Lexington: University Press of Kentucky, 2009), 8–14.

17. Richard Attenborough, introduction to Joseph E. Levine, *"A Bridge Too Far": Notes from a Filmmaker* (New York: Joseph E. Levine Presents, 1977), no pagination.

18. Peter Rosen to the author, personal correspondence, 6 February 2015.

19. Quoted in "Razzle Dazzle Showman," *New York Times,* 26 October 1965.

20. Paul O'Neil, "The Super Salesman of Super Colossals," *Life,* 27 July 1962.

21. Roy Frumkes, "Interview with Steve Reeves," *Perfect Vision*, 22 July 1994.

22. Interview with Tom Canford, *Hollow Square Press,* n.d., at http://www.hollowsquarepress.com/tattoo-1981.html (accessed 25 April 2016).

23. Quoted in Briget Byrne, "Jolting Joe Levine," *Women's Wear Daily,* 31 November 1981.

24. Tony Klinger to the author, personal correspondence, 13 August 2015.

25. Elizabeth Rosenberg to the author, personal correspondence, 5 September 2013.

26. Richard M. Nixon to Joseph E. Levine, 2 December 1968, Joseph E. Levine Collection, Howard Gotlieb Archival Research Center.

27. Quoted in Bob Sorolsky, "Whatever Became of All That Glamour?" *Philadelphia Bulletin,* 5 November 1978.

28. Maury Laws to the author, personal correspondence, 12 February 2014.

29. Tony Klinger to the author, 13 August 2015.

30. Quoted in Donna Rosenthal, "Self-Made Mogul Hangs On: Joseph E. Levine, 82, Is Still Wheeling and Dealing," *New York Times*, 5 July 1987.

31. Mort Drucker (artist) and Larry Siegal (writer), "*Mad* Visits Joe LeVenal: Hollywood's Latest Producing Genius," *Mad,* October 1961.

32. Harold Robbins, *The Inheritors* (New York: Pocket Books, 1971), 118, 122.

33. Quoted in Gary Arnold, "The Final Decision Will Be Mine: Joseph E. Levine Presents His 492d Movie Comeback," *Washington Post,* 15 June 1977, Style Sec.

34. Leo C. Rosten, *Hollywood: The Movie Colony, the Movie Makers* (New York: Harcourt, Brace, 1941), 163–64.

35. Philip Lopate, liner notes to *Contempt* (*Le Mépris,* 1963), DVD, Criterion Collection (New York: Criterion, 2002).

36. Paul Sherman, review of *Boccaccio 70* DVD, Turner Classic Movies (TCM), n.d., at http://www.tcmdb.com/title/title.jsp?stid=69274&atid=22766&category=Home%20Video%20Reviews&titleName=Boccaccio%20%6070&menuName=MAIN (accessed 21 January 2008).

37. J. W. Whitehead, *Mike Nichols and the Cinema of Transformation* (Jefferson, N.C.: McFarland, 2014), 36.

38. Dade Hayes and Jonathan Bing, *Open Wide: How Hollywood Box Office Became a National Obsession* (New York: Miramax Books, 2004), 232.

39. Ibid., 227–32; Steve Neale and Sheldon Hall, *Epics, Spectacles, and Blockbusters: A Hollywood History* (Detroit: Wayne State University Press, 2010); Pauline Small, *Sophia Loren: Moulding the Star* (Bristol, U.K.: Intellect Books, 2009); Tino Balio, *The Foreign Film Renaissance on American Screens, 1946–1973* (Madison: University of Wisconsin Press, 2010).

40. Sheldon Hall, *"Zulu": With Some Guts behind It—the Making of an Epic Movie* (Sheffield, U.K.: Tomahawk Press, 2005); P. B. Hurst, *The Most Savage Film: "Soldier Blue," Cinematic Violence, and the Horrors of War* (Jefferson, N.C.: McFarland, 2008).

41. Michael Caine, *What's It All About?* (London: Random House, 1992), 188.

42. Quoted in Arnold, "The Final Decision Will Be Mine."

43. Edward S. Feldman, with Tom Barton, *Tell Me How You Love the Picture: A Hollywood Producer's Hilarious Take on Life among the Stars* (Beverly Hills, Calif.: Creative Book Publishers International, 2007), 82.

44. Laws to the author, 12 February 2014.

45. Mel Brooks to the author, personal correspondence, 12 February 2014.

46. Brian Beacom, "The Bitch Is Back—but She's Not Scary at All," *Evening Times,* 6 March 2007.

47. Rosen to the author, 6 February 2015.

48. Quoted in Vernon Scott, "Movie Tycoon Shakes Off Retirement," *Nashua Telegraph,* 11 November 1974.

49. Klinger to the author, 13 August 2015.

50. Rosen to the author, 6 February 2015.

51. Feldman, *Tell Me How You Love the Picture,* 82.

52. Brooks to the author, 12 February 2014.

53. William Goldman, *The Story of "A Bridge Too Far"* (New York: Dell, 1977), unpaginated.

54. Quoted in James Powers, "Dialogue on Film," *American Film,* September 1979, 42.

55. Joseph E. Levine, "Ars Longa, Vita Brevis," *New York Times,* 8 October 1974.

56. Ibid., italics in the original.

1. Barefoot Boston Boy Becomes Movie Man

1. Quoted in Joseph A. MacDonald, "Report of the 11th Annual Dinner of the Old Time West Enders," Special Collections, West End Museum, Boston.

2. Quoted in Paul O'Neil, "The Super Salesman of Super Colossals," *Life,* 27 July 1962.

3. William A. Braverman, "The Emergence of a Unified Community, 1880–1917," in Jonathan D. Sarna, Ellen Smith, and Scott-Martin Kosofsky, eds., *The Jews of Boston* (New Haven, Conn.: Yale University Press, 2005), 66.

4. Quoted in Katherine Hamill, "The Supercolossal—Well, Pretty Good—World of Joe Levine," *Fortune,* March 1964.

5. MacDonald, "Report of the 11th Annual Dinner of the Old Time West Enders."

6. Quoted in Gay Talese, "Joe Levine Unchained: A Candid Portrait of a Spectacular Showman," *Esquire,* January 1961.

7. Quoted in Dick Griffin, "Levine: Huckster with a Heart," *Los Angeles Times,* 21 June 1966.

8. MacDonald, "Report of the 11th Annual Dinner of the Old Time West Enders."

9. Albert Maysles to the author, personal correspondence, 23 March 2007.

10. Quoted in O'Neil, "Super Salesman of Super Colossals."

11. Quoted in Hamill, "Supercolossal—Well, Pretty Good—World of Joe Levine."

12. Quoted in O'Neil, "Super Salesman of Supercolossals."

13. Quoted in Jonathan D. Sarna, "The Jews of Boston in Historical Perspective," in Sarna, Smith, and Kosofsky, *The Jews of Boston*, 9–10.

14. Ibid., 10–11.

15. Peter Dunn, "The Last Movie Mogul," *Sunday Times,* 5 February 1978.

16. Richard Attenborough and Diane Hawkins, *Entirely Up to You, Darling* (London: Hutchinson, 2008), 32–33.

17. Quoted in MacDonald, "Report of the 11th Annual Dinner of the Old Time West Enders."

18. Bernard F. Dick, *Hal Wallis: Producer to the Stars* (Lexington: University Press of Kentucky, 2004), 184–85.

19. Quoted in Talese, "Joe Levine Unchained."

20. Quoted in ibid.

21. Quoted in O'Neil, "Super Salesman of Super Colossals."

22. Quoted in Hamill, "Supercolossal—Well, Pretty Good—World of Joe Levine."

23. Quoted in Talese, "Joe Levine Unchained."

24. Quoted in ibid.

25. Quoted in Hamill, "Supercolossal—Well, Pretty Good—World of Joe Levine."

26. Quoted in Talese, "Joe Levine Unchained."

27. Quoted in O'Neil, "Super Salesman of Super Colossals."

28. Quoted in Hamill, "Supercolossal—Well, Pretty Good—World of Joe Levine."

29. Quoted in Talese, "Joe Levine Unchained."

30. Quoted in Hamill, "Supercolossal—Well, Pretty Good—World of Joe Levine."

31. Eric Schaeffer, *Bold! Daring! Shocking! True! A History of Exploitation Films, 1919–1959* (Durham, N.C.: Duke University Press, 1999), 111.

32. "Rosalie Gives Up Career for Joie," *Boston Times,* 20 June 1938.

33. Quoted in Hamill, "Supercolossal—Well, Pretty Good—World of Joe Levine."

34. Quoted in ibid.

2. Investing, Exploiting, Saturating

1. Elizabeth Rosenberg to the author, personal correspondence, 5 September 2013.

2. Hanson W. Baldwin, "Atom Bomb Wins Victory, but Sows Whirlwind," *Los Angeles Times,* 10 August 1945, 2.

3. Rosenberg to the author, 5 September 2013.

4. Quoted in "Old Movies Stand Test, Producer Says," *Rochester Times-Union,* 28 March 1946.

5. "Informing You," *Hartford Daily Courant,* 26 September 1945.

6. Untitled article, *Portland Evening Express,* 21 November 1945.

7. "Informing You."

8. Irv Kupcinent, "Kup's Column," *Chicago Times,* 29 October 1945.

9. G. K., "Old Times on Parade," *Los Angeles Times,* 8 June 1946.

10. Quoted in Paul O'Neil, "The Super Salesman of Super Colossals," *Life,* 27 July 1962.

11. Quoted in Katherine Hamill, "The Supercolossal—Well, Pretty Good—World of Joe Levine," *Fortune,* March 1964.

12. Quoted in ibid.

13. Quoted in Gay Talese, "Joe Levine Unchained: A Candid Portrait of a Spectacular Showman," *Esquire,* January 1961.

14. Quoted in O'Neil, "Super Salesman of Super Colossals."

15. Quoted in Talese, "Joe Levine Unchained."

16. Quoted in "Hollywood Inside," *Variety,* 14 April 1948.

17. Richard L. Coe, "Byrd–Marx Bill a Pair of Aces," *Washington Post,* 22 October 1948.

18. Bosley Crowther, "The Screen: Review of Byrd Voyage *The Secret Land,*" *New York Times,* 2 December 1948.

19. Frank Scully, "Scully's Scrapbook," *Variety,* 8 September 1948.

20. Quoted in Talese, "Joe Levine Unchained."

21. Eric Schaeffer, *Bold! Daring! Shocking! True! A History of Exploitation Films, 1919–1959* (Durham, N.C.: Duke University Press, 1999), 331.

22. Arthur L. Mayer, letter to the editor, *Los Angeles Times,* 24 November 1974.

23. Thomas Doherty, *Teenagers and Teenpics: The Juvenilization of American Movies in the 1950s* (Philadelphia: Temple University Press, 2002), 16–20.

24. Rosenberg to the author, 5 September 2013.

25. Quoted in Patrick Goldstein, "The Art of Horror Movies, from a King of the Genre," *Los Angeles Times,* 20 July 2003, at http://articles.latimes.com/2003/jul/29/entertainment/et-gold29.

26. For this rumor, see George Clarke, "Boy Film Star, 8, Has Fast Quip at Hub Greeting," *Boston Daily Record,* 14 December 1953.

27. Quoted in Robert Muller, "Breakfast with the Great Joe," *Daily Mail* (London), n.d. [c. 1961], clipping in the Joseph E. Levine File, British Film Institute, London, italics in original.

28. Quoted in O'Neil, "Super Salesman of Super Colossals."

29. Quoted in ibid.

30. Quoted in ibid.

31. Kerry Segrave, *Drive-In Theaters: A History from Their Inception in 1933* (Jefferson, N.C.: McFarland, 1993), 78.

32. Quoted in O'Neil, "Super Salesman of Super Colossals."

33. Talese, "Joe Levine Unchained."

34. Quoted in Sam Arkoff, with Richard Trubo, *Flying through Hollywood by the Seat of My Pants* (New York: Birch Lane Press, 1992), 39.

35. Quoted in Frank J. Taylor, "Big Boom in Outdoor Movies," in Gregory A. Waller, ed., *Moviegoing in America* (Malden, Mass.: Blackwell 2002), 251, originally published in *Saturday Evening Post,* 29 September 1956.

36. Arkoff, *Flying through Hollywood,* 7.

37. Ibid., 3.

38. Quoted in Jack Pitman, "The Saga of Joseph E. Levine: Brings Back Barnum Ballyhoo," *Variety,* 4 July 1962.

39. Quoted in Louella Parsons, "Joe Levine: How to Get into the Movie$," *Los Angeles Herald Examiner,* 20 September 1959, Pictorial Living Sec.

3. Monsters and Man-Gods

1. Lincoln Freeman, "The Comeback of the Movies," in Tino Balio, ed., *The American Film Industry* (Madison: University of Wisconsin Press, 1976), 377, originally published in *Fortune,* February 1955.

2. Quoted in "High Film Rentals Scored in Chicago: Goldenson Also Tells Theatre Owners' Meeting Shortage of Movies Hurts Industry," *New York Times,* 4 November 1953.

3. Steve Neale, "Hollywood Blockbusters: Historical Dimensions," in Julian Stringer, ed., *Movie Blockbusters* (London: Routledge, 2003), 48–52.

4. Berne Schneyer, "Showmanship: It Still Pays Off!" *Film Bulletin,* 20 July 1959, emphasis in original.

5. Ross Melnick, *American Showman: Samuel "Roxy" Rothafel and the Birth of the American Entertainment Industry, 1908–1935* (New York: Columbia University Press, 2012), 9.

6. Quoted in "Joe Unchained," *Time,* 24 February 1961, emphasis in original.

7. "Big Air Coin from Pix: *Hitler's Children* Seen as Starting New Bonanza with Ether Taking 40% of Budget," *The Billboard,* 8 May 1943.

8. Quoted in "Short Subjects," *Film Bulletin*, 25 August 1952.

9. Quoted in Dade Hayes and Jonathan Bing, *Open Wide: How Hollywood Box Office Became a National Obsession* (New York: Miramax Books, 2004), 149.

10. "Telecasting Notes," *Television Digest with Electronics Reports,* 2 May 1953.

11. "Unidentified Flying Objects," *Variety*, 25 April 1956.

12. Bosley Crowther, "Screen: Horror Import. *Godzilla,* a Japanese Film, Is at State," *New York Times,* 28 April 1956.

13. Quoted in Maria Matzer, "How *Godzilla* Made His Way to the US," *Los Angeles Times,* 22 May 1998.

14. Loren and Ponti were not fully married until 1966. They had a marriage ceremony in 1957, when Ponti was still married to his first wife, and they were not officially wed until 1966.

15. Louella Parsons, "Joe Levine: How to Get into the Movie$," *Los Angeles Herald Examiner,* 20 September 1959, Pictorial Living Sec. There are other accounts of the film's producers, Ponti and De Laurentiis, referring to *Attila* as "a dog"—see, for example, "A Simple Guy," *Newsweek,* 22 February 1960—yet one cannot discount the possibility that the story originated from Joe himself.

16. Bill Doll, "Boston's Joe Levine: A Profile," *Variety,* 1 April 1959.

17. "*Hercules* Reveals a Ballyhoo Strongman," *Film Bulletin,* 30 March 1959. "Watch charm" is a reference to Bert Metzger, a diminutive American football player who played in the guard position for the University of Notre Dame in the late 1920s.

18. Quoted in George W. Clarke, "TV to Exhaust All Films in 4 Yrs," *Boston Daily Record,* 19 April 1958.

19. Quoted in "A Simple Guy."

20. Quoted in Parsons, "Joe Levine."

21. Quoted in Art Cohn, *The Nine Lives of Mike Todd* (London: Hutchinson, 1959), 38, italics in original.

22. Oscar Godbout, "Hollywood Scene, Theatre-Owners Group Seeks Methods for More Profitable Exhibition," *New York Times,* 8 July 1956.

23. Quoted in "*Hercules* Reveals a Ballyhoo Strongman," emphasis in original.

24. Ibid.

25. Charles A. Aaronson, "Hard Sell 'Explodation' Party Gives *Hercules* Rousing Sendoff," *Motion Picture Herald,* 28 March 1959; "*Hercules* Reveals a Ballyhoo Strongman."

26. Quoted in Schneyer, "Showmanship."

27. Quoted in Aaronson, "Hard Sell 'Explodation' Party."

28. Quoted in "*Hercules* Reveals a Ballyhoo Strongman."

29. Aaronson, "Hard Sell 'Explodation' Party."

30. Quoted in ibid.

31. Ibid.

32. Dick Williams, "Muscular *Hercules* Is Raising Coin," *Mirror News,* 30 July 1959.

33. Quoted in Gay Talese, "Joe Levine Unchained: A Candid Portrait of a Spectacular Showman," *Esquire,* January 1961.

34. Quoted in Pat O'Haire, "This Levine Guy—He's a Real Joe," *Sunday News—New York's Picture Newspaper,* 29 September 1974. The only other change in Joe's spiel here is that "clerks" became "cab drivers."

35. Quoted in Robert Muller, "Breakfast with the Great Joe," *Daily Mail,* date illegible [c. 1961], clipping in the Joseph E. Levine File, British Film Institute, London.

36. Ibid.

37. Schneyer, "Showmanship."

38. Quoted in Aaronson, "Hard Sell 'Explodation' Party."

39. Philip K. Scheuer, "Meet Joe Levine, Super (Sales) Man!" *Los Angeles Times,* 27 July 1959.

40. Philip K. Scheuer, "This Hercules Just Tarzan in a Tunic," *Los Angeles Times,* 30 July 1959.

4. The Flim-Flam Man

1. Quoted in "A Simple Guy," *Newsweek,* 22 February 1960.

2. Quoted in "The Power of Cash," *Saturday Evening Post,* 30 December 1967.

3. Quoted in Steven M. L. Aronson, *Hype: The Names and Faces You Know so Well Will Never Look so Good to You Again* (New York: Morrow, 1983), 197. I have no figures for *Jack the Ripper;* it certainly did not do well, but, given Joe's fondness for hyperbole, it is possible that he could have been exaggerating the extent of its failure.

4. Robert E. Kapsis, *Hitchcock: The Making of a Reputation* (Chicago: University of Chicago Press, 1992), 23.

5. Quoted in "A Simple Guy."

6. Richard Nason, "*Hercules* Starts Flood Movies," *New York Times,* 24 October 1959.

7. Quoted in Katherine Hamill, "The Supercolossal—Well, Pretty Good—World of Joe Levine," *Fortune,* March 1964.

8. Robert Alden, "Advertising: Hard Sell for Motion Pictures," *New York Times,* 29 May 1960.

9. Mort Drucker (artist), and Larry Siegal (writer), "*Mad* Visits Joe LeVenal: Hollywood's Latest Producing Genius," *Mad,* October 1961.

10. "Hail Joe Levine, 'Pioneer of the Year,'" *Variety,* 16 August 1960.

11. Quoted in "Joe Levine: Pioneer of the Year," *Motion Picture Herald,* date illegible [c. November 1960], clipping in the Joseph E. Levine Collection, Howard Gotlieb Research Center, Boston University.

12. Tom Wolfe, introduction to *The Kandy-Kolored Tangerine-Flake Streamline Baby,* in Ronald Weber, ed., *The Reporter as Artist* (New York: Hastings House, 1974), 32–33.

13. Quoted in Gay Talese, "Joe Levine Unchained: A Candid Portrait of a Spectacular Showman," *Esquire,* January 1961.

14. Quoted in ibid.

15. Quoted in ibid.

16. Gay Talese to the author, personal correspondence, 25 April 2014.

17. Ibid.

18. Talese, "Joe Levine Unchained."

19. Drucker and Siegal, "*Mad* Visits Joe LeVenal," emphasis in original.

20. Ibid., emphasis in original.

21. Edward S. Feldman, with Tom Barton, *Tell Me How You Love the Picture: A Hollywood Producer's Hilarious Take on Life among the Stars* (Beverly Hills, Calif.: Creative Book Publishers International, 2007), 75.

22. Ibid., 75–82.

23. Bosley Crowther, "Putting Movies Across," *New York Times,* 12 April 1959.

24. Bosley Crowther, "Spears and Sandals: Flood of Cheap Costume Films Causes Dismay," *New York Times,* 12 March 1961.

25. Talese, "Joe Levine Unchained."

26. Quoted in David Nathan, "The Man Who Sold *Hercules,*" *Daily Herald* (London), 7 December 1960.

27. Ibid.

28. Mrs. N. I. Klien, letter to the editor, *Life,* 17 August 1962.

29. Skirmante Makaitis, letter to the editor, *Life*, 17 August 1962.

30. "Open Letter to Joseph E. Levine," *Variety,* 7 April 1965, Personals, emphasis and ellipses in original.

5. The Showman in the Art House

1. Pierre Bourdieu, *Distinction: A Social Critique of the Judgement of Taste* (Cambridge, Mass.: Harvard University Press, 2002), 56–57.

2. Art Cohn, *The Nine Lives of Mike Todd* (London: Hutchinson, 1959), 81–82.

3. Dick Griffin, "Levine: Huckster with a Heart," *Los Angeles Times,* 21 June 1966.

4. Bourdieu, *Distinction,* 57.

5. Eric Schaeffer, *Bold! Daring! Shocking! True! A History of Exploitation Films, 1919–1959* (Durham, N.C.: Duke University Press, 1999), 332–37.

6. Barbara Wilinsky, *Sure Seaters: The Emergence of Arthouse Cinema* (Minneapolis: University of Minnesota Press, 2001), 2.

7. "Metro Hypos Financing of Foreign Production," *Variety,* 26 April 1960.

8. Gay Talese, "Joe Levine Unchained: A Candid Portrait of a Spectacular Showman," *Esquire,* January 1961.

9. Howard Thompson, "Screen: *Where the Hot Wind Blows* Review," *New York Times,* 12 November 1960.

10. Philip K. Scheuer, "Hybrid *Hot Wind:* Art of Box Office?" *Los Angeles Times,* 9 October 1960.

11. Anna Magnani to Irving Lazar, telex, 30 July 1958, George Cukor Collection, Association of Motion Picture Arts and Sciences, Margaret Herrick Library, Beverly Hills, Calif.

12. Edward S. Feldman, with Tom Barton, *Tell Me How You Love the Picture: A Hollywood Producer's Hilarious Take on Life among the Stars* (Beverly Hills, Calif.: Creative Book Publishers International, 2007), 81.

13. Arthur Knight, "For Eggheads Only?" in Robert Hughes, ed., *Film Book 1: The Audience and the Filmmaker* (New York: Grove Press, 1959), 26.

14. Quoted in Paul O'Neil, "The Super Salesman of Super Colossals," *Life,* 27 July 1962.

15. Quoted in "Levine Going Arty; to Drop Spear and Sandals Films," *Variety,* 9 November 1961.

16. Review of *La Ciel et la boue, Variety,* 10 May 1961.

17. Stanley W. Penn, "New Movie Makers," *Wall Street Journal,* 17 January 1963.

18. Sam Lesner, "Levine on *8½,* Other Projects," *Chicago Daily News,* date illegible [c. 1963], clipping in the Joseph E. Levine Collection, Howard Gotlieb Research Center, Boston University.

19. Quoted in ibid.

20. Review of *Boccaccio 70, Hollywood Reporter,* 30 July 1962.

21. Catholic Legion of Decency, report on *Boccaccio 70,* 30 August 1962, Association of Motion Picture Arts and Sciences, Margaret Herrick Library.

22. Quoted in O'Neil, "Super Salesman of Super Colossals."

23. Dwight Macdonald, "Mr. Goldwyn and Mr. Levine," in *On Movies* (New York: De Capo Press, 1981), 131.

24. Dwight Macdonald, "Masscult and Midcult," in *Masscult and Midcult: Essays against the American Grain,* ed. John Summers (New York: New York Review of Books, 2011), 3–71.

25. Dwight Macdonald, "Films of the Quarter," *Film Quarterly* 16, no. 1 (1962): 62.

26. Dale Luciano, "*Long Day's Journey into Night:* An Interview with Sidney Lumet," *Film Quarterly* 25, no. 1 (1971): 20–29.

27. Quoted in Mark Harris, *Pictures at a Revolution: Five Movies and the Birth of the New Hollywood* (London: Penguin, 2008), 72.

28. Quoted in Macdonald, "Mr. Goldwyn and Mr. Levine," 130.

29. Dwight Macdonald, "No Art and No Box Office," *Esquire,* March 1959, 66.

30. Bourdieu, *Distinction,* 91.

31. Eugene Archer, "*Wonders of Aladdin* at Two Theatres," *New York Times,* 23 December 1961.

32. Bosley Crowther, "Screen: Sophia Loren in Old Form, She Is Impressive in de Sica's *Two Women,*" *New York Times,* 9 May 1961.

33. Bosley Crowther, "A Quizzical Paradox: Is It Really Boom or Is It Bust in the Field of Foreign Films?" *New York Times,* 7 June 1964.

34. "Takeoff Schedule on Embassy Pix," *Variety,* 6 March 1963.

35. "I'm sorry to disappoint Moravia, but I haven't read *Ulysses,*" was Fellini's response to the comparison (quoted in "Interview with Contanzo Costantini, 1963," in Charles Affron, ed., *Rutgers Films in Print: 8½* [New Brunswick, N.J.: Rutgers, 1987], 243).

36. "Joe Levine 'Shakes' on *La Dolce Vita* (*High Life Hobos*)," *Variety,* 12 October 1960.

37. "Astor Newest Claimant to US Rights to Controversial Italo Pic," *Variety,* 20 January 1961.

38. "For Immediate Release," *Variety,* 29 April 1963.

39. Bosley Crowther, "Screen: Fellini's Contemplation of a Director's Life; *8½* Is Showing at the Festival Theater; Japanese Film Opens at New Yorker," *New York Times,* 26 June 1963.

40. Dwight Macdonald, "Films of the Quarter," *Film Quarterly* 17, no. 1 (Autumn 1963): 51–55.

41. Quoted in Peter Dunn, "The Last Movie Mogul," *Sunday Times,* 5 February 1978.

42. Quoted in Steven M. L. Aronson, *Hype: The Names and Faces You Know so Well Will Never Look so Good to You Again* (New York: Morrow, 1983), 196–97, emphasis in original.

43. Quoted in ibid.

44. Anonymous source quoted in Calvin Tomkins, "Profiles: The Very Rich Hours of Joe Levine," *New Yorker,* 16 September 1967.

45. Wyndham Lewis, *The Apes of God* (New York: McBride, 1932), 255.

46. Stephen Taylor, "After the Nouvelle Vague," *Film Quarterly* 18, no. 3 (1965): 5.

47. F. W. Kent, *Lorenzo de Medici and the Art of the Magnificent* (Baltimore: Johns Hopkins University Press, 2007), 3.

48. Quoted in Murray Schumach, "Joseph E. Levine Says Making of Art Films for US Is Risky," *New York Times,* 6 December 1963.

49. Quoted in Harris, *Pictures at a Revolution,* 72.

50. Quoted in William Tusher, "Levine's Nix to Family Pix," *Film Daily,* 30 June 1967.

6. The Showman on the Screen

1. Quoted in Calvin Tomkins, "Profiles: The Very Rich Hours of Joe Levine," *New Yorker,* 16 September 1966, emphasis in original.

2. Peter Rosen to the author, personal correspondence, 6 February 2015.

3. Albert Maysles to the author, personal correspondence, 23 March 2007.

4. Quoted in "Instant Films," *Sunday Telegraph,* 23 February 1964.

5. Quoted in Maysles to the author, 23 March 2007.

6. Steven Alan Carr, *Hollywood and Anti-Semitism: A Cultural History 1880–1941* (Cambridge: Cambridge University Press, 2001), 283.

7. Maysles to the author, 23 March 2007.

8. Edward S. Feldman, with Tom Barton, *Tell Me How You Love the Picture: A Hollywood Producer's Hilarious Take on Life among the Stars* (Beverly Hills, Calif.: Creative Book Publishers International, 2007), 79.

9. Quoted in Peter Dunn, "The Last Movie Mogul," *Sunday Times,* 5 February 1978.

10. Jonas Mekas, "Movie Journal," *Village Voice,* 11 April 1963.

11. Ibid.

12. Quoted in Dunn, "The Last Movie Mogul."

13. Maysles to the author, 23 March 2007.

14. Gerald Peary, "The Maysles Brothers," *Boston Review,* October 1990, at http://www.geraldpeary.com/essays/mno/maysles.html.

15. Stephen Mamber, *Cinema Verite in America: Studies in Uncontrolled Documentary* (Cambridge, Mass.: MIT Press, 1974), 145.

16. Simon Plant, "The Watcher," *Herald-Sun* (Melbourne), 13 September 2003, Weekend Sec.

17. Jonathan B. Vogels, *The Direct Cinema of the Maysles Brothers* (Carbondale: Southern Illinois University Press, 2005), 30.

18. Maysles to the author, 23 March 2007.

19. Jacques Aumont, "The Fall of the Gods," in Susan Hayward and Ginette Vincendeau, eds., *French Film: Texts and Contexts* (London: Routledge, 1990), 176.

20. Edward S. Feldman, "A Look at Levine's Future Films," *Variety,* 8 February 1961.

21. "Joe Unchained," *Time,* 24 February 1961.

22. Quoted in Paul O'Neil, "The Super Salesman of Super Colossals," *Life*, 27 July 1962.

23. Christopher Frayling, *Sergio Leone: Something to Do with Death* (London: Faber and Faber, 2000), 114, 115.

24. Ibid., 115–16.

25. Alberto Moravia, *A Ghost at Noon* (1955; reprint, Middlesex, U.K.: Penguin, 1976); the novel's original title is *Il Disprezzo* (1954).

26. Robert Stam, commentary on *Contempt* (*Le Mépris,* 1963), DVD, Criterion Collection (New York: Criterion, 2002).

27. Moravia, *A Ghost at Noon,* 131, 66.

28. William MacAdams, *Ben Hecht: The Man behind the Legend* (New York: Scribner's, 1990), 260.

29. Frayling, *Sergio Leone,* 118.

30. Jean-Luc Godard, "*Le Mépris,*" in *Godard on Godard,* ed. Jean Narboni and Tom Milne, trans. Tom Milne (London: Secker and Warburg, 1972), 200–201, originally published in *Cahiers du Cinema* 146 (August 1963).

31. Quoted in Peter Lev, *The Euro-American Cinema* (Austin: University of Texas Press, 1993), 83.

32. Simone de Beauvoir, *Brigitte Bardot and the Lolita Syndrome* (New York: Reynal, 1960).

33. Interview with Raoul Coutard, *Contempt* Criterion DVD.

34. Moravia, *A Ghost at Noon,* 66.

35. James Verniere, "Film Shows Comic Contempt for the Industry," *Boston Herald,* 22 August 1997.

36. "Godard Only Knows" (review), *Observer,* 26 November 2000.

37. Todd Camp, "A Celluloid Contender: Dallas Film Festival Shows It's Ready to Play with the Big Boys," *Fort Worth Star-Telegram,* 18 April 1997.

38. Philip Lopate, liner notes to *Contempt* Criterion DVD.

39. Colin MacCabe, *Godard: Portrait of the Artist at 70* (London: Bloomsbury, 2004), 153.

40. Ibid., 154–55.

41. Ibid.

42. "Godard Deplores Distribs Tendency to Duck Film Festivals," *Variety,* 14 August 1963.

43. "Very Little Left for Production," *Variety,* 14 August 1963.

44. "Plot to Rub Out Dub," *Variety,* 14 August 1963.

45. Godard, "*Le Mépris,*" 209.

46. Review of *Contempt, New Republic,* 2 January 1965.

47. Review of *Contempt, Motion Picture Herald,* 23 December 1964.

48. Review of *Contempt, New Yorker,* 26 December 1964.

49. Review of *Contempt, Time,* 8 January 1965.

50. Review of *Contempt, New Republic.*

51. Godard, "*Le Mépris,*" 209.

52. Quoted in Mark Jenkins, "His Master's Voice: Joel E. Seigel 1940–2004," *Washington City Paper,* 19 March 2004, at http://www.washingtoncitypaper.com/articles/28253/his-masters-voice.

53. Quoted in Robert Lipsyte, "Museum Salutes Levine for Films," *New York Times,* 26 October 1965.

54. Quoted in Tomkins, "Profiles," emphasis in original.

55. Verniere, "Film Shows Comic Contempt for the Industry."

56. Desson Howe, "*Contempt* Film Fatale," *Washington Post,* 25 July 1997, Weekend Sec.

57. Lopate, liner notes to *Contempt* Criterion DVD.

7. Bad Taste in Hollywood

1. Edward S. Feldman, with Tom Barton, *Tell Me How You Love the Picture: A Hollywood Producer's Hilarious Take on Life among the Stars* (Beverly Hills, Calif.: Creative Book Publishers International, 2007), 107.

2. Mark A. Viera, "Horror Queens: Divas from Hollywood's Golden Age Rampage through the Sixties," *Bright Lights Film Journal,* 31 October 2004, at http://brightlightsfilm.com/46/horror.php#.U_2a7WPEkr4.

3. Feldman, *Tell Me How You Love the Picture,* 82.

4. Quoted in Hazel Flynn, "We Help Joe Levine Start *Where Love,*" *Citizen News,* 6 December 1964.

5. Quoted in "Producer-Distributor Levine Finds Two Hats Enough; to Sell Theatres," *Motion Picture Exhibitor,* 12 February 1964.

6. Quoted in Katherine Hamill, "The Supercolossal—Well, Pretty Good—World of Joe Levine," *Fortune,* March 1964.

7. Murray Schumach, "The Gaudy Career of Jonas Cord," *New York Times,* 25 June 1961.

8. Bernard F. Dick, *Engulfed: The Death of Paramount Pictures and the Birth of Corporate Hollywood* (Lexington: University Press of Kentucky, 2001), 80.

9. Murray Schumach, "Freeman Gives Up Paramount Post," *New York Times,* 18 May 1959.

10. Peter Bart, "Hollywood Package: Production Formation Probed by a Master," *New York Times,* 9 August 1964.

11. Andrew Wilson, *Harold Robbins: The Man Who Invented Sex* (London: Bloomsbury, 2008), 124.

12. Quoted in Andrew Wilson, *Harold Robbins: The Man Who Invented Sex* (London: Bloomsbury, 2008), 3.

13. "*Tropic Cancer* Like *Carpetbaggers* Covets Shurlock's Production Seal," *Variety,* 29 December 1962, 4.

14. Quoted in "They Yelled No!" *Los Angeles Herald Examiner,* 31 May 1964.

15. Quoted in "Robbins' Egg-Blue," *Newsweek,* 6 July 1964.

16. Quoted in Carroll Baker, *Baby Doll: An Autobiography* (London: Allen, 1984), 237.

17. Geoffrey M. Shurlock to Edward Schellhorn, 5 April 1963, Motion Picture Association of America Files, Association of Motion Picture Arts and Sciences (AMPAS), Margaret Herrick Library, Beverly Hills, Calif.

18. Geoffrey M. Shurlock to Edward Schellhorn, 13 April 1963, Motion Picture Association of America Files, AMPAS.

19. "Newsmakers," *Newsweek,* 8 July 1963.

20. "She's for Foreign Eyes Only," *Variety,* 15 July 1964.

21. Thomas Thompson, "Small-Bore Talents in Big Bore," *Life,* 26 June 1964.

22. Bosley Crowther, "Screen: *The Carpetbaggers* Opens: Adaptation of Book by Robbins in Debut," *New York Times,* 2 July 1964.

23. Susan Sontag, "Notes on Camp," in *Against Interpretation* (London: Penguin Classics, 2009), 289.

24. Philip K. Sheuer, "*Carpetbaggers* in Bad Taste as Film," *Los Angeles Times,* 5 June 1964.

25. "How to Start at the Top and Succeed," *Cosmopolitan,* June 1964.

26. Sontag, "Notes on Camp," 276.

8. Hollywood Undermined

1. Federico Fellini, "Open Letter to Joe Levine," *Variety,* 22 April 1964.

2. Vittorio de Sica, "Director's Idea of Typecasting," *Variety,* 22 April 1964.

3. Edward Dmytryk, "Director's Findings: Good Drama Made for Strong Merchandizing," *Variety,* 22 April 1964.

4. Stanley Baker, "A Handshake Deal That Paid Off," *Variety,* 22 April 1964.

5. George Weltner, "Par's Commercial for Joe Levine's Showmanship: A $30,000,000 Bankroll," *Variety,* 22 April 1964.

6. Geoffrey Shurlock to Sol Schwartz, 27 March 1963, Motion Picture Association of America (MPAA) Files, Association of Motion Picture Arts and Sciences (AMPAS), Margaret Herrick Library, Beverly Hills, Calif.

7. Quoted in "There'll Be a Nude (Natch) in Biopic of Polly Adler," *Variety,* 8 April 1964.

8. Bosley Crowther, "Moral Brinkmanship: Legion of Decency Makes a Point but Doesn't Support It Well," *New York Times,* 13 December 1964.

9. Peter Bart, "Producers Rush 3 Harlow Films: Carroll Baker Announced for Title Role by Levine," *New York Times,* 1 September 1964.

10. Quoted in "Now Hear This! Harlow Pic to Be in Good Taste—Levine," *Hollywood Reporter,* 17 December 1964.

11. Bosley Crowther, "Bad Taste in Films: More Cheapness and Vulgarity Appear," *New York Times,* 6 September 1964.

12. Bosley Crowther, "A Time to Face Facts," *New York Times,* 14 March 1965.

13. E. G. Dougherty, note to files, MPAA Office, Re: *Harlow,* 22 December 1964, MPAA Files, AMPAS.

14. Geoffrey Shurlock to Erwin Gelsey, 1 March 1964, MPAA Files, AMPAS.

15. Geoffrey M. Shurlock to Erwin Gelsey, 9 February 1965, MPAA Files, AMPAS.

16. Geoffrey M. Shurlock to Erwin Gelsey, 8 July 1964, MPAA Files, AMPAS.

17. Quoted in "Now Hear This! Harlow Pic to Be in Good Taste—Levine."

18. Minutes of *Harlow* story conference, 3 February 1965, Irene Kamp Collection, AMPAS.

19. Sydney Boehm to Mary Dorfman, 20 March 1965, Irene Kamp Collection, AMPAS, emphasis in original.

20. Richard G. Hubler, "*Harlow:* Script a 'Hack,'" *Los Angeles Times,* 28 June 1964.

21. Cecil Smith, "Crane Flying High Nightly," *New York Times,* 5 August 1964.

22. Hedda Hopper, "Jean Harlow New Literary Target," *Los Angeles Times,* 3 July 1964.

23. "Jean Harlow's Father Sues over Book," *New York Times,* 24 November 1964.

24. "$5 Million Damages Suit Filed over *Harlow* Book," *New York Times,* 1 May 1965.

25. "Shulman Tells All—or Nearly All," *Variety,* 27 January 1965.

26. "Shulman Shot an Arrow into the Air—Levine Brings It Down with a Flare," *Hollywood Reporter,* 25 February 1965.

27. Minutes of *Harlow* story conference, 3 February 1965, Irene Kamp Collection, AMPAS.

28. Eugene H. Frank, Paramount interoffice communication, 9 December 1964, Paramount Collection, AMPAS.

29. Quoted in "*Harlow* March Start on Electronovision," *Film Daily,* 19 January 1965.

30. Bill Ornstein, "Electronovision to Make 12 Pics at $7.5 Mil Cost," *Hollywood Reporter,* 19 January 1965.

31. Clipping of unknown article from *Life,* 7 May 1965, *Harlow* Clippings File, Margaret Herrick Library.

32. Quoted in Ronald Gold, "Levine Best Showman since L. B. Mayer," *Variety,* 14 April 1965.

33. Quoted in "Electronovision Has Ferrer for *Harlow,*" *Hollywood Reporter,* 25 February 1965.

34. Quoted in "Wallace Airs 'Harlow' Producers' Views on Juxtaposed Radio Tapes," *Variety,* 12 May 1965.

35. Howard W. Koch, Paramount interoffice memo, 5 October 1964, Paramount Collection, AMPAS.

36. Quoted in "Wallace Airs 'Harlow' Producers' Views."

37. Quoted in ibid.

38. Quoted in Philip K. Scheuer, "One + One Adds Up to Trouble," *Los Angeles Times,* 2 May 1965.

39. "NY Critics Rip into Electrono *Harlow,*" *Variety,* 19 May 1965.

40. Philip K. Scheuer, "Harlow Story—One Down, One to Go," *Los Angeles Times,* 12 May 1965.

41. Bosley Crowther, "Movie Based on Book by Shulman Opens," *New York Times,* 22 July 1965.

42. Minutes of *Harlow* story conference, 3 February 1965, Irene Kamp Collection, AMPAS.

43. Ibid.

44. Philip K. Scheuer, "*Harlow* Story Told Again—Less Cheaply," *Los Angeles Times,* 12 August 1965.

45. Ibid.

46. Quoted in Mike Fessier Jr., "Wheeling and Dealing with Bill Sargent," *Los Angeles Magazine,* 25 July 1965.

47. Richard Schickel, "Another Sock at an Aging Legend," *Life,* 25 March 1966.

48. Richard Davis, "Review of *The Oscar,*" *Films and Filming,* July 1966.

49. Philip K. Scheuer, "A Behind-Scenes View of What Makes *Oscar* Run," *Los Angeles Times,* 12 September 1965.

50. Philip K. Scheuer, "*Oscar* Runs Close Second to Sammy," *Los Angeles Times,* 16 February 1966.

51. Bosley Crowther, "Screen: *Oscar* Arrives," *New York Times,* 5 March 1966.

52. Bosley Crowther, "Is Hollywood Killing Itself?" *New York Times,* 13 March 1966.

9. The Scattergun Approach

1. Quoted in Katherine Hamill, "The Supercolossal—Well, Pretty Good—World of Joe Levine," *Fortune,* March 1964, 185.

2. Sheldon Hall, *"Zulu": With Some Guts behind It—the Making of the Epic Movie* (Sheffield, U.K.: Tomahawk Press, 2005), 131.

3. Quoted in Paul O'Neil, "The Super Salesman of Super Colossals," *Life,* 27 July 1962.

4. Quoted in Hall, *"Zulu,"* 83.

5. Ibid., 132.

6. Joseph E. Levine to Cy Endfield and Stanley Baker, 7 May 1963, Paramount Collection, Association of Motion Picture Arts and Sciences (AMPAS), Collections and Files, Margaret Herrick Library, Beverly Hills, Calif.

7. Stanley Baker to Joseph E. Levine, 16 May 1963, Paramount Collection, AMPAS.

8. R. H. Harrison to Jack Karp, 30 April 1963, Paramount Collection, AMPAS.

9. Colin Lesslie to Ken Hargreaves, telex, 25 April 1963, Paramount Collection, AMPAS.

10. Quoted in Hamill, "Supercolossal—Well, Pretty Good—World of Joe Levine."

11. Bosley Crowther, "Screen: *Darling* Is Selfish, Fickle, and Ambitious," *New York Times,* 4 August 1965.

12. Ray Galton and Alan Simpson to the author, personal correspondence, 23 May 2006.

13. Tino Balio, *United Artists: The Company That Changed the Film Industry* (Madison: University of Wisconsin Press, 1987), 231–32.

14. Paramount did distribute the U.K. production *Jack the Ripper* in 1960.

15. "Latest in Levine–Paramount Deals: Par Distribs Two Pix in Britain," *Variety,* 6 May 1964.

16. Dalton Trumbo to Joseph E. Levine, telegram, 18 February 1965, John Huston Collection, AMPAS.

17. John Huston to Jules Buck, 12 February 1966, John Huston Collection, AMPAS.

18. Quoted in "Embassy Expanding Operations; Levine Will Give More Time to Production," *Hollywood Reporter,* 2 August 1965.

19. Quoted in Bob Consadine, "Rosy Future for Films," *Los Angeles Herald Examiner,* 26 November 1969.

20. "Levine Budgets 8 Embassy Pix at $18 Mil in Next 6 Months," *Variety,* 10 August 1966.

21. Maury Laws to the author, personal correspondence, 12 February 2014.

22. Quoted in Wendy L. Marshall, *William Beaudine: From Silents to Television* (Lanham, Md.: Scarecrow Press, 2005), 280.

23. "Levine Plans 20 Low Budget Features to Be Made Here," *Hollywood Reporter,* 13 May 1965.

24. Charles Champlin, "TV Off and Running in High-Paying Movie Stakes," *Los Angeles Times,* 5 September 1965.

25. "Berle figures he was done in by CBS's new *Friday Night at the Movies* which teed off with *The Music Man* in two parts on successive evenings, the final one against Berle's second show of the season. Even if he had signed up Gen. Eisenhower, Bob Hope and the late Al Jolson as guests, says Berle, it wouldn't have done him any good" (Hal Humphrey, "Movies Bring End to Miltie's Return," *Los Angeles Times,* 3 November 1966).

26. Jack Gould, "Silver Screen Is a Gold Mine," *New York Times,* 7 January 1968.

27. Jack Gould, "TV Faces a Fight on Moviemaking," *New York Times,* 23 October 1967.

28. George W. Clarke, "TV to Exhaust All Films in 4 Yrs," *Boston Daily Record,* 19 April 1958.

29. Champlin, "TV Off and Running in High-Paying Movie Stakes."

30. "Embassy in Product Tie-Up with UK Firm," *Film Daily,* 24 March 1965. See also "Levine and Maxwell in Co-production Deal for Theaters, TV," *Hollywood Reporter,* 29 March 1965.

31. Bernard F. Dick, *Engulfed: The Death of Paramount Pictures and the Birth of Corporate Hollywood* (Lexington: University Press of Kentucky, 2001), 61.

32. Quoted in Charles Champlin, "Levine: Maestro of Hoopla, Hope," *Los Angeles Times,* 2 June 1967.

33. Minutes of *Harlow* story conference, 3 February 1965, Irene Kamp Collection, AMPAS.

10. Graduating Class

1. Sybil Burton, "Euripedes and the Establishment: Film Producer Puts His Money Where His (Legit) Enthusiasm Is," *Variety,* 22 April 1964.

2. Barney Lefferts, "Now the Mike Nichols Touch," *New York Times,* 22 November 1964.

3. Lawrence Turman to the author, personal correspondence, 8 March 2006.

4. "Levine Budgets 8 Embassy Pix at $18 Mil in Next 6 Months," *Variety,* 10 August 1966.

5. Ibid.

6. Quoted in Bert Cardullo, *Vittorio de Sica: Actor, Director, Auteur* (Newcastle-on-Tyne, U.K.: Cambridge Scholars Press, 2009), 192.

7. "Levine Has 'No Comment' on Mad Sq. Merger, Plenty on Other Topics," *Variety,* 29 March 1967.

8. Quoted in Mark Harris, *Pictures at a Revolution: Five Movies and the Birth of the New Hollywood* (London: Penguin, 2008), 71.

9. "The Producer: Joseph E. Levine," in Joseph McBride, ed., *Filmmakers on Filmmaking: The American Film Institute Seminars on Motion Pictures and Television* (Los Angeles: Tarcher, 1983), 30.

10. Larry Turman, *So You Want to Be a Producer?* (New York: Three Rivers Press, 2005), 195.

11. Turman to the author, 8 March 2006.

12. Julian Schlossberg, "Remembering Joe Levine," *Variety,* 28 October 1996. "Jack" refers to studio head Jack L. Warner.

13. Quoted in Calvin Tomkins, "Profiles: The Very Rich Hours of Joe Levine," *New Yorker,* 16 September 1967.

14. Quoted in Charles Champlin, "Levine, Maestro of Hoopla, Hope," *Los Angeles Times,* 2 June 1967.

15. Robert Sklar, *Movie-Made America: A Cultural History of American Movies* (New York: Vintage Books, 1994), 301.

16. Bosley Crowther, "Shoot-Em Up Film Opens World Fete: *Bonnie and Clyde* Cheered by Montreal First-Nighters," *New York Times,* 7 August 1967; "Screen: *Bonnie and Clyde* Arrives. Careers of Murderers Pictured as Farce," *New York Times,* 14 August 1967; and "Run *Bonnie and Clyde,*" *New York Times,* 3 September 1967, Arts and Leisure Sec.

17. Peter Biskind, *Easy Riders, Raging Bulls: How the Sex–Drugs–and–Rock 'n' Roll Generation Saved Hollywood* (London: Bloomsbury, 1999), 39–40.

18. Dwight Macdonald, "Films of the Quarter," *Film Quarterly* 17, no. 1 (1963): 55.

19. Quoted in Greg Kilday, "Influential Film Critic Andrew Sarris Dies at 83," *Hollywood Reporter*, 20 June 2012.

20. Quoted in William Tusher, "Levine's Nix to Family Pix," *Film Daily*, 30 June 1967.

21. "The Shock of Freedom in Films," *Time*, 8 December 1967, at http://www.time.com/time/magazine/article/0,9171,844256,00.html.

22. Turman to the author, 8 March 2006.

23. Turman, *So You Want to Be a Producer?* 210.

24. Stanley Kaufman, "Stanley Kaufman on Films," *New Republic*, 23 December 1967.

25. Andrew Sarris, review of *The Graduate*, *Village Voice*, 20 December 1973.

26. Hollis Alpert, "*The Graduate* Makes Out," *Saturday Review*, 6 July 1968.

27. Biskind, *Easy Riders, Raging Bulls*, 49.

28. "Embassy May Merge/Go Public," *Hollywood Reporter*, 31 May 1967.

29. Quoted in Abel Green, "Levine's Post-grad Aura: How a Hit Pic Restores Tone," *Variety*, 3 April 1968.

30. Turman to the author, 8 March 2006.

11. Selling Up and Winning Trophies

1. Vincent Canby, "And in Hollywood, Mergers Are Better Than Ever as Business Community Finds a New Area of Investment," *New York Times*, 9 January 1967.

2. Quoted in "Levine Has 'No-Comment' on Mad Sq. Merger, Plenty on Other Topics," *Variety*, 29 March 1967.

3. Peter Bart, "New Hollywood: New Riches, New Doubts," *New York Times*, 12 December 1966.

4. Quoted in Katherine Hamill, "The Supercolossal—Well, Pretty Good—World of Joe Levine," *Fortune*, March 1964.

5. James R. Kerr, "Billions Make a Nice Cushion or, AVCO Goes to Embassy Movies," *Variety*, 13 November 1968.

6. Tony Klinger to the author, personal correspondence, 13 August 2015.

7. Kerr, "Billions Make a Nice Cushion."

8. James Robert Parish, *It's Good to Be the King: The Seriously Funny Life of Mel Brooks* (Hoboken, N.J.: Wiley, 2007), 174.

9. Mel Brooks to the author, personal correspondence, 12 February 2014.

10. Ibid.

11. Parish, *It's Good to Be the King*, 174.

12. Quoted in Gene Wilder, *Kiss Me Like a Stranger: My Search for Love and Art* (New York: St Martin's Press, 2005), 103.

13. Quoted in Parish, *It's Good to Be the King*, 180.

14. Ibid., 181.

15. Renata Adler, review of *The Producers, New York Times,* 19 March 1968.

16. Brooks to the author, 12 February 2014.

17. Ibid.

18. Quoted in Guy Flatley, "Peter O'Toole, From 'Lawrence' to 'La Mancha,'" *New York Times,* 17 September 1972.

19. Kerr, "Billions Make a Nice Cushion."

20. "Embassy's Profits Estimated by Avco," *New York Times,* 21 May 1968.

21. Joyce Haber, "Joe Levine: Call Him Flamboyant," *Los Angeles Times,* 13 May 1968.

22. *Variety,* 13 November 1968.

12. The Corporate Gadabout

1. Quoted in Howard Kessel, "Joseph E. Levine Presents: Himself," *Women's Wear Daily,* 14 December 1973.

2. Tino Balio, "Introduction to Part II," in Tino Balio, ed., *Hollywood in the Age of Television* (London: Unwin Hyman, 1990), 259.

3. Thomas Schatz, "The New Hollywood," in Julian Stringer, ed., *Movie Blockbusters* (London: Routledge, 2003), 22.

4. Quoted in Hank Werba, "Joe Levine's Gearing More Pix for Those in 16–30 Age Bracket," *Variety,* 8 October 1969.

5. Quoted in Vernon Scott, "'I Dig Kids' Says Joe Levine," *Citizen News,* 2 May 1970.

6. Quoted in Calvin Tomkins, "Profiles: The Very Rich Hours of Joe Levine," *New Yorker,* 16 September 1967.

7. Michael Klinger to Joseph E. Levine, 29 March 1972, Michael Klinger Papers, University of the West of England, Bristol.

8. Examiner's report for *That Kind of Girl,* 5 April 1962, *That Kind of Girl* File, Papers, British Board of Film Classification, London.

9. Tony Klinger to the author, personal correspondence, 13 August 2015.

10. "Open points which have been a matter of discussion with Paul Baumgarten [of Avco-Embassy] to date," undated memo, 1968, Michael Klinger Papers.

11. Klinger to the author, 13 August 2015.

12. Linda Hayden, interview by the author and Andrew Spicer, 14 February 2011, London.

13. Ibid.

14. Klinger to the author, 13 August 2015.

15. Ibid.

16. James Brady, "Interview with Joe Levine," *New York Magazine,* 17 December 1973.

17. Quoted in Peter Dunn, "The Last Movie Mogul," *Sunday Times,* 5 February 1978.

18. "1911 Hupmobile and Other Antique Cars Bring $135,000 at Auction," *New York Times,* 23 November 1969.

19. Charlotte Curtis, "$15-Million Art Sale Falls Short," *New York Times,* 11 June 1969.

20. Robert Thomas Jr., "To Mrs. Levine, a Peacock Ball without Jewels," *New York Times,* 30 April 1971.

21. Quoted in Enid Nemy, "A Pleasure Ground Named Xanadu Welcomes Members to a Sunny Sea," *New York Times,* 30 November 1969.

22. Charlotte Curtis, "Off to Bermuda—for a Bite of Lunch," *New York Times,* 14 January 1972.

23. "Levine Aids Yale Theatre," *New York Times,* 18 January 1971.

24. Quoted in Iver Peterson, "Tourists Lose Place in Christina's World: Producer Builds Museum," *New York Times,* 21 July 1973.

25. Albin Krebs, "Notes on People: Rare Honor for Vietnam Veteran," *New York Times,* 22 January 1972.

26. Quoted in Guy Flatley, "Peter O'Toole, from 'Lawrence' to 'La Mancha,'" *New York Times,* 17 September 1972.

13. New Haven, 'Nam, Nichols, and Nazis

1. Andrew Spicer and A. T. McKenna, *The Man Who Got Carter: Michael Klinger, Independent Production, and the British Film Industry 1960–1980* (London: Tauris, 2013), 63–69.

2. Peter Rosen to the author, personal correspondence, 6 February 2015.

3. Bart Whiteman, "Yale University: Spring of 1970," *Chattanoogan*, 26 November 2005, at http://www.chattanoogan.com/2005/11/26/76466/Yale-University-Spring-of-1970.aspx.

4. Quoted in Joseph B. Treaster, "BREWSTER DOUBTS FAIR BLACK TRIALS; Yale President Is 'Skeptical' That Revolutionaries Can Obtain Justice in U.S.; Brewster Skeptical on Fairness of Trials Given Black Militant," *New York Times,* 25 April 1970.

5. Rosen to the author, 6 February 2015.

6. P. B. Hurst, *The Most Savage Film: "Soldier Blue," Cinematic Violence, and the Horrors of War* (Jefferson, N.C.: McFarland, 2008), 126.

7. Ibid., 138.

8. Ibid., 140.

9. Ralph Nelson, "Joe Levine: Supersalesman," *Variety,* 27 October 1971.

10. J. W. Whitehead, *Mike Nichols and the Cinema of Transformation* (Jefferson, N.C.: McFarland, 2014), 75.

11. Quoted in A. H. Weiler, "Nichols Meets Jules Feiffer," *New York Times,* 26 October 1969.

12. Gary Arnold, review of *Carnal Knowledge, Washington Post,* 2 July 1971.

13. Ibid.

14. "The Producer: Joseph E. Levine," in Joseph McBride, ed., *Filmmakers on Filmmaking: The American Film Institute Seminars on Motion Pictures and Television* (Los Angeles: Tarcher, 1983), 31.

15. A. H. Weiler, "Mike Nichols' *Dolphin*," *New York Times,* 12 March 1972.

16. Gavin Smith, "Interview with Mike Nichols," *Film Comment,* May 1999.

17. Quoted in "Joe Levine Has B'Way Legit Plans but Won't Be Specific, Unlike Giving Needle to Some Colleagues," *Variety,* 4 September 1974.

18. Quoted in "Disrespects Paid Scott by Levine," *Variety,* 13 November 1974.

19. Vernon Scott, "Movie Tycoon Shakes Off Retirement," *Nashua Telegraph,* 11 November 1974.

20. David Sheward, *Rage and Glory: The Volatile Life and Career of George C. Scott* (Milwaukee: Applause Theatre & Cinema Books, 2008), 236.

21. Quoted in "Joseph E. Levine Presents Himself: Takes Powder as AvEmb Official," *Variety,* 29 May 1974.

22. Quoted in Scott, "Movie Tycoon Shakes Off Retirement."

23. Quoted in Joseph McBride, "Levine Slaps Non-paying Exhibs, Press Agents for Industry Ills," *Variety,* 21 August 1974.

24. A. H. Weiler, "Screen: Encore Lelouch," *New York Times,* 22 March 1975; Kevin Thomas, "Lelouch Touches All Phases in 'Love,'" *Los Angeles Times,* 26 March 1975.

25. Quoted in "Joe Levine Warming Up Old-Style Promo Push for Porter," *Variety,* 19 June 1974.

26. Quoted in James Bacon, "Good and Bad Reviews," *Los Angeles Herald Examiner,* 1 November 1974.

27. Quoted in Charles Champlin, "He's Banking on the Last Laugh," *Los Angeles Times,* 1 November 1974.

28. Quoted in ibid.

29. Vincent Canby, "Turning a Negative Film Review into Good Ad Copy," *Los Angeles Herald Examiner,* 27 October 1974.

30. Quoted in Champlin, "He's Banking on the Last Laugh."

31. Canby, "Turning a Negative Film Review into Good Ad Copy," italics in original.

14. Joe's Baby

1. Quoted in Gary Arnold, "The Final Decision Will Be Mine: Joseph E. Levine Presents His 492d Movie Comeback," *Washington Post,* 15 June 1977, Style Sec.

2. John Higgins, "Richard Attenborough's Quest for an Indian Grail," *Times* (London), 24 July 1975.

3. Dorothy Manners, "Ike–Monty Saga to McCarthy," *Los Angeles Herald Examiner,* 29 September 1975.

4. Quoted in Calvin Tomkins, "Profiles: The Very Rich Hours of Joe Levine," *New Yorker,* 16 September 1967.

5. Charles Champlin, "Levine: Maestro of Hoopla, Hope," *Los Angeles Times,* 2 June 1967.

6. William Goldman, *Adventures in the Screen Trade* (London: Futura, 1985), 279–80.

7. Richard Attenborough, *In Search of Gandhi* (London: Bodley Head, 1983), 159.

8. William Goldman, *The Story of "A Bridge Too Far"* (New York: Dell, 1977), unpaginated.

9. William E. Chaikin, Avco, to Joseph E. Levine, 11 November 1975, Joseph E. Levine (JEL) Collection, Howard Gotlieb Research Center, Boston University.

10. Quoted in Goldman, *Story of "A Bridge Too Far,"* unpaginated.

11. Richard Attenborough to Joseph E. Levine, telex, 8 December 1975, JEL Collection.

12. Goldman, *Story of "A Bridge Too Far,"* unpaginated.

13. Joseph E. Levine Presents Inc. to Wildwood Enterprises, telex, 22 January 1976, and Wildwood Enterprises to Joseph E. Levine Presents Inc., telex, 26 January 1976, JEL Collection.

14. Rosalie Levine, diary, undated entry, JEL Collection.

15. "A Budget Too Big," *Economist,* 29 May 1976.

16. Arthur Krim to Richard Attenborough, telex, n.d. [c. April or May 1976], JEL Collection.

17. "UA to Release *Bridge,*" *Hollywood Reporter,* 18 May 1976.

18. David Robinson, *Richard Attenborough* (London: National Film Theatre, 1992), 58.

19. Joseph E. Levine to Richard Attenborough, telex, n.d. [c. April 1976], JEL Collection.

20. Rosalie Levine, diary, undated entry [c. April 1976], JEL Collection.

21. Attenborough, *In Search of Gandhi,* 158.

22. Joseph E. Levine to Richard Attenborough, telex, n.d. [c. April or May 1976], JEL Collection.

23. Richard Attenborough to Joseph E. Levine, telex, n.d [c. April or May 1976], JEL Collection.

24. William Goldman to Richard Attenborough, telex, n.d. [c. April or May 1976], JEL Collection.

25. Joseph E. Levine to Richard Attenborough, n.d. [c. early 1977], JEL Collection.

26. Sean Connery to Joseph E. Levine, letter, 2 November 1976, JEL Collection.

27. Quoted in Victor Davies, "How the Bridge at Arnhem Came to Be Paved with Gold," *Daily Express* (London), 7 February 1977.

28. Quoted in Earl Wilson, "One Filmmaker Recreates War," *Los Angeles Herald Examiner,* 5 June 1977.

29. Quoted in Guy Flatley, "'I Have Butterflies' Says Joseph E. Levine. *ABTF* Opening Has Him Nervous," *Los Angeles Herald Examiner,* 18 June 1977.

30. Quoted in "Joe's Epic War Tale," *Los Angeles Herald Examiner,* 29 May 1977.

31. Barry Powell, "Scapegoat General," *News of the World,* 25 May 1977.

32. Cornelius Ryan, *A Bridge Too Far* (London: Hodder and Staunton, 1977), 93–94.

33. Powell, "Scapegoat General"; Richard Attenborough and Diane Hawkins, *Entirely Up to You, Darling* (London: Hutchinson, 2008), 152–53.

34. John Sandilands, "Tanks, David Darling," *Observer* (London), 27 March 1977.

35. Colonel John Waddy, "The Making of *A Bridge Too Far,*" *After the Battle,* no. 17 (1977): 30–52.

36. Quoted in Powell, "Scapegoat General."

37. Douglas Orgill, "A Bridge Too Far from the Truth," *Daily Express* (London), 5 July 1977.

38. Patrick Gibbs, "Arnhem through the Smoke," *Daily Telegraph* (London), 24 June 1977.

39. Richard Schickel, "Clumping around Market Garden," *Time,* 13 June 1977.

40. Andrew Sarris, "Films in Focus: A War Picture to End All War Pictures," *Village Voice,* 27 June 1977.

41. Earl Wilson, "The Last Hustler," *Dallas Morning News,* 23 October 1978.

42. Joe Baltake, "Fun? Flops? Levine Has 'Em," *Detroit Free Press,* 23 November 1978.

43. Goldman, *Story of "A Bridge Too Far,"* unpaginated.

44. Frederick M. Esry, "Film Pirates," letter to the editor, *New York Times,* 2 August 1977.

45. Joseph E. Levine, *"A Bridge Too Far": Notes from a Filmmaker* (New York: Joseph E. Levine Presents, 1977).

15. Leaving the Exploitation Business

1. Quoted in Gary Arnold, "The Final Decision Will Be Mine: Joseph E. Levine Presents His 492d Movie Comeback," *Washington Post,* 15 June 1977, Style Sec.

2. Quoted in Fred Ferretti, "The Evening Hours," *New York Times,* 28 November 1980.

3. "The Producer: Joseph E. Levine," in Joseph McBride, ed., *Filmmakers on Filmmaking: The American Film Institute Seminars on Motion Pictures and Television* (Los Angeles: Tarcher, 1983), 36.

4. Mike Hutner (national publicity director for 20th Century Fox, distributors of *Magic*) to Joseph E. Levine, 13 October 1978, Joseph E. Levine (JEL) Collection, Howard Gotlieb Research Center, Boston University.

5. Quoted in Joe Baltake, "Levine: Hollywood's Lion Roars," *Chicago Tribune*, 10 December 1978, sec. 6.

6. James Monaco, *American Film Now* (New York: Oxford University Press, 1979), 124.

7. John Desplas, "Moving Pictures: *Magic*," *Figaro*, 22 November 1978, sec. 2.

8. Richard Attenborough and Diane Hawkins, *Entirely Up to You, Darling* (London: Hutchinson, 2008), 32–33.

9. Joseph E. Levine to Peter Rosen, 14 February 1979, JEL Collection.

10. Quoted in Arnold, "The Final Decision Will Be Mine."

11. Bob Brooks to Joseph E. Levine, 16 March 1981, JEL Collection.

12. Bob Brooks to Joseph E. Levine, 30 May 1981, JEL Collection.

13. Both Leidholdt and Joe are quoted in Sal Manna, "Levine Revels in *Tattoo* Scars: Producer Says Feminist Uproar over Posters Is Bound to Boost Box Office," *Los Angeles Herald Examiner*, 10 April 1981.

14. Quoted in ibid.

15. Quoted in Bob Thomas, "Star Watch: Joseph E. Levine and *Tattoo*," Associated Press, 30 October 1981.

16. Quoted in Manna, "Levine Revels in *Tattoo* Scars."

17. Quoted in Pat O'Haire, "This Levine Guy —He's a Real Joe," *Sunday News—New York's Picture Newspaper*, 29 September 1974.

18. Quoted in Donna Rosenthal, "Self-Made Mogul Hangs On: Joseph E. Levine, 82, Is Still Wheeling and Dealing," *New York Times*, 5 July 1987.

19. Quoted in ibid.

20. Quoted in ibid.

21. Nan Robertson, "Joseph E. Levine, a Towering Figure in Movie Making, Is Dead," *New York Times*, 1 August 1987.

22. Jack Jones, "Self-Made Movie Mogul Joseph E. Levine, 81, Dies," *Los Angeles Times*, 1 August 1987.

Epilogue

1. Ross Melnick, *American Showman: Samuel "Roxy" Rothafel and the Birth of the Entertainment Industry 1908–1935* (New York: Columbia University Press, 2012), passim. In 1919, Rothafel released *The Rothapfel Unit Program* in forty-five cities in America. Rothafel was still using the original spelling of his surname, Rothapfel, at this time (ibid., 175–76).

2. John Waters, "Whatever Happened to Showmanship?" in *Crackpot: The Obsessions of John Waters* (New York: Scribner, 2003), 13–24.

3. Quoted in "Levine's Many Sided Exploitation," *Variety*, 19 August 1964.

4. Quoted in Bridget Byrne, "Jolting Joe Levine," *Women's Wear Daily,* 3 November 1981.

5. Tom Schatz, "The Studio System and Conglomerate Hollywood," in Paul McDonald and Janet Wasko, eds., *The Contemporary Hollywood Film Industry* (Oxford: Blackwell, 2008), 29.

6. Waters, "Whatever Happened to Showmanship?" 13.

7. Quoted in Alisa Perren, *Indie, Inc.: Miramax and the Transformation of Hollywood in the 1990s,* Kindle ed. (Austin: University of Texas Press, 2012), location 719.

8. Brian Jacks, "Anthony Hopkins on Flying in the 'Slipstream,' Going 'Psycho,' and Why New Age Hippies Don't Make Sense," Movies, MTV.com, 5 November 2007, at http://www.mtv.com/news/2429362/anthony-hopkins-on-flying-in-the-slipstream-going-psycho-and-why-new-age-hippies-dont-make-sense/.

9. Peter Rosen to the author, personal correspondence, 6 February 2015.

10. John Thornton Caldwell, *Production Culture: Industrial Reflexivity and Critical Practice in Film and Television* (Durham, N.C.: Duke University Press, 2008), 203–10.

11. Ibid., 205.

12. Ibid., 204, 205–6.

13. Pierre Bourdieu, *Distinction: A Social Critique of the Judgement of Taste* (Cambridge, Mass.: Harvard University Press, 2002), 56–57.

Bibliography

Archival Sources

Association of Motion Picture Arts and Sciences. Margaret Herrick Library, Beverly Hills, Calif.
George Cukor Collection.
Harlow Clippings File.
Irene Kamp Collection.
John Huston Collection.
Motion Picture Association of America Files.
Paramount Collection.

British Board of Film Classification Papers. London.

Joseph E. Levine Collection. Howard Gotlieb Research Center, Boston University.

Joseph E. Levine File. British Film Institute, London.

Michael Klinger Papers. University of the West of England, Bristol.

West End Museum Special Collections. Boston.

Secondary Sources

"$5 Million Damages Suit Filed over *Harlow* Book." *New York Times,* 1 May 1965.

"1911 Hupmobile and Other Antique Cars Bring $135,000 at Auction." *New York Times,* 23 November 1969.

Aaronson, Charles A. "Hard Sell 'Explodation' Party Gives *Hercules* Rousing Sendoff." *Motion Picture Herald,* 28 March 1959.

Adler, Renata. Review of *The Producers. New York Times,* 19 March 1968.

Alden, Robert. "Advertising: Hard Sell for Motion Pictures." *New York Times,* 29 May 1960.

Alpert, Hollis. "*The Graduate* Makes Out." *Saturday Review,* 6 July 1968.

Archer, Eugene. "*Wonders of Aladdin* at Two Theatres." *New York Times,* 23 December 1961.

Arkoff, Sam, with Richard Trubo. *Flying through Hollywood by the Seat of My Pants.* New York: Birch Lane Press, 1992.

Arnold, Gary. "The Final Decision Will Be Mine: Joseph E. Levine Presents His 492d Movie Comeback." *Washington Post,* 15 June 1977, Style Sec.

———. Review of *Carnal Knowledge*. *Washington Post*, 2 July 1971.

Aronson, Steven M. L. *Hype: The Names and Faces You Know so Well Will Never Look so Good to You Again*. New York: Morrow, 1983.

"Astor Newest Claimant to US Rights to Controversial Italo Pic." *Variety*, 20 January 1961.

Attenborough, Richard. *In Search of Gandhi*. London: Bodley Head, 1983.

Attenborough, Richard, and Diane Hawkins. *Entirely Up to You, Darling*. London: Hutchinson, 2008.

Aumont, Jacques. "The Fall of the Gods." In Susan Hayward and Ginette Vincendeau, eds., *French Film: Texts and Contexts*, 174–89. London: Routledge, 1990.

Bacon, James. "Good and Bad Reviews." *Los Angeles Herald Examiner*, 1 November 1974.

Baker, Carroll. *Baby Doll: An Autobiography*. London: Allen, 1984.

Baker, Stanley. "A Handshake Deal That Paid Off." *Variety*, 22 April 1964.

Baldwin, Hanson W. "Atom Bomb Wins Victory, but Sows Whirlwind." *Los Angeles Times*, 10 August 1945.

Balio, Tino, ed. *The American Film Industry*. Madison: University of Wisconsin Press, 1976.

———. *The Foreign Film Renaissance on America Screens, 1946–1973*. Madison: University of Wisconsin Press, 2010.

———, ed. *Hollywood in the Age of Television*. London: Unwin Hyman, 1990.

———. "Introduction to Part II." In Tino Balio, ed., *Hollywood in the Age of Television*, 259–96. London: Unwin Hyman, 1990.

———. *United Artists: The Company That Changed the Film Industry*. Madison: University of Wisconsin Press, 1987.

Baltake, Joe. "Fun? Flops? Levine Has 'Em." *Detroit Free Press*, 23 November 1978.

———. "Levine: Hollywood's Lion Roars." *Chicago Tribune*, 10 December 1978, sec. 6.

Bart, Peter. "Hollywood Package: Production Formation Probed by a Master." *New York Times*, 9 August 1964.

———. "New Hollywood: New Riches, New Doubts." *New York Times*, 12 December 1966.

———. "Producers Rush 3 Harlow Films: Carroll Baker Announced for Title Role by Levine." *New York Times*, 1 September 1964.

Beacom, Brian. "The Bitch Is Back—but She's Not Scary at All." *Evening Times*, 6 March 2007.

"Big Air Coin from Pix: *Hitler's Children* Seen as Starting New Bonanza with Ether Taking 40% of Budget." *The Billboard*, 8 May 1943.

Biskind, Peter. *Easy Riders, Raging Bulls: How the Sex-Drugs-and-Rock 'n' Roll Generation Saved Hollywood*. London: Bloomsbury, 1999.

Bourdieu, Pierre. *Distinction: A Social Critique of the Judgement of Taste.* Translated by Richard Nice. Cambridge, Mass.: Harvard University Press, 2002.

Brady, James. "Interview with Joe Levine." *New York Magazine,* 17 December 1973.

Braverman, William A. "The Emergence of a Unified Community, 1880–1917." In Jonathan D. Sarna, Ellen Smith, and Scott-Martin Kosofsky, eds., *The Jews of Boston,* 65–86. New Haven, Conn.: Yale University Press, 2005.

"A Budget Too Big." *Economist,* 29 May 1976.

Burton, Sybil. "Euripedes and the Establishment: Film Producer Puts His Money Where His (Legit) Enthusiasm Is." *Variety,* 22 April 1964.

Byrne, Bridget. "Jolting Joe Levine." *Women's Wear Daily,* 31 November 1981.

Caine, Michael. *What's It All About?* London: Random House, 1992.

Caldwell, John Thornton. *Production Culture: Industrial Reflexivity and Critical Practice in Film and Television.* Durham, N.C.: Duke University Press, 2008.

Camp, Todd. "A Celluloid Contender: Dallas Film Festival Shows It's Ready to Play with the Big Boys." *Fort Worth Star-Telegram,* 18 April 1997.

Canby, Vincent. "And in Hollywood, Mergers Are Better Than Ever as Business Community Finds a New Area of Investment." *New York Times,* 9 January 1967.

———. "Turning a Negative Film Review into Good Ad Copy." *Los Angeles Herald Examiner,* 27 October 1974.

Cardullo, Bert. *Vittorio de Sica: Actor, Director, Auteur.* Newcastle-on-Tyne, U.K.: Cambridge Scholars Press, 2009.

Carr, Steven Alan. *Hollywood and Anti-Semitism: A Cultural History 1880–1941.* Cambridge: Cambridge University Press, 2001.

Champlin, Charles. "He's Banking on the Last Laugh." *Los Angeles Times,* 1 November 1974.

———. "Levine: Maestro of Hoopla, Hope." *Los Angeles Times,* 2 June 1967.

———. "TV Off and Running in High-Paying Movie Stakes." *Los Angeles Times,* 5 September 1965.

Clarke, George W. "Boy Film Star, 8, Has Fast Quip at Hub Greeting." *Boston Daily Record,* 14 December 1953.

———. "TV to Exhaust All Films in 4 Yrs." *Boston Daily Record,* 19 April 1958.

Coe, Richard L. "Byrd–Marx Bill a Pair of Aces." *Washington Post,* 22 October 1948.

Cohn, Art. *The Nine Lives of Mike Todd.* London: Hutchinson, 1959.

Consadine, Bob. "Rosy Future for Films." *Los Angeles Herald Examiner,* 26 November 1969.

Contempt (*Le Mépris,* 1963). DVD. Criterion Collection. New York: Criterion, 2002.

Crowther, Bosley. "Bad Taste in Films: More Cheapness and Vulgarity Appear." *New York Times,* 6 September 1964.

———. "Cinematic *Tom Jones:* Fielding's Classic Novel Made into Great Film. Bold Method *Wuthering Heights." New York Times,* 13 October 1963, Art and Leisure Sec.

———. "Is Hollywood Killing Itself?" *New York Times,* 13 March 1966.

———. "Moral Brinkmanship: Legion of Decency Makes a Point but Doesn't Support It Well." *New York Times,* 13 December 1964.

———. "Movie Based on Book by Shulman Opens." *New York Times,* 22 July 1965.

———. "Putting Movies Across." *New York Times,* 12 April 1959.

———. "A Quizzical Paradox: Is It Really Boom or Is It Bust in the Field of Foreign Films?" *New York Times,* 7 June 1964.

———. "Run *Bonnie and Clyde." New York Times,* 3 September 1967, Arts and Leisure Sec.

———. "Screen: *Blow-Up* Arrives at Coronet; Hero Switches between Luxury and Squalor." *New York Times,* 19 December 1966, 52.

———. "Screen: *Bonnie and Clyde* Arrives. Careers of Murderers Pictured as Farce." *New York Times,* 14 August 1967.

———. "Screen: *The Carpetbaggers* Opens: Adaptation of Book by Robbins in Debut." *New York Times,* 2 July 1964.

———. "Screen: *Darling* Is Selfish, Fickle, and Ambitious." *New York Times,* 4 August 1965.

———. "Screen: Fellini's Contemplation of a Director's Life; *8½* Is Showing at Festival Theatre; Japanese Film Opens at New Yorker." *New York Times,* 26 June 1963.

———. "Screen: Horror Import. *Godzilla,* a Japanese Film, Is at State." *New York Times,* 28 April 1956.

———. "Screen: A Man Who Would Be an Ape; *Morgan!* British Film, Begins Sutton Run." *New York Times,* 5 April 1966.

———. "Screen: *Oscar* Arrives." *New York Times,* 5 March 1966.

———. "The Screen: Review of Byrd Voyage *The Secret Land." New York Times,* 2 December 1948.

———. "Screen: Sophia Loren in Old Form; She Is Impressive in de Sica's *Two Women." New York Times,* 9 May 1961.

———. "Shoot-Em Up Film Opens World Fete: *Bonnie and Clyde* Cheered by Montreal First-Nighters." *New York Times,* 7 August 1967.

———. "Spears and Sandals. Flood of Cheap Costume Films Causes Dismay." *New York Times,* 12 March 1961.

———. "A Time to Face Facts." *New York Times,* 14 March 1965.

Curtis, Charlotte. "$15-Million Art Sale Falls Short." *New York Times,* 11 June 1969.

———. "Off to Bermuda—for a Bite of Lunch." *New York Times,* 14 January 1972.

Davies, Victor. "How the Bridge at Arnhem Came to Be Paved with Gold." *Daily Express* (London), 7 February 1977.

Davis, Richard. "Review of *The Oscar.*" *Films and Filming,* July 1966.

De Beauvoir, Simone. *Brigitte Bardot and the Lolita Syndrome.* New York: Reynal, 1960.

De Sica, Vittorio. "Director's Idea of Typecasting." *Variety,* 22 April 1964.

Desplas, John. "Moving Pictures: *Magic.*" *Figaro,* 22 November 1978, sec. 2.

Dick, Bernard F. *Engulfed: The Death of Paramount Pictures and the Birth of Corporate Hollywood.* Lexington: University Press of Kentucky, 2001.

———. *Hal Wallis: Producer to the Stars.* Lexington: University Press of Kentucky, 2004.

———. *The Merchant Prince of Poverty Row: Harry Cohn of Columbia Pictures.* Lexington: University Press of Kentucky, 2009.

"Disrespects Paid Scott by Levine." *Variety,* 13 November 1974.

Dmytryk, Edward. "Director's Findings: Good Drama Made for Strong Merchandizing." *Variety,* 22 April 1964.

Doherty, Thomas. *Teenagers and Teenpics: The Juvenilization of American Movies in the 1950s.* Philadelphia: Temple University Press, 2002.

Doll, Bill. "Boston's Joe Levine: A Profile." *Variety,* 1 April 1959.

Drucker, Mort (artist), and Larry Siegal (writer). "*Mad* Visits Joe LeVenal: Hollywood's Latest Producing Genius." *Mad,* October 1961.

Dunn, Peter. "The Last Movie Mogul." *Sunday Times,* 5 February 1978.

"Electronovision Has Ferrer for *Harlow.*" *Hollywood Reporter,* 25 February 1965.

"Embassy Expanding Operations; Levine Will Give More Time to Production." *Hollywood Reporter,* 2 August 1965.

"Embassy in Product Tie-Up with UK Firm." *Film Daily,* 24 March 1965.

"Embassy May Merge/Go Public." *Hollywood Reporter,* 31 May 1967.

"Embassy's Profits Estimated by Avco." *New York Times,* 21 May 1968.

Esry, Frederick M. "Film Pirates" (letter to the editor). *New York Times,* 2 August 1977.

Feldman, Edward S. "A Look at Levine's Future Films." *Variety,* 8 February 1961.

Feldman, Edward S., with Tom Barton. *Tell Me How You Love the Picture: A Hollywood Producer's Hilarious Take on Life among the Stars.* Beverly Hills, Calif.: Creative Book Publishers International, 2007.

Fellini, Federico. "Open Letter to Joe Levine." *Variety,* 22 April 1964.

Ferretti, Fred. "The Evening Hours." *New York Times,* 28 November 1980.

Fessier, Mike, Jr. "Wheeling and Dealing with Bill Sargent." *Los Angeles Magazine,* 25 July 1965.

Flatley, Guy. "At the Movies." *New York Times,* 10 June 1977.

———. "Cary—from Mae to September." *New York Times,* 22 July 1973.

———. "'I Have Butterflies' Says Joseph E. Levine. *ABTF* Opening Has Him Nervous." *Los Angeles Herald Examiner,* 18 June 1977.

———. "Peter O'Toole, from 'Lawrence' to 'La Mancha.'" *New York Times,* 17 September 1972.

Flynn, Hazel. "We Help Joe Levine Start *Where Love.*" *Citizen News,* 6 December 1965.

"For Immediate Release." *Variety,* 29 April 1963.

Frayling, Christopher. *Sergio Leone: Something to Do with Death.* London: Faber and Faber, 2000.

Freeman, Lincoln. "The Comeback of the Movies." In Tino Balio, ed., *The American Film Industry,* 371–85. Madison: University of Wisconsin Press, 1976. Originally published in *Fortune,* February 1955.

Frumkes, Roy. "Interview with Steve Reeves." *Perfect Vision,* 22 July 1994.

Gibbs, Patrick. "Arnhem through the Smoke." *Daily Telegraph* (London), 24 June 1977.

G. K. "Old Times on Parade." *Los Angeles Times,* 8 June 1946.

Godard, Jean-Luc. "*Le Mépris.*" In *Godard on Godard,* edited by Jean Narboni and Tom Milne, translated by Tom Milne, 161–244. London: Secker and Warburg, 1972. Originally published in *Cahiers du Cinema* 146 (August 1963).

"Godard Deplores Distribs Tendency to Duck Film Festivals." *Variety,* 14 August 1963.

"Godard Only Knows" (review). *Observer* (London), 26 November 2000.

Godbout, Oscar. "Hollywood Scene, Theatre-Owners Group Seeks Methods for More Profitable Exhibition." *New York Times,* 8 July 1956.

Gold, Ronald. "Levine Best Showman since L. B. Mayer." *Variety,* 14 April 1965.

Goldman, William. *Adventures in the Screen Trade.* London: Futura, 1985.

———. *The Story of "A Bridge Too Far."* New York: Dell, 1977.

Goldstein, Patrick. "The Art of Horror Movies, from a King of the Genre." *Los Angeles Times,* 20 July 2003. At http://articles.latimes.com/2003/jul/29/entertainment/et-gold29.

Gould, Jack. "Silver Screen Is a Gold Mine." *New York Times,* 7 January 1968.

———. "TV Faces a Fight on Moviemaking." *New York Times,* 23 October 1967.

Green, Abel. "Levine's Post-grad Aura: How a Hit Pic Restores Tone." *Variety,* 3 April 1968.

Griffin, Dick. "Levine: Huckster with a Heart." *Los Angeles Times,* 21 June 1966.

Haber, Joyce. "Joe Levine: Call Him Flamboyant." *Los Angeles Times,* 13 May 1968.

"Hail Joe Levine, 'Pioneer of the Year.'" *Variety,* 16 August 1960.

Hall, Sheldon. "*Zulu*": *With Some Guts behind It—the Making of the Epic Movie.* Sheffield, U.K.: Tomahawk Press, 2005.

Hamill, Katherine. "The Supercolossal—Well, Pretty Good—World of Joe Levine." *Fortune,* March 1964.

"*Harlow* March Start on Electronovision." *Film Daily,* 19 January 1965.

Harris, Mark. *Pictures at a Revolution: Five Movies and the Birth of the New Hollywood.* London: Penguin, 2008.

Harris, Neil. *Humbug: The Art of P. T. Barnum.* Chicago: University of Chicago Press, 1973.

Hayes, Dade, and Jonathan Bing. *Open Wide: How Hollywood Box Office Became a National Obsession.* New York: Miramax Books, 2004.

Hayward, Susan, and Ginette Vincendeau, eds. *French Film: Texts and Contexts.* London: Routledge, 1990.

"*Hercules* Reveals a Ballyhoo Strongman." *Film Bulletin,* 30 March 1959.

Higgins, John. "Richard Attenborough's Quest for an Indian Grail." *Times* (London), 24 July 1975.

"High Film Rentals Scored in Chicago: Goldenson Also Tells Theatre Owners' Meeting Shortage of Movies Hurts Industry." *New York Times,* 4 November 1953.

"Hollywood Inside." *Variety,* 14 April 1948.

Hopper, Hedda. "Jean Harlow New Literary Target." *Los Angeles Times,* 3 July 1964.

"How to Start at the Top and Succeed." *Cosmopolitan,* June 1964.

Howe, Desson. "*Contempt* Film Fatale." *Washington Post,* 25 July 1997, Weekend Sec.

Hubler, Richard G. "*Harlow:* Script a 'Hack.'" *Los Angeles Times,* 28 June 1964.

Hughes, Robert, ed. *Film Book 1: The Audience and the Filmmaker.* New York: Grove Press, 1959.

Humphrey, Hal. "Movies Bring End to Miltie's Return." *Los Angeles Times,* 3 November 1966.

Hurst, P. B. *The Most Savage Film: "Soldier Blue," Cinematic Violence, and the Horrors of War.* Jefferson, N.C.: McFarland, 2008.

"Informing You." *Hartford Daily Courant,* 26 September 1945.

"Instant Films." *Sunday Telegraph* (London), 23 February 1964.

"Interview with Contanzo Costantini, 1963." In Charles Affron, ed., *Rutgers Films in Print: 8½,* 243–48. New Brunswick, N.J.: Rutgers, 1987.

Interview with Tom Canford. *Hollow Square Press,* n.d. At http://www.hollowsquarepress.com/tattoo-1981.html. Accessed 25 April 2016.

Jacks, Brian. "Anthony Hopkins on Flying in the 'Slipstream,' Going 'Psycho,' and Why New Age Hippies Don't Make Sense." Movies, MTV.com, 5 November 2007, at http://www.mtv.com/news/2429362/anthony-hopkins-on-flying-in-the-slipstream-going-psycho-and-why-new-age-hippies-dont-make-sense/.

"Jean Harlow's Father Sues over Book." *New York Times,* 24 November 1964.

Jenkins, Mark. "His Master's Voice: Joel E. Seigel 1940–2004." *Washington City Paper,* 19 March 2004. At http://www.washingtoncitypaper.com/special/joel0319.html. Accessed 25 April 2016.

"Joe Levine Has B'Way Legit Plans but Won't Be Specific, Unlike Giving Needle to Some Colleagues." *Variety,* 4 September 1974.

"Joe Levine 'Shakes' on *La Dolce Vita* (*High Life Hobos*)." *Variety,* 12 October 1960.

"Joe Levine Warming Up Old-Style Promo Push for Porter." *Variety,* 19 June 1974.

"Joe's Epic War Tale." *Los Angeles Herald Examiner,* 29 May 1977.

"Joe Unchained." *Time,* 24 February 1961.

Jones, Jack. "Self-Made Movie Mogul Joseph E. Levine, 81, Dies." *Los Angeles Times,* 1 August 1987.

"Joseph E. Levine Presents Himself: Takes Powder as AvEmb Official." *Variety,* 29 May 1974.

Kapsis, Robert E. *Hitchcock: The Making of a Reputation.* Chicago: University of Chicago Press, 1992.

Kaufman, Stanley. "Stanley Kaufman on Films." *New Republic,* 23 December 1967.

Kent, F. W. *Lorenzo de Medici and the Art of the Magnificent.* Baltimore: Johns Hopkins University Press, 2007.

Kerr, James R. "Billions Make a Nice Cushion or, AVCO Goes to Embassy Movies." *Variety,* 13 November 1968.

Kessel, Howard. "Joseph E. Levine Presents: Himself." *Women's Wear Daily,* 14 December 1973.

Kilday, Greg. "Influential Film Critic Andrew Sarris Dies at 83." *Hollywood Reporter,* 20 June 2012.

Klien, Mrs. N. I. Letter to the editor. *Life,* 17 August 1962.

Knight, Arthur. "For Eggheads Only?" In Robert Hughes, ed., *Film Book 1: The Audience and the Filmmaker,* 24–34. New York: Grove Press, 1959.

Kramer, Chuck. "You Seen My Art Pitchas?" *Phoenix Star,* May 1970.

Krebs, Albin. "Notes on People: Rare Honor for Vietnam Veteran." *New York Times,* 22 January 1972.

Kupcinent, Irv. "Kup's Column." *Chicago Times,* 29 October 1945.

"The Last of the Movie Barons." *Newsweek,* 2 May 1966.

"Latest in Levine–Paramount Deals: Par Distribs Two Pix in Britain." *Variety,* 6 May 1964.

Lefferts, Barney. "Now the Mike Nichols Touch." *New York Times,* 22 November 1964.

Lev, Peter. *The Euro-American Cinema.* Austin: University of Texas Press, 1993.
Levine, Joseph E. "Ars Longa, Vita Brevis." *New York Times,* 8 October 1974.
———. *"A Bridge Too Far": Notes from a Filmmaker.* New York: Joseph E. Levine Presents, 1977.
"Levine Aids Yale Theatre." *New York Times,* 18 January 1971.
"Levine and Maxwell in Co-production Deal for Theaters, TV." *Hollywood Reporter,* 29 March 1965.
"Levine Budgets 8 Embassy Pix at $18 Mil in Next 6 Months." *Variety,* 10 August 1966.
"Levine Going Arty; to Drop Spear and Sandals Films." *Variety,* 9 November 1961.
"Levine Has 'No Comment' on Mad Sq. Merger, Plenty on Other Topics." *Variety,* 29 March 1967.
"Levine Plans 20 Low Budget Features to Be Made Here." *Hollywood Reporter,* 13 May 1965.
"Levine Prepping 4 'Family' Pix; Hopes to Improve Image." *Variety,* 26 January 1965.
"Levine's Many Sided Exploitation." *Variety,* 19 August 1964.
Lewis, Wyndham. *The Apes of God.* New York: McBride, 1932.
Lipsyte, Robert. "Museum Salutes Levine for Films." *New York Times,* 26 October 1965.
Luciano, Dale. "*Long Day's Journey into Night:* An Interview with Sidney Lumet." *Film Quarterly* 25, no. 1 (1971): 20–29.
MacAdams, William. *Ben Hecht: The Man behind the Legend.* New York: Scribner's, 1990.
MacCabe, Colin. *Godard: Portrait of the Artist at 70.* London: Bloomsbury, 2004.
Macdonald, Dwight. "Films of the Quarter." *Film Quarterly* 16, no. 1 (1962): 60–65.
———. "Films of the Quarter." *Film Quarterly* 17, no. 1 (1963): 51–55.
———. "Masscult and Midcult." In *Masscult and Midcult: Essays against the American Grain,* John Summers, ed., 3–71. New York: New York Review of Books, 2011.
———. "Mr. Goldwyn and Mr. Levine." In *On Movies,* 130–32. New York: De Capo Press, 1981.
———. "No Art and No Box Office." *Esquire,* March 1959.
Makaitis, Skirmante. Letter to the editor. *Life,* 17 August 1962.
Mamber, Stephen. *Cinema Verite in America: Studies in Uncontrolled Documentary.* Cambridge, Mass.: MIT Press, 1974.
Manna, Sal. "Levine Revels in *Tattoo* Scars: Producer Says Feminist Uproar over Posters Is Bound to Boost Box Office." *Los Angeles Herald Examiner,* 10 April 1981.

Manners, Dorothy. "Ike–Monty Saga to McCarthy." *Los Angeles Herald Examiner,* 29 September 1975.

Marshall, Wendy L. *William Beaudine: From Silents to Television.* Lanham, Md.: Scarecrow Press, 2005.

Matzer, Maria. "How *Godzilla* Made His Way to the US." *Los Angeles Times,* 22 May 1998.

Mayer, Arthur L. Letter to the editor. *Los Angeles Times,* 24 November 1974.

McBride, Joseph, ed. *Filmmakers on Filmmaking: The American Film Institute Seminars on Motion Pictures and Television.* Los Angeles: Tarcher, 1983.

———. "Levine Slaps Non-paying Exhibs, Press Agents for Industry Ills." *Variety,* 21 August 1974.

McDonald, Paul, and Janet Wasko, eds. *The Contemporary Hollywood Film Industry.* Oxford: Blackwell, 2008.

Mekas, Jonas. "Movie Journal." *Village Voice,* 11 April 1963.

Melnick, Ross. *America Showman: Samuel "Roxy" Rothafel and the Birth of the Entertainment Industry 1908–1935.* New York: Columbia University Press, 2012.

"Metro Hypos Financing of Foreign Production." *Variety,* 26 April 1960.

Monaco, James. *American Film Now.* New York: Oxford University Press, 1979.

Moravia, Alberto. *A Ghost at Noon.* 1955. Reprint. Middlesex, U.K.: Penguin, 1976.

Narboni, Jean, and Tom Milne, eds. *Godard on Godard.* Translated by Tom Milne. London: Secker and Warburg, 1972.

Nason, Richard. "*Hercules* Starts Flood Movies." *New York Times,* 24 October 1959, 13.

Nathan, David. "The Man Who Sold *Hercules.*" *Daily Herald* (London), 7 December 1960.

Neale, Steve. "Hollywood Blockbusters: Historical Dimensions." In Julian Stringer, ed., *Movie Blockbusters,* 46–60. London: Routledge, 2003.

Neale, Steve, and Sheldon Hall. *Epics, Spectacles, and Blockbusters: A Hollywood History.* Detroit: Wayne State University Press, 2010.

Nelson, Ralph. "Joe Levine: Supersalesman." *Variety,* 27 October 1971.

Nemy, Enid. "A Pleasure Ground Named Xanadu Welcomes Members to a Sunny Sea." *New York Times,* 30 November 1969.

"Newsmakers." *Newsweek,* 8 July 1963.

"Now Hear This! Harlow Pic to Be in Good Taste—Levine." *Hollywood Reporter,* 17 December 1964.

"NY Critics Rip into Electrono *Harlow.*" *Variety,* 19 May 1965.

O'Haire, Pat. "This Levine Guy—He's a Real Joe." *Sunday News—New York's Picture Newspaper,* 29 September 1974.

"Old Movies Stand Test, Producer Says." *Rochester Times-Union,* 28 March 1946.

O'Neil, Paul. "The Super Salesman of Super Colossals." *Life*, 27 July 1962.
"Open Letter to Joseph E. Levine." *Variety*, 7 April 1965, Personals.
Orgill, Douglas. "A Bridge Too Far from the Truth." *Daily Express* (London), 5 July 1977.
Ornstein, Bill. "Electronovision to Make 12 Pics at $7.5 Mil Cost." *Hollywood Reporter*, 19 January 1965.
Parish, James Robert. *It's Good to Be the King: The Seriously Funny Life of Mel Brooks*. Hoboken, N.J.: Wiley, 2007.
Parsons, Louella. "Joe Levine: How to Get into the Movie$." *Los Angeles Herald Examiner*, 20 September 1959, Pictorial Living Sec.
Peary, Gerald. "The Maysles Brothers." *Boston Review*, October 1990. At http://www.geraldpeary.com/essays/mno/maysles.html.
Penn, Stanley W. "New Movie Makers." *Wall Street Journal*, 17 January 1963.
Perren, Alisa. *Indie, Inc.: Miramax and the Transformation of Hollywood in the 1990s*. Austin: University of Texas Press, 2012.
———. "Sex, Lies, and Marketing: Miramax and the Development of the Quality Indie Blockbuster." *Film Quarterly* 55, no. 2 (2001): 30–39.
Peterson, Iver. "Tourists Lose Place in Christina's World: Producer Builds Museum." *New York Times*, 21 July 1973.
Pitman, Jack. "The Saga of Joseph E. Levine: Brings Back Barnum Ballyhoo." *Variety*, 4 July 1962.
Plant, Simon. "The Watcher." *Herald-Sun* (Melbourne), 13 September 2003, Weekend Sec.
"Plot to Rub Out Dub." *Variety*, 14 August 1963.
Powell, Barry. "Scapegoat General." *News of the World*, 25 May 1977.
"The Power of Cash." *Saturday Evening Post*, 30 December 1967.
Powers, James. "Dialogue on Film." *American Film*, September 1979, 40–46.
"The Producer: Joseph E. Levine." In Joseph McBride, ed., *Filmmakers on Filmmaking: The American Film Institute Seminars on Motion Pictures and Television*, 27–39. Los Angeles: Tarcher, 1983.
"Producer-Distributor Levine Finds Two Hats Enough; to Sell Theatres." *Motion Picture Exhibitor*, 12 February 1964.
Quarles, Mike. *Down and Dirty: Hollywood's Exploitation Filmmakers and Their Movies*. Jefferson, N.C.: McFarland Classics, 2001.
"Razzle Dazzle Showman." *New York Times*, 26 October 1965.
Review of *Boccaccio 70*. *Hollywood Reporter*, 30 July 1962.
Review of *La Ciel et la Boue*. *Variety*, 10 May 1961.
Review of *Contempt*. *Motion Picture Herald*, 23 December 1964.
Review of *Contempt*. *New Republic*, 2 January 1965.
Review of *Contempt*. *New Yorker*, 26 December 1964.
Review of *Contempt*. *Time*, 8 January 1965.

Robbins, Harold. *The Inheritors.* New York: Pocket Books 1971.
"Robbins' Egg-Blue." *Newsweek,* 6 July 1964.
Robertson, Nan. "Joseph E. Levine, a Towering Figure in Movie Making, Is Dead." *New York Times,* 1 August 1987.
Robinson, David. *Richard Attenborough.* London: National Film Theatre, 1992.
"Rosalie Gives Up Career for Joie." *Boston Times,* 20 June 1938.
Rosenthal, Donna. "Self-Made Mogul Hangs On: Joseph E. Levine, 82, Is Still Wheeling and Dealing." *New York Times,* 5 July 1987.
Rosten, Leo C. *Hollywood: The Movie Colony, the Movie Makers.* New York: Harcourt, Brace, 1941.
Ryan, Cornelius. *A Bridge Too Far.* London: Hodder and Staunton, 1977.
Sandilands, John. "Tanks, David Darling." *Observer* (London), 27 March 1977.
Sarna, Jonathan D. "The Jews of Boston in Historical Perspective." In Jonathan D. Sarna, Ellen Smith, and Scott-Martin Kosofsky, eds., *The Jews of Boston,* 3–20. New Haven, Conn.: Yale University Press, 2005.
Sarna, Jonathan D., Ellen Smith, and Scott-Martin Kosofsky, eds. *The Jews of Boston.* New Haven, Conn.: Yale University Press, 2005.
Sarris, Andrew. "Films in Focus: A War Picture to End All War Pictures." *Village Voice,* 27 June 1977.
———. Review of *The Graduate. Village Voice,* 20 December 1973.
Schaeffer, Eric. *Bold! Daring! Shocking! True! A History of Exploitation Films, 1919–1959.* Durham, N.C.: Duke University Press, 1999.
Schatz, Thomas. "The New Hollywood." In Julian Stringer, ed., *Movie Blockbusters,* 15–44. London: Routledge, 2003.
———. "The Studio System and Conglomerate Hollywood." In Paul McDonald and Janet Wasko, eds., *The Contemporary Hollywood Film Industry,* 13–42. Oxford: Blackwell, 2008.
Scheuer, Philip K. "A Behind-Scenes View of What Makes *Oscar* Run." *Los Angeles Times,* 12 September 1965.
———. "*Carpetbaggers* in Bad Taste as Film." *Los Angeles Times,* 5 June 1964.
———. "Harlow Story—One Down, One to Go." *Los Angeles Times,* 12 May 1965.
———. "*Harlow* Story Told Again—Less Cheaply." *Los Angeles Times,* 12 August 1965.
———. "Hybrid *Hot Wind:* Art of Box Office?" *Los Angeles Times,* 9 October 1960.
———. "Meet Joe Levine, Super (Sales) Man!" *Los Angeles Times,* 27 July 1959.
———. "One + One Adds Up to Trouble." *Los Angeles Times,* 2 May 1965.
———. "*Oscar* Runs Close Second to Sammy." *Los Angeles Times,* 16 February 1966.
———. "This Hercules Just Tarzan in a Tunic." *Los Angeles Times,* 30 July 1959.
Schickel, Richard. "Another Sock at an Aging Legend." *Life,* 25 March 1966.

———. "Clumping around Market Garden." *Time,* 13 June 1977.

Schlossberg, Julian. "Remembering Joe Levine." *Variety,* 28 October 1996.

Schneyer, Berne. "Showmanship: It Still Pays Off!" *Film Bulletin,* 20 July 1959.

Schumach, Murray. "Freeman Gives Up Paramount Post." *New York Times,* 18 May 1959.

———. "The Gaudy Career of Jonas Cord." *New York Times,* 25 June 1961.

———. "Joseph E. Levine Says Making of Art Films for US Is Risky." *New York Times,* 6 December 1963.

Scott, Vernon. "'I Dig Kids' Says Joe Levine." *Citizen News,* 2 May 1970.

———. "Movie Tycoon Shakes Off Retirement." *Nashua Telegraph,* 11 November 1974.

Scully, Frank. "Scully's Scrapbook." *Variety,* 8 September 1948.

Segrave, Kerry. *Drive-In Theaters: A History from Their Inception in 1933.* Jefferson, N.C.: McFarland, 1993.

Sherman, Paul. Review of *Boccaccio 70* DVD. Turner Classic Movies (TCM), n.d. At http://www.tcmdb.com/title/title.jsp?stid=69274&atid=22766&category=Home%20Video%20Reviews&titleName=Boccaccio%20%6070&menuName=MAIN. Accessed 21 January 2008.

"She's for Foreign Eyes Only." *Variety,* 15 July 1964.

Sheward, David. *Rage and Glory: The Volatile Life and Career of George C. Scott.* Milwaukee: Applause Theatre & Cinema Books, 2008.

"The Shock of Freedom in Films." *Time,* 8 December 1967. At http://www.time.com/time/magazine/article/0,9171,844256,00.html.

"Short Subjects." *Film Bulletin,* 25 August 1952.

"Shulman Shot an Arrow into the Air—Levine Brings It Down with a Flare." *Hollywood Reporter,* 25 February 1965.

"Shulman Tells All—or Nearly All." *Variety,* 27 January 1965.

"A Simple Guy." *Newsweek,* 22 February 1960.

Sklar, Robert. *Movie-Made America: A Cultural History of American Movies.* New York: Vintage Books, 1994.

Small, Pauline. *Sophia Loren: Moulding the Star.* Bristol, U.K.: Intellect Books, 2009.

Smith, Cecil. "Crane Flying High Nightly." *New York Times,* 5 August 1964.

Smith, Gavin. "Interview with Mike Nichols." *Film Comment,* May 1999.

Sontag, Susan. "Notes on Camp." In *Against Interpretation,* 275–93. London: Penguin Classics, 2009.

Sorolsky, Bob. "Whatever Became of All That Glamour?" *Philadelphia Bulletin,* 5 November 1978.

Spicer, Andrew, and A. T. McKenna. *The Man Who Got Carter: Michael Klinger, Independent Production, and the British Film Industry 1960–1980.* London: Tauris, 2013.

Stringer, Julian, ed. *Movie Blockbusters.* London: Routledge, 2003.

Talese, Gay. "Joe Levine Unchained: A Candid Portrait of a Spectacular Showman." *Esquire,* January 1961.

Taylor, Frank J. "Big Boom in Outdoor Movies." In Gregory A. Waller, ed., *Moviegoing in America,* 247–51. Malden, Mass.: Blackwell, 2002. Originally published in *Saturday Evening Post,* 29 September 1956.

Taylor, Stephen. "After the Nouvelle Vague." *Film Quarterly* 18, no. 3 (1965): 5–9.

"Telecasting Notes." *Television Digest with Electronics Reports,* 2 May 1953.

"There'll Be a Nude (Natch) in Biopic of Polly Adler." *Variety,* 8 April 1964.

"They Yelled No!" *Los Angeles Herald Examiner,* 31 May 1964.

Thomas, Bob. "Star Watch: Joseph E. Levine and *Tattoo.*" Associated Press, 30 October 1981.

Thomas, Kevin. "Lelouch Touches All Phases in 'Love.'" *Los Angeles Times,* 26 March 1975.

Thomas, Robert, Jr. "To Mrs. Levine, a Peacock Ball without Jewels." *New York Times,* 30 April 1971.

Thompson, Howard. "Screen: *Where the Hot Wind Blows* Review." *New York Times,* 12 November 1960.

Thompson, Thomas. "Small-Bore Talents in Big Bore." *Life,* 26 June 1964.

Tomkins, Calvin. "Profiles: The Very Rich Hours of Joe Levine." *New Yorker,* 16 September 1967.

Treaster, Joseph B. "BREWSTER DOUBTS FAIR BLACK TRIALS; Yale President Is 'Skeptical' That Revolutionaries Can Obtain Justice in U.S.; Brewster Skeptical on Fairness of Trials Given Black Militant." *New York Times,* 25 April 1970.

"*Tropic Cancer* Like *Carpetbaggers* Covets Shurlock's Production Seal." *Variety,* 29 December 1962.

Turman, Larry. *So You Want to Be a Producer?* New York: Three Rivers Press, 2005.

Tusher, William. "Levine's Nix to Family Pix." *Film Daily,* 30 June 1967.

"UA to Release *Bridge.*" *Hollywood Reporter,* 18 May 1976.

"Unidentified Flying Objects." *Variety,* 25 April 1956.

Verniere, James. "Film Shows Comic Contempt for the Industry." *Boston Herald,* 22 August 1997.

"Very Little Left for Production." *Variety,* 14 August 1963.

Viera, Mark A. "Horror Queens: Divas from Hollywood's Golden Age Rampage through the Sixties." *Bright Lights Film Journal,* 31 October 2004. At http://brightlightsfilm.com/46/horror.php#.U_2a7WPEkr4.

Vogels, Jonathan B. *The Direct Cinema of the Maysles Brothers.* Carbondale: Southern Illinois University Press, 2005.

Waddy, Colonel John. "The Making of *A Bridge Too Far.*" *After the Battle,* no. 17 (1977): 30–52.

"Wallace Airs 'Harlow' Producers' Views on Juxtaposed Radio Tapes." *Variety,* 12 May 1965.

Waller, Gregory A., ed. *Moviegoing in America.* Malden, Mass.: Blackwell, 2002.

Waters, John. "Whatever Happened to Showmanship?" In *Crackpot: The Obsessions of John Waters,* 13–24. New York: Scribner, 2003.

Weiler, A. H. "Mike Nichols' *Dolphin.*" *New York Times,* 12 March 1972.

———. "Nichols Meets Jules Feiffer." *New York Times,* 26 October 1969.

———. "Screen: Encore Lelouch." *New York Times,* 22 March 1975.

Weltner, George. "Par's Commercial for Joe Levine's Showmanship: A $30,000,000 Bankroll." *Variety,* 22 April 1964.

Werba, Hank. "Joe Levine's Gearing More Pix for Those in 16–30 Age Bracket." *Variety,* 8 October 1969.

Whitehead, J. W. *Mike Nichols and the Cinema of Transformation.* Jefferson, N.C.: McFarland, 2014.

Whiteman, Bart. "Yale University: Spring of 1970." *Chattanoogan,* 26 November 2005. At http://www.chattanoogan.com/2005/11/26/76466/Yale-University-Spring-of-1970.aspx.

Wilder, Gene. *Kiss Me Like a Stranger: My Search for Love and Art.* New York: St. Martin's Press, 2005.

Wilinsky, Barbara. *Sure Seaters: The Emergence of Arthouse Cinema.* Minneapolis: University of Minnesota Press, 2001.

Williams, Dick. "Muscular *Hercules* Is Raising Coin." *Mirror News,* 30 July 1959.

Wilson, Andrew. *Harold Robbins: The Man Who Invented Sex.* London: Bloomsbury, 2008.

Wilson, Earl. "The Last Hustler." *Dallas Morning News,* 23 October 1978.

———. "One Filmmaker Recreates War." *Los Angeles Herald Examiner,* 5 June 1977.

Wolfe, Tom. Introduction to *The Kandy-Kolored Tangerine-Flake Streamline Baby.* In Ronald Weber, ed., *The Reporter as Artist: Readings on the New Journalism Controversy,* 32–33. New York: Hastings House, 1974.

Index

Screen Classics

Screen Classics is a series of critical biographies, film histories, and analytical studies focusing on neglected filmmakers and important screen artists and subjects, from the era of silent cinema to the golden age of Hollywood to the international generation of today. Books in the Screen Classics series are intended for scholars and general readers alike. The contributing authors are established figures in their respective fields. This series also serves the purpose of advancing scholarship on film personalities and themes with ties to Kentucky.

Series Editor

Patrick McGilligan

Books in the Series

Mae Murray: The Girl with the Bee-Stung Lips
Michael G. Ankerich
Hedy Lamarr: The Most Beautiful Woman in Film
Ruth Barton
Rex Ingram: Visionary Director of the Silent Screen
Ruth Barton
Conversations with Classic Film Stars: Interviews from Hollywood's Golden Era
James Bawden and Ron Miller
Von Sternberg
John Baxter
Hitchcock's Partner in Suspense: The Life of Screenwriter Charles Bennett
Charles Bennett, edited by John Charles Bennett
My Life in Focus: A Photographer's Journey with Elizabeth Taylor and the Hollywood Jet Set
Gianni Bozzacchi with Joey Tayler
Hollywood Divided: The 1950 Screen Directors Guild Meeting and the Impact of the Blacklist
Kevin Brianton
Ziegfield and His Follies: A Biography of Broadway's Greatest Producer
Cynthia Brideson and Sara Brideson
The Marxist and the Movies: A Biography of Paul Jarrico
Larry Ceplair
Dalton Trumbo: Blacklisted Hollywood Radical
Larry Ceplair and Christopher Trumbo
Warren Oates: A Wild Life
Susan Compo
Crane: Sex, Celebrity, and My Father's Unsolved Murder
Robert Crane and Christopher Fryer
Jack Nicholson: The Early Years
Robert Crane and Christopher Fryer
Being Hal Ashby: Life of a Hollywood Rebel
Nick Dawson
Bruce Dern: A Memoir
Bruce Dern with Christopher Fryer and Robert Crane
Intrepid Laughter: Preston Sturges and the Movies
Andrew Dickos
John Gilbert: The Last of the Silent Film Stars
Eve Golden

Stuntwomen: The Untold Hollywood Story
Mollie Gregory
Saul Bass: Anatomy of Film Design
Jan-Christopher Horak
Hitchcock Lost and Found: The Forgotten Films
Alain Kerzoncuf and Charles Barr
Pola Negri: Hollywood's First Femme Fatale
Mariusz Kotowski
Sidney J. Furie: Life and Films
Daniel Kremer
Albert Capellani: Pioneer of the Silent Screen
Christine Leteux
Mamoulian: Life on Stage and Screen
David Luhrssen
Maureen O'Hara: The Biography
Aubrey Malone
My Life as a Mankiewicz: An Insider's Journey through Hollywood
Tom Mankiewicz and Robert Crane
Hawks on Hawks
Joseph McBride
Showman of the Screen: Joseph E. Levine and His Revolutions in Film Promotion
A. T. McKenna
William Wyler: The Life and Films of Hollywood's Most Celebrated Director
Gabriel Miller
Raoul Walsh: The True Adventures of Hollywood's Legendary Director
Marilyn Ann Moss
Veit Harlan: The Life and Work of a Nazi Filmmaker
Frank Noack
Charles Walters: The Director Who Made Hollywood Dance
Brent Phillips
Some Like It Wilder: The Life and Controversial Films of Billy Wilder
Gene D. Phillips
Ann Dvorak: Hollywood's Forgotten Rebel
Christina Rice
Arthur Penn: American Director
Nat Segaloff
Claude Rains: An Actor's Voice
David J. Skal with Jessica Rains
Buzz: The Life and Art of Busby Berkeley
Jeffrey Spivak
Victor Fleming: An American Movie Master
Michael Sragow
Hollywood Presents Jules Verne: The Father of Science Fiction on Screen
Brian Taves
Thomas Ince: Hollywood's Independent Pioneer
Brian Taves
Carl Theodor Dreyer and Ordet: *My Summer with the Danish Filmmaker*
Jan Wahl

CPSIA information can be obtained at www.ICGtesting.com
Printed in the USA
BVOW02*0732100916

461586BV00001B/2/P

9 780813 168715